The Other Roots

RECENT TITLES FROM THE HELEN KELLOGG INSTITUTE SERIES ON DEMOCRACY AND DEVELOPMENT

Scott Mainwaring, series editor

The University of Notre Dame Press gratefully thanks the Helen Kellogg Institute for International Studies for its support in the publication of titles in this series.

Barry S. Levitt
Power in the Balance: Presidents, Parties, and Legislatures in Peru and Beyond (2012)
Sérgio Buarque de Holanda
Roots of Brazil (2012)
José Murilo de Carvalho
The Formation of Souls: Imagery of the Republic in Brazil (2012)
Douglas Chalmers and Scott Mainwaring, eds.
Problems Confronting Contemporary Democracies: Essays in Honor of Alfred Stepan (2012)
Peter K. Spink, Peter M. Ward, and Robert H. Wilson, eds.
Metropolitan Governance in the Federalist Americas: Strategies for Equitable and Integrated Development (2012)
Natasha Borges Sugiyama
Diffusion of Good Government: Social Sector Reforms in Brazil (2012)
Ignacio Walker
Democracy in Latin America: Between Hope and Despair (2013)
Laura Gómez-Mera
Power and Regionalism in Latin America: The Politics of MERCOSUR (2013)
Rosario Queirolo
The Success of the Left in Latin America: Untainted Parties, Market Reforms, and Voting Behavior (2013)
Erik Ching
Authoritarian el Salvador: Politics and the Origins of the Military Regimes, 1880–1940 (2013)
Brian Wampler
Activating Democracy in Brazil: Popular Participation, Social Justice, and Interlocking Institutions (2015)
J. Ricardo Tranjan
Participatory Democracy in Brazil: Socioeconomic and Political Origins (2016)
Tracy Beck Fenwick
Avoiding Governors: Federalism, Democracy, and Poverty Alleviation in Brazil and Argentina (2016)
Alexander Wilde
Religious Responses to Violence: Human Rights in Latin America Past and Present (2016)

For a complete list of titles from the Helen Kellogg Institute for International Studies, see http://www.undpress.nd.edu

THE OTHER ROOTS

Wandering Origins in *Roots of Brazil* and the Impasses of Modernity in Ibero-America

PEDRO MEIRA MONTEIRO

Translated by
Flora Thomson-DeVeaux

University of Notre Dame Press
Notre Dame, Indiana

University of Notre Dame Press
Notre Dame, Indiana 46556
undpress.nd.edu
All Rights Reserved

Published in the United States of America

English translation copyright © University of Notre Dame

Translated by Flora Thomson-DeVeaux from *Signo e desterro: Sérgio Buarque de Holanda e o Brasil* by Pedro Meira Monteiro (with revisions), published by Hucitec, São Paulo (2015), and as an e-book by e-galáxia, São Paulo (2016).
Copyright © 2014 by Pedro Meira Monteiro.

Library of Congress Cataloging-in-Publication Data

Names: Monteiro, Pedro Meira author. | Thomson-DeVeaux, Flora translator.
Title: The other roots : wandering origins in roots of Brazil and the impasses of modernity in Ibero-America / Pedro Meira Monteiro ; translated by Flora Thomson-DeVeaux.
Other titles: Signo e desterro. English
Description: Notre Dame, Indiana : University of Notre Dame Press, 2017. | Series: Helen Kellogg Institute series on democracy and development | Includes bibliographical references and index. |
Identifiers: LCCN 2017024316 (print) | LCCN 2017032328 (ebook) | ISBN 9780268102357 (pdf) | ISBN 9780268102364 (epub) | ISBN 9780268102333 (hardcover : alk. paper) | ISBN 9780268102340 (pbk. : alk. paper) | ISBN 0268102341 (pbk. : alk. paper)
Subjects: LCSH: Holanda, Sérgio Buarque de, 1902-1982—Criticism and interpretation.
Classification: LCC PQ9697.B88 (ebook) | LCC PQ9697.B88 Z76 2017 (print) | DDC 981—dc23
LC record available at https://lccn.loc.gov/2017024316

∞ *This paper meets the requirements of ANSI/NISO Z39.48-1992 (Permanence of Paper)*

For Déa, love of my life

Inside, we are still not American.
—Sérgio Buarque de Holanda, *Roots of Brazil*, 1936

Contents

Acknowledgments ix

Preface to the North American Edition xi

Introduction 1

PART I. FAMILIAL POLITICS

CHAPTER 1. Marking the Starting Point:
Readings of Sérgio Buarque de Holanda 19

CHAPTER 2. A Familial Tragedy (in Hegel's Shadow) 37

CHAPTER 3. Rural Roots of the Brazilian Family:
Sérgio Buarque de Holanda and Gilberto Freyre 49

PART II. THE NONEXISTENT AMERICAN

CHAPTER 4. Wandering Origins:
The Impertinence of Belonging 79

CHAPTER 5. Seeking America:
The Impasses of Liberalism (1) 99

CHAPTER 6. "*El hombre cordial*" and Specular Poetics:
The Impasses of Liberalism (2) 117

PART III. WORDS AND TIME

CHAPTER 7. Cordiality and Power:
The President and Politics between Film and Essay 143

CHAPTER 8. Sérgio Buarque de Holanda and Words,
or Evoking Wittgenstein   161

CHAPTER 9.   In a Thread of Time:
Chico, Sérgio, and Benjamin   175

Epilogue.   Roots of the Twenty-First Century:
Wisnik and the Horizons of the Essay   183

Appendix: Excerpts from *Roots of Brazil*   207

Notes   217

Works Cited   261

Index   285

Acknowledgments

Many people helped me think through the themes proposed here. The hypotheses presented in this book were elaborated and re-elaborated over the course of the past two decades, during which I shared my arguments and anguishes in private conversations, email exchanges, revisions and discussions of texts, talks, classes, and workshops in various countries. I am deeply grateful to all those I had the pleasure of including in that network. I will not list them here, but I hope that each will recognize him- or herself in these pages, even when my conclusions may diverge from theirs.

I should also note that the journeys that allowed me to split my time between research and academic events, as well as the translation of this book to English, were made possible by funds from Princeton University, those of the Department of Spanish and Portuguese and the Program in Latin American Studies, as well as from the University Committee on Research in the Humanities and Social Sciences. A crucial part of the writing came years ago, during a postdoctoral fellowship at the Universidade Estadual de Campinas (Unicamp), under the supervision of Joaquim Brasil Fontes.

I would like to thank Scott Mainwaring for suggesting the publication of this book in the Helen Kellogg Institute Series on Democracy and Development of the University of Notre Dame Press. I also thank Stephen Little, acquisitions editor, and most especially Eli Bortz, senior acquisitions editor of the UND Press, for their invaluable help. This book was also, of course, made possible by the talents of Flora Thomson-DeVeaux, who translated my work into English with exceptional diligence and creativity.

Finally, to my colleagues, as well as to my students in and outside Brazil, a special and hearty *muito obrigado!*

Preface to the North American Edition

Writing is a way of creating realities. Often we do not realize that we seem to be in a novel, looking for all the world like characters in a plot written by who knows what author. But can the real subject live with the idea that there is a plot guiding her, beyond her control? How can the autonomous individual bear the weight of a narrative in which he is merely a character? In *The Other Roots* I examine a fundamental work in which history, sociology, anthropology, and literature are joined, flowing together in discreet and illuminating prose. That work is *Roots of Brazil*, by Sérgio Buarque de Holanda, a book that, it would be no exaggeration to say, has invented a country. Whether they like it or not, or whether they know it or not, Brazilians are all Buarque de Holanda's characters.

Translated into countless languages over recent decades after its original publication in Brazil in 1936, *Roots of Brazil* was not published in English until 2012. When I wrote the foreword to the English-language edition, I emphasized the fact that this was a long-awaited translation that had finally come at an important juncture, at a moment when Brazil seemed on the verge of occupying an important place in the world as a whole. If that possibility holds water, then the time is ripe to revisit classic narratives around the country—although without supposing that such narratives can comprise a seamless national entity. On the contrary, despite the "roots" in its title, Buarque de Holanda's book suggests the insufficiency of any discourse looking to address the whole of a collectivity and contain it in a single sign. The "roots" here are free-flying, contradictory and paradoxical; it is unclear where they are coming from or where they are going. The essayistic imagination so characteristic of lettered Latin America in the first decades of the twentieth century allowed for the confection of a provocatively unstable vision, one perennially recalling that Brazilian history—like that of any country, for that matter—cannot cling to a precise origin frozen in a remote past.

While the "roots of Brazil" turn our gaze to the Iberian Peninsula, from whence the Spanish and Portuguese colonizers set off, Buarque de Holanda's vision cannot be understood without the African and American continents—not to mention the fact that the Portuguese colonial world included Asia as well, a place that would produce many elements of the culture that is sometimes called, in an obsessive nativist fantasy, "Brazilian."

The Other Roots: Wandering Origins in Roots of Brazil *and the Impasses of Modernity in Ibero-America* is the translation of a book recently published in Portuguese (*Signo e desterro: Sérgio Buarque de Holanda e a imaginação do Brasil*), in which I analyze Buarque de Holanda's work in the context of the great "essays of national interpretation," but where I also investigate the limits of national discourse itself. That said, in Brazil a book like mine is aimed at readers already familiar with *Roots of Brazil*, which is an academic best seller. A reader less well-versed in the debates that the book presents, or less acquainted with the history of Brazil, might not recognize references that would seem quite natural to a Brazilian. In order to address this issue, I have made small changes in this edition, trying to attain a balance between specialization and generalization. Moreover, in the appendix, readers will find a few key passages from *Roots of Brazil* that may help guide them.

* * *

A quick contextualization of the author and his work may be useful, at the very least up to the publication of *Roots of Brazil* in 1936. This may help to clarify Buarque de Holanda's importance as an essayist, even before he would find acclaim as Brazil's greatest historian and one of its most important literary critics.

Sérgio Buarque de Holanda (1902–1982) was born in São Paulo at a time when the city was establishing itself as a hub of an economy in transformation, spurred on by both industrialization and the capital flowing from coffee production. The setting here is that of a typical provincial city in the Americas in the process of modernization, where the signs of a past idealized by writers and poets mingled with the signs of a progress whose glories would be sung by other poets and writers (or sometimes the same ones). While at that point the city did not boast an Afro-Brazilian presence as significant as that of Rio de Janeiro or Salvador, São Paulo had been host to some of the abolitionist clashes that led to the eradication of slavery in 1888 and the end of the Empire in the following year. Above all, it was the city that received the most immigrants, especially Europeans, who headed for the agricultural frontier farther inland in the state or stayed right there in the city, stoking the factories and forever changing the social landscape of what had once been a sleepy provincial city.

This is, in short, the setting that would produce the generation of the "modernists": caught between the vibrant economy, the promises of the future, and the limits imposed by the past. Unlike late-nineteenth-century Hispanic-American modernism, Brazilian modernism emerged around 1920, tied to European vanguards and seduced by the velocity and hypersensitivity induced by metropolises across the world. Figures such as Oswald de Andrade, Anita Malfatti, Menotti del Picchia, Tarsila do Amaral, and Mário de Andrade would assume a new place on the arts scene, sharply pushing back against anything considered *passadista*, or backwards looking. In 1922 the Teatro Municipal in São Paulo would host the Modern Art Week, which became a symbolic milestone of the modernist movement. That same year, a young Sérgio Buarque de Holanda moved to Rio de Janeiro (then the nation's capital), where he became the representative of the São Paulo modernist magazine *Klaxon* (1922–1923). While in Rio, as a law student and journalist, he joined forces with Prudente de Moraes Neto to found *Estética* magazine (1924–1925), inspired by T.S. Eliot's *The Criterion*. By 1927, when he relocated to another state for a short stint as a prosecutor, Buarque de Holanda had made a name for himself as one of the most important modernist critics around, and also as one of the most important critics *of* modernism.

Brazilian modernism—or perhaps we should say São Paulo's modernism—has a curious side to it: its original, iconoclastic, libertarian drive, determined to bring about a renewal of the artistic field, soon found itself faced with the impasse of construction. In a country that was still feeling out its place in the modern world, it was not enough to simply rattle the foundations of old mentalities; rather, one had to find new foundations upon which to erect the columns of a new social and political edifice. This, of course, is the paradox of all avant-garde movements: when the bonds of imagination are broken, as the surrealists would have it, will there not inevitably come a moment when imagination itself is called upon to conjure up a stable plateau where one can stop, rest, and finally erect something? At the moment when it is fixed on paper or on the canvas, does not language—meant as a liberating force—morph surreptitiously into a prison? But if Brazilian modernism was grappling with the paradox common to all vanguards, what made it singular?

I think that here we may understand how Buarque de Holanda stood at the eye of the hurricane, and how *Roots of Brazil*, published in 1936 and extensively revised in later editions, is a tentative response to the impasse faced by modernism, as well as a reaction to the international political context. During the 1920s and 1930s, as it so happens, the desire for construction that the vanguards tended to repress would grow increasingly stronger, and in the Brazilian case would soon ally itself to nationalistic ideas, which often drifted into utterly authoritarian fantasies around a new order for politics and culture. Imagining how the country ought to be frequently led to a new orthodoxy, opening the way for authoritarianism and leaving little space for spontaneity.

The positive side of this framework for imagining Brazil is that the 1930s would bring a new and greater appreciation of the country's Afro-Brazilian heritage, and even the experience of postcolonial ethnic mixing, thus exorcising the specters of racist thought that had haunted the first decades of the twentieth century. From this bubbling broth came the valorization of *miscigenação* (or *mestizaje* in the Hispanic-American world), as well as the foundations for the idea of a mestizo national culture, which would soon become state policy under the administration of President Getúlio Vargas (1930–1945), particularly so in the dictatorial context of the Estado Novo (1937–1945). This, not coincidentally, is the period of the "invention" of the national symbols that pursue Brazilians to this day, whether they like it or not, making them characters in a grand and luminous narrative where they inhabit the country of Carnaval, samba, and soccer. A strange symbol-making machine, this, able to turn spontaneity into formulas, fixing the shapes of that which by definition should never be fixed. Nor was it by chance that in the 1930s, Gilberto Freyre's production (whose similarities and differences with Buarque de Holanda's I will discuss in this book) laid the groundwork for the thinking that would later crystallize in an expression that took on special appeal in the postwar period. To this day, "racial democracy" remains a thorn in the side of those addressing racism, the cruel reality of which flies daily in the face of the fable wherein individuals of different colors and classes coexist in perfect harmony in Brazil.

This gigantic jigsaw rooted in the 1930s offers us the puzzle pieces we need to understand culture and politics in Brazil, and it remains crucial today—especially in the discussion around affirmative action, for example, and in the negotiation of social inclusion, when one attempts to address racism and the overwhelming prejudice against the poor (independent of color) in a society with slaveholding origins. But this complex state of affairs, where exclusion and inclusion go hand in hand, is also made possible by the narratives that seek to give history meaning. Like warped mirrors, these narratives project places for individuals, forcing them to position themselves on a discursive plane whenever they seek to bring their own projects and wills to the fore. In short, and once again, social agents are characters in search of an author.

* * *

We know that Buarque de Holanda devised some of the arguments in *Roots of Brazil* during the period he spent in Berlin (1929–1930), in the twilight of the Weimar Republic, as Germany's democratic experiment began quaking at the approach of that which would become one of history's greatest nightmares from 1933 onward: the rise of Nazism. As will be seen here, the discussion of authoritarianism in *Roots of Brazil* heralds an impasse that may only be understood in the context of the interwar period.

On one hand, "spontaneity" in the Brazilian historical experience (supposedly more ductile than others) indicated a future that would move away from authoritarianism, specifically from totalitarianism. Employing a concept in *Roots of Brazil* that would become tremendously controversial—the "cordial man"—Buarque de Holanda broadened the possibility of conceiving a world more open to differences, less drawn on by the irresistible pull of civilization's advance and ironclad visions of the future. As a counterpoint for this supposedly more porous Brazilian history, one might take in large part the experience of Puritan North America, less malleable and more obsessed with the uplifting of the community of the Elect. As we shall see, by the way, the United States is an inescapable mirror in the Brazilian imagination, and for Latin America in general.

On the other hand, 1936, the year *Roots of Brazil* was released, was already witness to the clear development of authoritarian tendencies, which would lead those responsible for public policy under the Vargas era to project out a one-size-fits-all "Brazilian culture" over the nation as a whole, standing as a kind of irresistible answer to the turbulent contemporary world that was then set to conjuring the specter of a new world war (as we know in retrospect). Buarque de Holanda vigorously rejected the totalitarian solution that was slowly taking over Europe, but he also rejected the Brazilian authoritarian solution, quickly spotting the fascist streaks in the regime that would become the Brazilian Estado Novo just the next year, in 1937. The problem was complex: unlike European totalitarianism, which succumbed to fantasies around the mythic origins of a single, unique people (think of the ideal Rome of Italian fascism, to say nothing of the Aryan roots imagined by Nazism), Brazil offered up the myth of the bloodless meeting of races, a world without conflicts, where differences would be attenuated and fuse together almost magically. How to resist the song of these sirens?

As the reader will see, Buarque de Holanda is writing between authoritarianisms, spurning both the domestic authoritarian solution, with its hues of tolerance, and the totalitarianism blooming in Europe. However, one point makes the picture even more complicated: his study of the Peninsular origins of Brazil suggests that the political pact in Iberian America resists the principles of liberalism, which assume both an ethic of privacy and dedication to the exhausting daily work at the basis of collective advancement. In this vision, the Iberian Peninsula planted in American soil a different framework for the political pact, one predating "modern" forms of the social contract. The cordial man, in this sense, is the figure who snubs transcendental aims in favor of the here-and-now of his closest relationships. To paint in strokes so broad they verge on cartoonish, it is as if Carnaval and soccer were the *polis* itself, with salvation hinging not on the personal work ethic of the individual but on the carnivalesque appearance of a savior, a sovereign Father able to restore lost order: gracious and welcoming, tolerant but firm. *Roots of Brazil* cannot be conceived of without the specter of populism in Latin America, as we will also see here.

In short, Buarque de Holanda was a fierce critic of authoritarianism but also had his reservations as to the liberal pact. None of the solutions at hand satisfied him: neither the foundational mythology of Nazi fascism; nor the local authoritarianism formulated on the idea of a mixed-race nation; nor liberalism, with its calls for impersonality and neutrality. All impasses, in sum, where no option was embraced with conviction. One has only to recall that today, with World War II behind us, we can choose among our options with greater security, precisely because the liberal pact may strike us as the safeguard of a freedom threatened by the emergence of personalist power in the political arena. But during the interwar period, the dilemma was felt more keenly, and political uncertainty, such as in Buarque de Holanda's case, reveals that the principles opposing liberalism could not be summarily discarded either. While this idea may seem strange, if not alarming, to us today, it is because we are thinking from a present in which this dilemma has already taken on sharper contours, driving us—all those with at least a minimal penchant for democracy—to confidently support the control of all personalist power. The reading of *Roots of Brazil*, as I hope to suggest in this book, can help us learn to relive the impasses of a time foreign to our own, when today's political certainties had not yet crystallized.

As we shall see, in *Roots of Brazil* this impasse also takes shape in the dramatization of politics. The cordial man, in this case, lives off the proximity of everything he is familiar with to such an extent that any ritualistic form that distances him from those he is capable of recognizing will strike him as ominous. That is to say, political representation—the basis for modern notions of the liberal pact—is fundamentally foreign to the cordial man. After all, the masks that allow the individual to play the part of representative for collective projects and desires are alien to the cordial man, as are the formulas that defend privacy and make bodies untouchable. Once again running the risk of drawing a caricature, imagine the trouble faced by a Brazilian arriving in the United States and suddenly finding herself in a world where hugs and kisses are limited to the most intimate circles. Cordiality is the husk around this Brazilian individual who feels herself close to others, always "living through others," as we read in *Roots of Brazil*. But that husk can just as easily become a prison, a sort of smiling mask that blocks access to any real intimacy. The extreme version of this concept of the subject is, as we will see, the absence of interiority and the superficiality haunting the cordial man: in the illusion of sincerity and proximity, and the festive body's occupation of space, he is nothing more than a hollow mask, eternal and weightless joy.

* * *

Between the publication of the Brazilian version of this book in early 2015 and the finalizing of the manuscript in English, early in 2017, plenty of water roiled over the dam of politics in Brazil. The impeachment of President Dilma Rousseff in 2016 was the result of a sweeping conservative maneuver, but it could also be chalked up to the political inability of both the president herself and the Workers' Party, with which she'd won election in 2010 and reelection in 2014. The parliamentary coup d'état that resulted in Rousseff's impeachment availed itself of a veneer of "legality" that barely served to disguise the illegitimacy of the means it employed, which ran the gamut from turning justice into a spectacle to the scandalously selective choice of its initial targets. In the end, those who survived the shipwreck of the administration were its most conservative members, symbolized by the vice president, Michel Temer, who currently occupies the presidency and is facing down a political and economic crisis without precedent in Brazilian history.

In 1980, as Brazil began to shift out of yet another dictatorship, an ailing, elderly Sérgio Buarque de Holanda became a founding member of the Workers' Party (Partido dos Trabalhadores, or PT), which would become one of the most interesting experiments in the Left in Latin America and across the world. While the author of *Roots of Brazil*, who died in 1982, would never see the ascension of the Workers' Party with the election of Luiz Inácio Lula da Silva to the presidency in 2002, his reflections continue to shed light on the history of the nation, now heir to the contradictions of what may be called the "Lula era" (2003–2010).

Though it is true that since Lula's election, a massive swath of the Brazilian population was pulled away from the poverty line and into the world of consumption, it is no less true that the key social policies of his administration did nothing to shake the power of financial capital and apparently failed to even scratch the endemic corruption plaguing the state and society. Those with even a minimal familiarity with Brazil are aware that the lines between "informality" and the space regulated by law are always flexible, and that the ability to strike deals when the law fails (or when it is simply absent) is one of the most relevant traits of the Brazilian political and cultural tradition. In *Roots of Brazil*, as I will discuss in this book, Brazilian citizens' failure to internalize the law is a theme developed at some length.

While Buarque de Holanda's book, over a variety of editions, speaks to contexts that are quite different from the current one, it may lead us to questions that are crucial for understanding the dilemmas of contemporary politics in Brazil. To what extent have law and order been internalized by the country's citizens? What internal reins, meant to regulate and control action, have individuals developed or failed to develop in societies of Iberian origin? What are the consequences on a national level of the prevalence of an ethics of personal relationships that makes individuals feel protected by their clans from the logic of the state, which they often see as distant and incomprehensible? What notions of collectivity and public space can arise in a country where general law is external and quite often alien to the political subject?

Roots of Brazil, as will be made evident in *The Other Roots*, points to countless paradoxes. One of them, which is key to understanding contemporary Brazil, suggests that distance from and the daily flouting of law make individuals kowtow, suddenly subservient, when that law is embodied by a savior of the nation. In this context, the execution of law turns into personal wrath: a vengeful judge may embody justice itself and send out arrest warrants willy-nilly, applauded by a collectivity baying for an exemplary punishment. At the same time, prevailing anxiety at the prospect of seeing law enforced—that messianically awaited-for law that individuals are incapable of respecting in everyday life—gives rise to a scapegoat to be immolated on the altar of the media, bringing peace and tranquility to all.

This is not a matter of defending the honesty of this or that individual (it would fall to justice to do so, duly sheltered from media spectacle), but rather of simply noting that the scant internalization of law and order by the subject, and the subsequent clan logic and political godparenting, lead not infrequently to the expectation that law be enforced in the blink of an eye, as if a Judgment Day were the ultimate, sole solution for the impasses of politics.

The problem is that judgment must fall upon flesh-and-blood figures. Within the dynamic of social class currently at play in Brazil, it is precisely he who has done the most to eradicate poverty who is running the risk of immolation. The ongoing persecution of former president Lula by the media and the judiciary attests, in short, to a mechanism examined in depth in *Roots of Brazil*. One must recall that one of the central thrusts of Buarque de Holanda's book—as we will see here—is the macabre persistence of oligarchy within the Republic, hampering and stifling radical agendas.

The irony of recent Brazilian political history is precisely this: he who may have contributed the most to breaking the oligarchical cycle is falling victim to the poison that that very oligarchy helped (not alone, it should be said) to perfect, in its dodging and weaving around the ever-flexible limits of the law. The extent to which former president Lula allowed himself to be molded by that flexibility, obeying a clannish logic that avoids head-on confrontation and attempts to shield all political agents, is a question for which only the unfolding of history will eventually be able to provide an answer. Until then, while public and private interests remain undifferentiated and while the law remains something external to the citizen—something that he or she awaits with obstinate anxiety—*Roots of Brazil* will remain current, even at age eighty.

Princeton, NJ, January 2017

Introduction

It has already been noted how difficult it is to say where books begin. There are two points, however, without which this book would not exist, at least not in its current form.

The first goes back twenty-five years when, in a seminar on sociological theory in Brazil, I heard Octavio Ianni (1926–2004) lament the absence of a detailed study of the presence of Max Weber in *Roots of Brazil* (1936), the classic essay by historian and literary critic Sérgio Buarque de Holanda (1902–1982). His point was intriguing, since Ianni himself came from that lineage of intellectuals from the Universidade de São Paulo who had cast a suspicious gaze over the essayistic work produced in the 1930s, of which *Roots of Brazil* is one of the most notable examples. But whether from the fascination exerted by the "essay as form," in Adorno's phrasing, or his interest in Weberian criticism, the fact is that Ianni saw it as urgent to return to Buarque de Holanda at that moment, deepen the understanding of his work, and place it back in the contemporary debate in social sciences in Brazil and Latin America.

It is true that *Roots of Brazil* had hardly been languishing up until then. Ever since 1936, when it was first published as the inaugural volume of the Documentos brasileiros [Brazilian Documents][1] collection directed by Gilberto Freyre for the publishing house José Olympio, the essay has inspired ardent reactions. But it is not less true that, between the 1960s and the 1980s in Brazil, Buarque de Holanda's debut book was the target of harsh critiques that tagged it as "ideological," a label that seems to suffer from a kind of curse. How ideology can be a motive for suspicion is something that evades my aims and interests here. But we would do well to recall that these accusations, even when not made material in critical texts, hung in the air. Sérgio Buarque de Holanda was suspect.

The reaction to this suspicion led to my own interest in *Roots of Brazil* and steered me to write my first book, published almost twenty years ago, in which I sought to feel out the Weberian counterpoint in the composition of the analytical categories drawn up by Buarque de Holanda.[2] Today I believe that in that book, the discussion of those "sociological" categories left unanswered questions around the metaphorical field opened up by the organic imaginary that helped to shape *Roots of Brazil*, especially when we insert it into the framework of Latin American (or Latin Americanist) thought about "America." Perhaps precisely the use of its metaphors (the "adventurer," the "cordial man," the Iberian "roots," etc.) had sparked the suspicions of scholars such as those from the Universidade de São Paulo and thus—while I did not fully realize it at the time—stood at the origin of my own reflection. I may call the book that the reader now holds a continuation of my first book, although its development and its objects are different, more "literary"—not to conjure up an unyielding divide between fields and perspectives, as if social sciences and history stood on one side and literature on another.[3]

The reference to literary studies brings us to the second point where this book's origin becomes clear, one inconceivable without many years of experience outside Brazil. It was through contact with the North American university system, especially in terms of Latin American Studies, oscillating between literature and intellectual history, that many of the texts that comprise the following chapters would be initially developed.

This is not, however, the simple defense of a perspective "from the outside," as if scholars of Brazil should necessarily seek out the airing-out of ideas provided by experience abroad. Rather, I wish to recognize the importance of a field of study whose legitimacy is constantly sub judice. The fact is that, once transported to North American academia, the study of Brazilian literature becomes something else entirely. For one thing, the theoretical debate changes, because there is no more "Brazilian" literature without Latin America— a space more symbolic than it is geographic, in which Brazil is included to a greater or lesser extent, depending on the theoretical or political interests at work. On the other hand, our objects of study fall into a field whose very constitution is intensely problematic. I won't recount the history of Latin American studies in the United States, which would lead to a discussion of the emergence of area studies during the Cold War and the constitution of a complex gaze cast on the country's neighbors to the south, one shot through with strangenesses. This very gaze produces a new form of "orientalism"—in a somewhat flexible usage of Edward Said's illustrious category, not by chance another product of the same intellectual environment, outside Latin American studies, but still within a comparative perspective.[4]

"We" are an "other" when we mingle with "them": the trap set by these pronouns reveals the complexity of a relationship that not only has personal consequences, but also resonates profoundly on an epistemological level. The constitution of the object shifts. In the binomen Brazilian literature, both "literature" and "Brazilian" are destabilized as immediately comprehensible categories when one is outside Brazil. This is not to say that, when one is in Brazil, studies on Brazilian literature constitute a field that does not question itself or does not formulate questions about the very possibility of its existence. What I am suggesting is a difference of degree. In the North American academic environment, assigned to the field of Latin American studies or slotted into a department of foreign languages and literatures, the subject of knowledge is faced with the need to justify her object on an almost daily basis (to herself and to the academic institution), the object thus becoming the focus of an arduous intellectual task. What is "literature"? Is it the same in Brazilian academia (and in which part of Brazil, incidentally?) and on the North American scene, one generally quite marked by cultural studies? But what is "Brazilian" here? Is it the same in Brazil, where "Latin American" is frequently tied to "Hispanic American," and in the United States, where Brazil is aligned with a series of expectations that place it as the tail end of (Hispanic-American) traditions with which we in Brazilian academia are barely familiar? And who are we, or what is this "we"?

One way or another, the "we" and the "them" are subject to a zone of instability, which is the contradictory space from which one may form a discourse on one's objects, whether understood in terms of identity-based and theoretical categories or from administrative perspectives, and where it may often be difficult to make out the political narrative below the classification of fields and themes. Not to forget, of course, that these battles are fought with a powerful weapon: languages. But who are "we"? Brazilians, or Latin Americans? Or both? And who are "they"? North Americans or Hispanic Americans? Or just North Americans? Or are we all "Americans," and are "they" Europeans? But which Europe? Northern Europe or continental Europe, and on which side of the Pyrenees?

Categories cannot rest in an environment such as this. They become different, defamiliarized, in the language and even in the constitution of a legitimizable and respectable environment for study. In short, "Brazil" is another "Brazil" when enunciated from outside. Let us abandon the quotation marks, however (Sérgio Buarque de Holanda jokingly called them "little horns," as we shall see), and let the ink run and explain my work.

The work is split into two stages: first, a reaction to the suspicions around Buarque de Holanda in Brazil; second, my own suspicions around the Brazilian specificity of *Roots of Brazil*, this time in the framework of a debate where Brazil alone cannot suffice.

I hope that the "wandering origins" in the book's title may slowly become clearer. Perhaps they refer to the only question possible in the face of a legacy: the one posed when there is a shift in relation to the space of origin, when that space has become strange—the moment in which our roots ultimately provoke astonishment and doubt.

* * *

The primary aim of this book is to help understand how a book— *Roots of Brazil*—may determine the imagination of a country. Sérgio Buarque de Holanda's work—beyond his debut book, of course, although marked by it—shapes the way in which Brazil is thought of, conceived alternately as radically different from and surprisingly similar to other countries. It may help to revisit and question this imaginary Brazil, not simply because many Brazilians identify with precisely this vision of the country, but also because the question as to the explanatory power of a book called *Roots of Brazil* may lead to a better understanding of a period like ours, in which discussions around supraindividual principles related to identity oscillate between the systematic negation of a national discourse and the constant resurgence of collective hopes and fears. Between the "farewell" to national frontiers, which informs much of contemporary thought, and the dogged power of discourse around the nation, there lies a reflection on the power of identification wielded by the national sign, the word *Brazil*—a word like any other, after all.

I do not seek here to place myself at either extreme, affirming or negating the principle, or even a national "instinct," as Machado de Assis would put it. I simply wish to look into the survival of Buarque de Holanda's book, offering up some reasons as to why it continues to speak to us and provoke us, at a time when the grand national narratives have entered into crisis, although they continually threaten to return. *Roots of Brazil* is not infrequently evoked by Brazilians as one of the most important models for interpreting "our reality." At other times, Buarque de Holanda's work may serve to kindle interpretations of "Brazilian culture," without an explicit reference to the author or, at times, without the thinker in question even realizing that *Roots of Brazil* is providing the tools to put together a self-image that, like all self-images, is a precarious one. In a somewhat provocative tone, one might say that *Roots of Brazil* and its concept of the cordial man (which will be discussed here) already belong to Brazil's collective unconscious. But in strictly psychoanalytic terms, it can never hurt to recall that, when it emerges, the unconscious bursts through and interrogates the coherent self-image that the subject vainly tries to hold up. In short, Brazil is always more (or less) than that which Brazilians say about it and about themselves.

The heritage of a book like *Roots of Brazil* is vast. Like any heritage, it also poses a problematic legacy, mobilizing the heirs and creating peculiar situations in which the "original" is called upon to say more than it actually said. The latencies at its origin allow for the creation of histories from a starting point whose location, or even its existence, may be called into question. Apropos of such entanglements, I might recall the relationship that I propose in this book between Sérgio Buarque de Holanda and North American historian Richard Morse, or even Brazilian critic and musician José Miguel Wisnik. In both cases, the aim is not to explore necessarily explicit connections but to investigate to what extent the identity principle behind Morse's and Wisnik's analyses is a more or less conscious response to problems raised in *Roots of Brazil*. After all, don't Morse's "Ibero-American" principle and the "place outside ideas" that Wisnik proposes, different as they are, both wend back to the *Iberian deviation* presupposed in *Roots of Brazil*? As we shall see in the following chapters, both reflections reaffirm, albeit with differing degrees of intensity, the imaginary frontiers of "another" Europe (the Iberian Peninsula), the source of "another" America (Ibero-America). But this opens up a new and fascinating problem: what to do with the triangulation between Europe, America, and Africa, the basis for the imagination and the supposed novelty of the American continent? These considerations may easily take in other works, of course, beyond *Roots of Brazil*. For that matter, as I hope to suggest, *Roots of Brazil* cannot be understood without the proximity of Gilberto Freyre, another Brazilian essayist (and anthropologist himself) who rose to prominence in the 1930s, and whose influence on the understanding of Brazil remains enormous as well.

There are still other remainders, other kinds of legacies. I might recall the Buarquian framework present in João Moreira Salles's documentary on President Lula, or even the way in which the discussion around history and its "end" appears, transformed by fiction, in Chico Buarque's contemporary novels. Not to forget, of course, that the discussion about "cordiality" always rears its head whenever the debate on affirmative action policies slides into a revisiting and imagining of the differences apparently shearing America into North and South—the basis for the prevailing notion that issues of race are substantially different in the United States, with its one-drop rule, and Brazil, apparently more malleable in its understanding of colors. This imaginary divide between North and South America is discussed at greater length in the second part of this book, with center stage taken up by the confrontation between Brazil and the United States, or between Latin America and the United States of America. An America whose very existence, or whose symbolic unity, may and should be put into question.

I hope, in the end, that my reflections may allow the reader to follow how some of the most persistent self-images of Brazil have been processed over the last seven or eight decades, allowing both Brazilians and foreigners to still recognize themselves in those images. This recognition is inevitable, and perhaps even necessary. But it is curious that, as a book investigating Brazil, *Roots of Brazil* should allow this principle of identity to reveal both its strength and its weakness—its power, but also its impotence. This is the case because ultimately, as we will see, *Roots of Brazil* shakes the foundations of any thought constructed on the placid difference between "us" and "them."

* * *

The first part of this book ("Familial Politics") is divided into three chapters. In the first, "Marking the Starting Point: Readings of Sérgio Buarque de Holanda," I discuss how the analyses of literary critic Antonio Candido constructed an image of the author of *Roots of Brazil* that has hung over the understanding of his work ever since and which I seek to critique. On one hand, Candido's imagination helps us in shaping an understanding of the broader period that produced Buarque de Holanda's debut book; on the other, the return to the closely entangled bonds of social studies and literary criticism, especially starting in the 1940s, lets us see how a totalizing approach to culture slowly falls apart, revealing its own limits in the establishment of a national framework for understanding Brazilian literature. Within Buarque de Holanda's work as a literary critic, there emerge the fissures in the foundations of an idea of "Brazilian culture." These texts confront the problematic nature of any and all origins and envision a growing feeling of unbelonging, perhaps tied congenitally to the national condition. Finally, I seek to schematically define how Sérgio Buarque de Holanda's work has been understood, from at least the preface that Antonio Candido wrote for *Roots of Brazil* in the 1960s to the more recent publication of practically all of Buarque de Holanda's literary criticism in *O espírito e a letra* [The Spirit and the Letter].[5]

In the second chapter, "A Familial Tragedy (in Hegel's Shadow)," I begin with the epigraph from the first edition of *Roots of Brazil* (1936), which announced the discussion of the cordial man, suggesting that the metaphor of the *heart* ("cordial" comes from the Latin *cor*, *cordis*—that is, heart, or *coração*) is central to understanding the conflict that, in rising between the public and private spheres, expresses the individual dimension of the suffering wrought by the loss of meaning in the metropolis, be it the São Paulo of the 1930s or the Chicago of the early twentieth century, as will be seen. In either case, individuals, tossed into the whirlwind of the city, discover that they are incapable of recomposing the universe of relationships that once brought them the comfort of the just and unquestionable values present in the logic of the family. In this chapter, I shall briefly run down some of the sociological founts from which Buarque de Holanda is drinking—Pareto, Thomas, and Znaniecki—and analyze the tragic form he lends to the conflict between public and private, through a singular reading of Sophocles's *Antigone*. I should note that *Roots of Brazil*'s take on the Greek tragedy is markedly Hegelian, with a clash between two clearly opposed ethics: the "natural" scope of the family and the "universal" ethic of the polis. In submitting Sophocles to a Hegelian reading, I propose that *Roots of Brazil* loses the play's most precious and paradoxical assets: the irresolution of that conflict between family and polis and the muddying of its message, both adding to a certain fascination with the familial roots that persist in the city's breast. In this chapter, I also hope to clarify how I diverge from the interpretations of Antonio Candido, returning to his studies on the interior of the state of São Paulo in order to recall how the clash between the familial and the urban is a Buarquian theme within Candido's own critical imagination.

In the third chapter, "Rural Roots of the Brazilian Family: Sérgio Buarque de Holanda and Gilberto Freyre," I propose a parallel reading of *Roots of Brazil*, by Buarque de Holanda, and *Sobrados e mucambos* [The Mansions and the Shanties],[6] by Freyre, both published in 1936 and extensively revised in their second editions. I suggest that the two authors' having come together as youths, in the Bohemia of 1920s Rio de Janeiro, hides important differences between them that come into clearer focus in the wake of Buarque de Holanda's criticisms of the second edition of *Sobrados e mucambos* in 1951. Chief among them is his discomfort at the empathetic approach to the country's patriarchal past, which Freyre took as a repository of positive values. I should observe, however, that the critique of the metaphysical side of Freyre's analysis, which tended to sugarcoat Brazil's colonial period, comes from Sérgio Buarque de Holanda the historian, the author of *Monções* [Monsoons] (1945), and not from the younger and more eclectic author of *Roots of Brazil*. In the discussion of a starting point for understanding the formation of Brazilian culture, there resurfaces the tension between "Iberianism" and "Americanism."[7] As for the imbalance wrought by urbanization, in Buarque de Holanda *conflict* is the mark of an insoluble impasse, while in Freyre *compromise* reemerges on the political scene in the vision of a "cordial mulatto," supposedly a product of the nineteenth century in Brazil. In attenuating the political impasse subsumed by the concept of the cordial man, Freyre lends Buarque de Holanda's concept a moral character, projecting the Brazilian as broadly "good" and, in this, falling into step with the analyses of Cassiano Ricardo, one of the most important intellectuals of the so-called Estado Novo in Brazil (1937–1945), the period of Getúlio Vargas's dictatorial stint in the presidency. The promise of the cordial mulatto evidences the seduction that Freyre's theses can inspire to this day, amidst heated discussions in Brazil around affirmative action and the perennially thorny topics of miscegenation and racism.[8]

The second part ("The Nonexistent American") opens with the fourth chapter, "Wandering Origins: The Impertinence of Belonging," in which displacement sets the tone, showing how it is only through movement that the subject can speak of a space of belonging. In terms of language, this space will be the postulation of an imaginary geography, of a place that has been abandoned and threatens to fall apart, fostering the projection of difference: a point in which identity discourses take off, founded on a simultaneously urgent and impossible search for one's origins. I suggest that the investigation of Brazil's "roots" is also a question about the power of language: what does Brazil as a linguistic sign reveal, dissemble, and conceal? A fragment from Saussure on the indeterminacy of the symbol will help us to comprehend the undecidability at the core of the production of meaning, revealing that the search for roots is also the stuff of signification. The national label is shown to be insufficient and witnesses the sliding away of identification as the subject realizes that belonging is impossible, and that one's "I" is necessarily constituted in an "other" after the abandonment of the origin and, thus, after the clearing of the field of language. Rimbaud's provocative syntagma (*"Je est un autre,"* "the I is an Other") will ultimately open up into a brief analysis of the allegorization of belonging in a short story by Minas Gerais–born writer João Guimarães Rosa, "The Third Bank of the River." Through this analysis, we can ask—what is the national symbol that slides between the banks of meaning? And why does the subject move alternately to and away from this sign of origin, as if from a compromising vision?

In the fifth chapter, "Seeking America: The Impasses of Liberalism (1)," I look to examine the handful of metaphors in *Roots of Brazil* that herald a deep investigation, inherent in examining the roots of a civilization of Iberian origin. The suggestion of a mental universe set apart from that of Europe beyond the Pyrenees allows for us to imagine two "Americas," like separate branches of the colonizing advance. As a symbolic frontier, the Pyrenees, dividing the Iberian Peninsula from the "rest" of Europe, are seen to reappear in the New World, establishing the line that separates South from North, like two sides of a single European mirror reflected on American soil. I also address the issue of *authority* and *revelation*, setting the mentality of the Protestant Reformation against a Counter-Reformationist view of the role played by tradition in directing the collectivity and thus demonstrating that the religious debate is intimately tied to the foundation of the political pact. I also propose a brief comparison with Richard Morse, suggesting that his *Prospero's Mirror*,[9] published in the 1980s, is a sort of exaggerated reading of Buarque de Holanda's *Roots of Brazil*. It is almost as if the North American historian had succumbed in that moment to the enchantment seeping through from the other side of the mirror, which his Brazilian colleague had inadvertently helped to uncover; in short, Morse's disenchantment with the North American world feeds into the analysis that locates the promise of a new civilization in the "Other" to the South. In contrast with this optimism, *Roots of Brazil* lays out the impasses of the formation of citizenship in a society that, through its emphasis on the disaggregating force of the person, managed to avoid the formation of intimacy, the modern conception of which is heavily indebted (in Buarque de Holanda's case) to the formulations of Max Weber. Richard Morse, then, might have found the extreme end of a veiled civilizational promise in *Roots of Brazil*, which may be understood, as we shall see, when one superimposes the 1936 essay on Buarque de Holanda's modernist critiques from the previous decade. This chapter may also be read as an invitation to evaluate *Roots of Brazil* within Latin American essayism as a whole, leaving the complex issue of the Brazilian modernists' imagination of "America" hanging in the air.[10]

In the sixth chapter, "'*El hombre cordial*' and Specular Poetics: The Impasses of Liberalism (2)," I discuss in greater detail the Latin American phantasm of the *arielista* imagination and its influence on Buarque de Holanda. I recall that, in taking the metaphor of the mirror to its limits, Richard Morse exalted the Iberian choice, taking his inspiration from the same Shakespearean motifs that allowed the Uruguayan writer José Enrique Rodó to publish his famous work *Ariel* (1900), which in addition to serving as a great landmark in the Hispanic-American literature of the turn of the twentieth century, would also spark the interest and admiration of a young Buarque de Holanda in the early 1920s in Brazil.[11] In this sense, *Prospero's Mirror*, by Morse, is yet another step in the longstanding Latin Americanist passion shared by authors as different as Rubén Darío in Nicaragua; Rodó himself in Uruguay; José Carlos Mariátegui in Peru; and writers such as Manoel Bonfim, Sérgio Buarque de Holanda, and Gilberto Freyre in Brazil. In essays, these thinkers conceive of "another" America, felt or imagined in the sense of a difference, with the United States as its inescapable referent. This difference, moreover, suggests a separate quality altogether, and thus we might say that *Roots of Brazil* is still an heir to the nineteenth century in its frequent flirtations with the Romantic ideas of a "national character" and of unshakable differences between peoples. At the same time, Buarque de Holanda's book allows for a move toward the project of "another modernity," one able to subvert that original mirroring, supposing that the future of civilization is indeed a secret kept by the South (whose social and political experience would repel liberalism's most basic principles) and proposing a model for society in which individuals do not close themselves off in their own individuality and privacy. Here we see the construction of dreams of alternative epistemologies and a broad perspectivism, which for its part ballasts the "South-South" dialogues (or the so-called Global South) that have taken on such prominence in the international academic sphere. This is not merely a battle against the big brother to the north, but full-blown war against an entire paradigm of civilization. Taken to its most extreme consequences by Richard Morse in *Prospero's Mirror*, this war allows us to rediscover the array of promises latent in *Roots of Brazil*, a work that, while rejecting essentialisms, still postulates a difference that is an unresolved problem in and of itself. I also sketch a possible genealogy of "cordiality," indicating the first usages of the expression in Hispanic America, starting with Rubén Darío, Mexican writer José Vasconcelos, and Brazilian writer Rui Ribeiro Couto in his dialogue with Alfonso Reyes, also of Mexico. This angle raises another question, which I do not develop here and which would imply another research project: in its reference to the "ebb and flow" of the social organism, *Roots of Brazil* points toward an imaginary formed out of the reaction to the "decadence" observed in Europe. Vico and Spengler are hidden, but perhaps powerful, voices in the constitution of an American space in Sérgio Buarque de Holanda's imagination.[12]

The third part ("Words and Time") opens with the seventh chapter, "Cordiality and Power: The President and Politics between Film and Essay." Here, a few threads spun out by the previous chapters meet and intertwine in order to shed light on the permanence (and propriety) of Buarquian themes in contemporary artistic reflections about Brazil. A brief history of *Roots of Brazil* and the various visions of cordiality precedes a reflection on João Moreira Salles's documentary *Intermissions*, focusing on the action behind the scenes in the campaign that would lift Luiz Inácio Lula da Silva into the presidency of Brazil in 2002, in a cinematographic framing that has cordiality as a clear measure for understanding politics. The attention paid to the private sphere—which the concept of cordiality opens up—helps in understanding the importance of intimate gestures in the formation of a public personality. In the tension between privilege (literally, private law) and collective rights, Lula's central, agonic issue is exposed. The documentary thus joins sociology and literature in searching for the intimate moments of the subject, giving new life to the debate on the tension between public and private, in its suggestion that the political leader's greatest crisis, as underscored in *Roots of Brazil*, lies in his abandoning the comfort of collective solutions. That comfort would be the hallmark of the individual still chained to the pleasant image that intimates and courtiers alike project around him, holding him hostage to a familial phantasm that only truly representative politics would be able to overcome. This is the new president's predicament, as seen through the lens of Salles's documentary.

In the eighth chapter, "Sérgio Buarque de Holanda and Words, or Evoking Wittgenstein," I discuss Buarque de Holanda's tart criticism of historian Carlos Guilherme Mota in the early 1970s, directed at his "superstition" around the "pure word." This critique unfolds within a broader discussion about language, with the return to a number of debates from the period of Brazilian modernism in the 1920s, woven into a reflection on the historian's craft and his or her condition as a writer. Inspired by Wittgenstein, Buarque de Holanda discusses the complexity of language, situational and transitory as it is, through a focus on syntax, vigorously rejecting the notion of an "unequivocal" word. In his reaction to Mota, I suppose that Buarque de Holanda was exacting a sort of revenge: in his response to his colleague's criticism, he was also reacting to the distrust that his oeuvre, *Roots of Brazil* in particular, could still provoke in the 1970s, under the sway of social psychologist Dante Moreira Leite's earlier interpretation of the "ideological" and therefore reprehensible nature of the grand essays of national interpretation.[13] The label "ideological," let us recall, was never disassociated, in the case of the suspicions hanging over Buarque de Holanda, from the eclecticism of his language. I thus seek to clarify that the constitution of language, which had so concerned Buarque de Holanda the literary critic in the 1920s, would continue to bother Buarque de Holanda the historian through his old age, by which time he finally felt able to unashamedly say everything he thought in a combination of sarcasm and melancholy, without taking the distrust or scorn of his rivals to heart.

The ninth chapter, "In a Thread of Time: Chico, Sérgio, and Benjamin," may strike the reader at first glance as a complementary essay. Nevertheless, I believe that it is a key part of my arguments in this book. In briefly analyzing *Benjamin*, the novel by Francisco Buarque de Holanda, I suggest that his central problem has to do with the impotence of writing when faced with that which his father, Sérgio Buarque de Holanda, had identified as the "breaking point with life." The rupture in the epic register, as I argue, separates Chico Buarque (as the musician and novelist is known both in Brazil and elsewhere) from the Colombian writer Gabriel García Márquez, suggesting that the death at the start of the narrative in Chico's *Benjamin* (1995) simply announces the nonsense of the present, while in *One Hundred Years of Solitude* (1967), by García Márquez, death and curses swirl around the family as it makes and unmakes itself mythically in a sort of joyous circular alchemy. However, in Chico Buarque, a curse shuts the titular character into the brief delirium that is his failed life, which as the reader discovers, is nothing more than the narrative of *Benjamin* the book. Intertwined temporal relations connect Sérgio Buarque de Holanda's considerations to the narrative created by his son. The excessive "visual focus" that the Brazilian historian saw in Leopold von Ranke would eventually emerge in the shaping of the *instant*, in which Benjamin's story unfolds; the protagonist, living amidst the ruins of the last Brazilian dictatorship (1964–1985), sees the future simply vanish. Instead of reconstituting itself in a mythical time, the past stakes itself on the field of the postdictatorial narrative, announcing the absurd absence of any end and pulling the reader into a crisis that is simultaneously political and literary.

The epilogue, "Roots of the Twenty-First Century: Wisnik and the Horizons of the Essay," is simultaneously a destination and a jumping-off point. Beyond simply inserting *Veneno remédio: O futebol e o Brasil* [Poison/Cure: Soccer and Brazil] (2008), by Brazilian critic and musician José Miguel Wisnik, into the lineage of the great hermeneutical essays that includes *Roots of Brazil*, I examine how, in updating and lending a new scale to the central issues of Brazilian essayism of the 1930s, Wisnik takes up Sérgio Buarque de Holanda's ambivalence in *Roots of Brazil*, conceiving of it as a middle ground between the running optimism of Gilberto Freyre's oeuvre and the bleak affirmation of the scars of development from the colony onward, as seen in the work of historian Caio Prado Júnior, author of the 1942 classic *The Colonial Background of Modern Brazil*. As we shall see, in examining the nonrectilinear form that, in 1970, filmmaker Pier Paolo Pasolini saw in the way South Americans played soccer "in poetry," *Veneno remédio* opens up an array of issues that call into question the positive hues taken on by peripheral experience in the *dialética da malandragem* (dialectic of malandroism) conceived by critic Antonio Candido around the same period. From soccer to literature, the eternal, winking "malandros" of the Brazilian tradition,[14] living between the law and the contravention of it, are reread by essayists and serve as a counterpoint to the stern internalization of the Law in the Protestant tradition. This, in turn, brings us back to the initial intuitions in *Roots of Brazil*, transforming them into a framework for understanding the impasses of development and modernization of a country with Iberian origins and a slaveholding past, from our vantage point in the twenty-first century.

* * *

Finally, let me recall an idea that will appear with some insistence here: *Roots of Brazil* does not illuminate the self-image of a motley people open to differences; on the contrary, Sérgio Buarque de Holanda's book may reveal the impossibility of collective definition, or at least the limits of our fantasies around any sort of singularity. It is precisely that singularity that this book will attempt to suspend, even if just for a moment.

PART I

Familial Politics

CHAPTER 1

Marking the Starting Point

Readings of Sérgio Buarque de Holanda

Since the preface to the fifth Brazilian edition of *Roots of Brazil* in 1969, where Antonio Candido (b. 1918) reinforced the importance of Max Weber in understanding the book, the discussion of Sérgio Buarque de Holanda's German influences has remained a central one.[1] We would do well to recall, however, that the German theorists to which Candido refers are not limited to the heirs of the modern hermeneutics, with Max Weber, the author of *The Protestant Ethic and the Spirit of Capitalism*, as an illustrious representative. Candido argues that, in bowing to the softening of Buarque de Holanda's "dialectical" inspiration, the Weberian streak in *Roots of Brazil* has lost much of its original rigidity. It would take until the early 1990s, however, for a sharp-eyed reader of Antonio Candido to elevate that dialectic to the level of sentiment, casting it as a constitutive part of the Brazilian intellectual experience.[2] And only in the decade to follow would Candido's work be understood in terms of the influence of the German tradition of Romance studies, and Auerbach in particular—an author who would leave deep marks on Buarque de Holanda's imagination.[3]

If there is a "sentiment of dialectic" in Buarque de Holanda as well, the issue will demand a painstaking investigation, one that overspills the scope of this book. For now, I will simply register the idea that after the 1970s, *Roots of Brazil* is virtually inseparable from Candido's reading. Hence the *boutade* from Wanderley Guilherme dos Santos (declaring that the Sérgio Buarque de Holanda "of the book

Roots of Brazil is an invention of Antonio Candido's"[4]) is somewhat illuminating: the preface's questions have left an indelible mark on the text, with all subsequent readers working under the sign of that interpretation. This becomes even more ironic when one is aware that Candido himself, in another important preface, would declare provocatively that "the common denominator amongst most prefaces is their lack of necessity."[5]

The reading sketched out in that preface is often reproduced in academic environments in Brazil and abroad, sometimes in the form of the hypothesis of ideal types built in pairs—broadening the old dichotomy in Latin American thought, stretching back to Euclides da Cunha and Domingo Faustino Sarmiento.[6] The observation that *Roots of Brazil* apparently lacks the rigidity of the framework that unyieldingly pits civilization against barbarity opened up a modernist territory in the critical imagination. From this view, European heritage and all its associated values would receive the impact of something beyond local color—the very possibility of reimagining the order of that heritage. It is as if from the entrails of an "other" (being none other than "we" Brazilians, in the perspective constructed by the modernists in the 1920s and transformed into an allegory by the tropicalists in the 1960s), there emerged a new reading and the formidable rediscovery of the modern. Here we have the new forms of modernity in the tropics: the "million-dollar contribution of all our mistakes," in Oswald de Andrade's avant-garde phrasing from the 1920s, or the "advantages of backwardness," in the formulation that was so key for the Brazilian sociological imagination.[7]

In terms of Buarque de Holanda and his imagination of Brazil, this was a matter of turning a skeptical gaze on the imported formulas of a liberalism that continued to justify itself ideologically and which by 1936 was evoking dreams of an economic thrust that might finally cast out the specter of social dissolution from the political horizon. This phantasm was not merely the communism that had been prowling around Europe since the previous century, but also, and more importantly, the specter of the debacle that had shaken New York in 1929, and which in Brazil, with the crisis in coffee prices on the international market, had revealed the deep fissures in a venerable, prodigious political and economic structure. The 1930s brought a widespread renegotiation within the Brazilian elites, forcing the coffee heavyweights offstage or at least into new roles, they having been the first patrons of the young vanguard and those who would also help to shape the modern Brazilian university, sprung of the illusion of a still-mighty São Paulo.[8] In the heat of the period, national and international politics were discussed with a focus on the debate over the virtues and vices of capitalism, an advanced capitalism that Buarque de Holanda had seen and studied in his German years. In the twilight of the Weimar Republic, from 1929 to 1930, the late Weber's name still shone as an insuperable reference for the new generations of academic intellectuals around the young Brazilian journalist in Berlin. This is the background to the conception of *Roots of Brazil*—a half-German book, as we tend to put it.[9]

Antonio Candido's preface both validated and suggested a reading that, after the late 1960s, would highlight method in *Roots of Brazil* (ideal types ordered in dialectical pairs), while it also underscored the magnitude of the political problem: with the nation's Iberian roots revealed, how to seek out practical solutions for Brazil? In other words, which resonate some of the preoccupations that would keep so many generations of Latin American economists and sociologists busy, one might ask: how to imagine and propose the development of a country of Iberian origin?[10]

In his preface, Antonio Candido sketched out a veritable map of interpretative possibilities. Hence posterior studies from researchers of a number of generations, who although they may at times seem to distance themselves from or simply steer around his concerns, ultimately provide responses to questions that appear, albeit in embryonic form, in that preface. The preface does not stand alone in this regard, however. The critical reception of Sérgio Buarque de Holanda's work cannot be understood outside the framework of an editorial effort where Antonio Candido's name must be cited, although not exclusively. In the late 1980s, Maria Amélia Alvim Buarque de Holanda, Sérgio's widow, discovered a trove of unpublished material that Candido would evaluate, edit, and publish under the title *Capítulos de literatura colonial* [Chapters of Colonial Literature].[11]

The "Introduction" to this posthumously published book painstakingly details the story of the recently discovered manuscript: this was Buarque de Holanda's contribution to a failed project from Álvaro Lins, who had planned to publish a *História da literatura brasileira* [History of Brazilian Literature] (through Rio publishing house José Olympio) in fifteen volumes, with Gilberto Freyre and a number of other intellectuals as collaborators. Buarque de Holanda himself would take on the seventh volume, dedicated to colonial literature. The story of the book's conception and the planning of the collection—which would produce just two volumes, one on oral literature by Luís da Câmara Cascudo and another on prose fiction from 1870 to 1920 by Lúcia Miguel Pereira—is symptomatic, providing us with a rare map of the intellectual field that demonstrates the indissociability of literature and social studies in the critical imagination of the time.

The collection, perhaps overly eclectic to our contemporary eyes, was first proposed (as Candido tells us) in the early 1940s, which brings up two important issues in our understanding of Buarque de Holanda's thought.[12] First of all, the studies for the volume on colonial literature, which would be written for the most part in the following decade, reveal that the project came to stand as an important and perhaps even an essential part of Sérgio Buarque de Holanda's research, which by then had grown beyond the investigation of the westward push from the highlands of São Paulo—this vein had already produced the 1945 book *Monções* and would later lead to *Caminhos e fronteiras* [Paths and Frontiers] in 1957, while it also took in the Italian Renaissance, Luso-Brazilian *arcadismo*, and the Iberian baroque. This would lead Candido to speak of an "Italian phase" in Buarque de Holanda's work from 1952 to 1954, namely the years he spent teaching at the University of Rome, an experience that bolstered the conception and composition of the thesis behind his 1958 masterwork *Visão do paraíso* [Vision of Paradise], as well as a "German phase," covering his time in Berlin from 1929 to 1930.[13] Second, beyond the story of Buarque de Holanda's research, we can imagine what it might mean to compile a "history of Brazilian literature" in the 1940s and 1950s with such a wide array of collaborators. This was a highly specialized field (a specialization that Buarque de Holanda himself, a fixture in newspapers' literary sections, could speak to with great competence and refinement), but one that also demanded a critical imagination with a vast scope. We contemporary readers frequently reject this vastness, given our stockpile of qualms around grand theories. But these syntheses, generally viewed with distrust, when not scorn, and which would be nearly inconceivable today, anchored an intellectual horizon that could resist academic departmentalization and the fragmentation of knowledge, engaging with the public sphere in ways that we are hard-pressed to understand today. The notion of the *public*, or at least the reading public, was entirely different, as it presupposed an audience thirsty for interdisciplinary work—this, much before our current quest for interdisciplinary studies, which can be understood as a reaction to the compartmentalization of knowledge that has shaped contemporary disciplines and fields.

The scene described by Candido in his "Introduction" to Buarque de Holanda's posthumous book is itself an intervention that refers to and rues the specialization of the field of literary studies but also recalls a taste for synthesis that, we may imagine, serves as a profound link between the two authors: the one who left the manuscripts and the one editing them. In this sense, we can better understand the brilliant phrasing of the title: "I proposed *Capítulos de literatura colonial*," Antonio Candido writes, "with the famous book by Capistrano de Abreu [*Capítulos de história colonial* (Chapters of Colonial History)] in mind, but particularly recalling a less systematic work, by Alfonso Reyes: *Capítulos de Literatura Española* [Chapters of Spanish Literature]."[14]

The reference to Capistrano de Abreu (1853–1908) suggests the fertile presence of historical studies within literary reflections, exposing the very intersection that produces Sérgio Buarque de Holanda's reflections.[15] Evoking Alfonso Reyes (1889–1959), on the other hand, is an indication of a more complex relationship, one that Candido may well have had in mind. Not only did the Mexican writer play a role in the invention of the cordial man, as we shall see, but we must also recall that the "non-systematic" nature of this "too-disperse work," the *Capítulos de Literatura Española*, mingles in Reyes's oeuvre with a profound sense of the organic nature of the *latinoamericano*.

The same year that Buarque de Holanda published his *Roots of Brazil*, three years before the appearance of the first volume of *Capítulos de Literatura Española* in Mexico, and after six years spent as Mexican ambassador in Rio de Janeiro (then the nation's capital), Alfonso Reyes presented his "Note on American Intelligence" in Buenos Aires. Here, the organic imaginary stands out emphatically:

> To speak of American civilization would be, in this case, inappropriate: that would take us to archeological regions outside of the topic at hand. To speak of American culture would be something of an error: that would make us think of a branch from a European tree transplanted in American soil. We may, however, speak of American intelligence, the American vision of life and action in life. This will allow us to define, albeit provisionally, the tone of America.[16]

This American "tone" or hue may be less a clearly established quantity than a speculative finding, the precarious nature of which comes through in Reyes's prose, in his "provisional definition," which is all that any interpreter of "America" can aspire to. Not only do both succumb to the allure of organic metaphors, but in both cases the train of thought also runs into the same doubt as to America as an entity. In the cutting terms of *Roots of Brazil*, "Inside, we are still not American."[17]

A reading of Antonio Candido's introduction to *Capítulos de literatura colonial* allows us, in short, to understand that we are standing before a vast map on which the broad lines of the imagining of the new American space can be sketched, this place at once *ciudad letrada* and *carte de Tendre* for the ranks of Brazilian intellectuals—or Latin American intellectuals, from a wider angle.[18]

The late 1980s would bring yet another attempt to reconstruct the critical memory of Buarque de Holanda—to wit, the book edited by Francisco de Assis Barbosa, *Raízes de Sérgio Buarque de Holanda* [Roots of Sérgio Buarque de Holanda]. A partial collection of the articles published prior to *Roots of Brazil* (up until 1935, that is), it includes two studies, true prefaces, by Barbosa ("Sérgio antes de

Berlim" [Sérgio before Berlin]) and, once again, Candido ("Sérgio em Berlim e depois" [Sérgio in Berlin and Afterwards]).[19] The former provides a firsthand testimony of the early years of the restless, immature critic—Buarque de Holanda's "apprenticeship," as Barbosa puts it—based on the recollections of friends and colleagues, revealing from the start that this world cannot be understood outside one's circle of personal and emotional ties, ones which join the prefacers and the prefaced in ways that are often quite complex. Barbosa's study and editorial work are thus one of the first serious attempts at a critical mapping of what might be called a prehistory of *Roots of Brazil*. Or, to recall George Avelino Filho's astute turn of phrase, a search for the "roots of *Roots of Brazil*."[20]

This interest in the early history of *Roots of Brazil* lets us imagine an investigation in which the very making of thought takes center stage, where the scholar seeks both that which is revealed and that which the thought-in-progress hides from view. In the case of such procedures, Walter Benjamin's metaphor of a move "against the grain" is always welcome.[21] To put it in terms that may be more familiar to our contemporary sensibility, we might evoke the need for a genealogical effort in analyzing thought, recalling that the coherence of a discourse is ultimately constructed after it, and that its meaning is always, inescapably, up for debate. The search for that which lurks beneath the more visible, refined part of discourse is something of an archaeological task, which prefaces both can and should undertake.[22] This genealogical mission, however, with its furious drive to discover the power dynamics implicit in the interpretations of a body of thought, is not itself a neutral procedure. This may be the meaning of Baudrillard's well-known diatribe: Foucault is the "last of the dinosaurs" because his investigation is still indebted to the very conceptual constellation that he seeks to destroy.[23]

I wish to address just a part of the controversy: the reminder that the dismantling of a thought in the attempt to comprehend it may still retain the elements that the critical imagination seeks to break down and which resist despite all attempts to subdue them. Within my investigation, an uncomfortable question abides: Doesn't the very attention paid to the organic aspects of imagination in Sérgio

Buarque de Holanda reinforce the imaginary that we ultimately wish to free ourselves from? What to do with the contemporary critiques of "foundations" when faced with a book in which "roots" are an inevitable signifier? Or should we twist the sense of the word and, à la Deleuze, seek out the "rhizomes" where experience yokes the man to the landscape? But are these "roots" simply the sign of an anxiety around unmooring and drifting, as if expressing an unspoken desire to return to the ward of authority, when the Law stood supreme and explanations found definite endings?[24]

Let us return, however, to the terrain where *Roots of Brazil* situates itself, so as to formulate other questions that will pursue us throughout this book: Isn't the organic imaginary developed in Sérgio Buarque de Holanda's essay precisely part of the secret of Antonio Candido's critical undertaking? Aren't Buarque de Holanda's coherence and his progressive political attitude already part of a desire to detect exemplary personalities—to wit, the "radicals" that Candido studies and admires?[25]

If we examine the preface to *Roots of Brazil*, but also Antonio Candido's other prefaces (to *Capítulos de literatura colonial* and the "German" part of *Raízes de Sérgio Buarque de Holanda*), we can glimpse the gradual construction of a field of interpretation around Buarque de Holanda that takes *Roots of Brazil* as its jumping-off point and argues for (or constructs) a profound political and conceptual coherence on the part of the author.[26] The question that pursues me is the following: isn't this "radical" Sérgio Buarque de Holanda, which we are used to seeing, a character that emerges from Antonio Candido's interpretations? An author who looked right and left on the political spectrum, only to move resolutely straight ahead with the writing of *Roots of Brazil*? Let us see.

After identifying Buarque de Holanda as the stylist who, à la Spitzer or Simmel, could extrapolate from an empirical fact with an illuminating touch, Candido recalls that, while in the Germany of the Weimar Republic, the future author of *Roots of Brazil* was exposed to the still-recent legacy of Weber, which itself retained something of that "mental attitude" able to meld utter scientific rigor to an incredible literary audacity. But Candido recalls that an attraction to types and a use of broad, culture-defining characteristics could also lead, and had indeed led, to a dangerous fantasy: there bubbled the literary and scientific stew that would produce Nazism, with its "'cultural morphology,' the dualism of 'blood and earth,' race-differentiating psychology, and the appeal to 'obscure forces.'"[27] Buarque de Holanda, nevertheless, is seen to have reacted correctly to the negative aspects of this cultural environment, the breeding ground for the nightmare of the Third Reich:

> But the rectitude of his spirit, his young but solid formation, and the correct orientation of his political instincts led him to something surprising: from this cultural broth, which could go from conservative to reactionary, from mystical to apocalyptical, he extracted the elements of a personal formula for a progressive interpretation of his country, forging an exemplary combination of a demystifying interpretation of the past and a democratic sense of the present. The "empathy," a trust in a certain mysticism of "types"—all this was purged of any vestiges of irrationality and ground up in his peculiar fashion, and [then] flowed into an open, extremely critical and radical interpretation.[28]

The great Enlightenment battle rears its head in this scene of reading: the young critic shedding the uncomfortable burden of irrationality.[29] Even so, it would be rash to seek out in Buarque de Holanda the opposite of what Candido sees in him. And my own intentions are very far indeed from aligning the author of *Roots of Brazil* to any conservative thread of Brazilian social thought. My aim, which I hope to make clear over the course of this book, is to revisit, or perhaps simply imagine, the tension that hums acutely in the writer's consciousness as the writing is conceived and brought about.

At the moment when *Roots of Brazil* is being produced (and I hope to make it clear over the following chapters why I often turn to the book's first edition, from 1936), the prediction of a democratic route for Brazil is not guided by a fearless vision of some Western democratic future, nor by any sympathy for the socialist model, which Buarque de Holanda would, incidentally, make an unsuccessful attempt to see in place.[30] On the contrary, here we see the intimate and turbulent space of his consciousness, which is also the place where the writing is conceived, shot through with profound and brutal doubts. What I read in *Roots of Brazil*, as I seek to suggest, is more the torment with which the critic approaches politics than the clarity with which he addresses its challenges and dilemmas. I am drawn to the waverings and the sinuous questions that must have torn at the writer rather than the answers and the coherence of a perfectly correct political posture.

The political realm is not, for the author of *Roots of Brazil*, a field of unequivocal options able to unlock the paradise of some final solution for the collectivity (and Candido is with him on this count). Rather, for Sérgio Buarque de Holanda, politics is the realm in which the individual is reduced to debating impotently, faced with alternatives whose promises seem inevitably insufficient, if not utterly terrifying. In our secularized modernity, we often forget the religious roots of torment. In Buarque de Holanda's case, one cannot say that the trope of "demons" is a metaphor like any other. He knew what he was talking about when, at the end of *Roots of Brazil*, he suggested that a "perfidious and pretentious" demon appears to cover our eyes whenever we seek the political order that will save us in the end.[31]

It is against the eschatological and finalist horizon of the authoritarian imagination that Sérgio Buarque de Holanda will rise up. But the alternative horizon that he envisions is not a rational solution nor a well-organized alternative to the dilemmas of the collectivity. Rather, it is wracked by doubt, and ultimately by the affliction of knowing oneself to be abandoned by precisely the figure who ought to bear the solution. After all, behind the authoritarian solution on the political scene, Latin America was incubating the long-term phenomenon and the specter of populism. It is above all in this sense that *Roots of Brazil* is a creature of the 1930s.

* * *

For Buarque de Holanda, the clarity of reason, whether more or less tinged with liberal colors, cannot be enough. To make things worse, from a somehow Nietzschean angle, hopes of a final, peaceable redemption have faded away on the horizon. His world is *modern*, in the fullest sense of the word: no salvation, no moral certainty. This is an intricate, complex world where the individual is forsaken somewhere between solitude and solidarity.

It will come as no surprise when, from a few years after the publication of *Roots of Brazil* to at least the 1950s, Buarque de Holanda himself turns to a blind obsession with the nature of the modern novel. From his 1941 "Notas sobre o romance" [Notes on the Novel], published in the *Diário de Notícias* in Rio de Janeiro, to the reflections on the fiction prose in his beautiful "Em volta do círculo mágico" [Around the Magic Circle], for example, published in the same newspaper in 1950, what stands out is his investigation into the elements in the very form of the novel that destabilize any pretension of aesthetic perfection. These elements create conflict-ridden situations that, especially in the American case, lend the characters their tragic aspect and the anguish that comes from their knowing themselves to be in "permanent exile," as in the expression that Buarque de Holanda borrows from Henry James.[32]

The problem of "roots" is also central in the discussion of literature. To keep on "living" and "coexisting," in a space that emerges far from the European center, meant facing and expressing distance in relation to an aesthetic ideal, ultimately pushing the writer to an "essentially prosaic and relatively impure type of art." Buarque de Holanda is thinking of Gogol's and Dostoevsky's Russia, where "the irruption of ideas and lifestyles which are alien to ancestral patterns and tend to dilute them" opened the way for the "dramatic conflicts where the art of fiction seems to find its ideal sustenance."[33] The peripheral condition, Russia being an exemplary case, had an American dimension to it, however:

> In our America, the profound transformations that these almost alluvial societies underwent around the same period also doubtless presented a problematic or tragic aspect. While the protagonists of the drama found ready-made models, gestures copied at a distance (in space and somewhat in time, as well) refused to take on the natural and inevitable tone here that they must have

had in their places of origin. In other words, we were a peripheral world: the true center lay in Paris or London. One of our statesmen, who served the Empire and the Republic, expressed this in words for the ages: in us, he declared, the sentiment is Brazilian, the imagination European.[34]

The invocation of the statesman Joaquim Nabuco (1849–1910), and the reference to the "ineluctable continental destiny" that had haunted politicians and writers alike, leads the critic over to the other part of America (still America nonetheless)—the United States, and its relationship with England. Henry James's caricature of the "American" is thus brought in to bear witness to a discomfort ripe for fiction, while it is also, and above all, fodder for social reflection. In Buarque de Holanda's imagination, at the time of the writing, two possibilities seemed to remain open: either Brazilians could give themselves over to the "simple valorization" of national and regional motifs, writing in a "liana-wreathed" style, or—as in the rare case of Machado de Assis (1839–1908)–these merely "superficial decorations" might give way to an investigation capable of revealing "the conditions of [one's] time in [one's] country."

I will abstain here from the complex discussion around Machado de Assis. I should clarify that the critic was referring to what was then a recently released book by Lúcia Miguel Pereira, itself a part of that collection organized by Álvaro Lins, which conceived of the Machado de Assis of recent critical investigations as a "special case."[35] Expatriation—the state of feeling oneself in tension with a center that is at once close and intangible—refers to a problem of a fictional order, which has a historical and sociological side to it as well. "Roots" are an extremely powerful *topos* in Buarquian prose (from both the critic and the historian, insofar as the differences between them are meaningful), where the reading always leaves a tang of irresolution, of an attempt at something, of successive advances and retreats, where the horizon of a "Brazilian literature" is never fully revealed.

We might ultimately ask if there isn't something in Sérgio Buarque de Holanda beyond what Antonio Candido's profound criticism allows us to see. As I have sought to suggest thus far, Candido seeks out a political coherence in his friend that one cannot honestly deny but to which I would add an element of doubt—to wit, the inconstancy inherent in any and all matter constructed over time, as is of course the case of thought. In short, Buarque de Holanda's "radicalism" may not completely explain *Roots of Brazil*, in which, to use a melancholy metaphor, the black ink of suspicion around liberal theses has been laid on darkly and resists any attempt to erase it.

This is not merely an attempt to lend greater substance to the interpretation of the political proposal behind *Roots of Brazil*. Rather, I am attempting to see whether the book's very conception of Brazil rejects essentialisms (as recent critical production may suggest, incidentally). Of course Candido himself never proposed a static or essentialist image of Buarque de Holanda's work, nor would he. However, it seems to me that in terms of a discourse on what is national—that is, the fundamentally "Brazilian" aspects of those roots—Buarque de Holanda has fewer certainties than doubts; fewer proposals than apprehensions; less hope than a sinuous, at times simply discreet, melancholy.[36] Or, to move beyond mere impressions, there is a deep sense of *unbelonging* in *Roots of Brazil*, a feeling of incompleteness that stands as an ineluctable condition, or the opposite of an essence: "no Brazil exists," in the poetic formulation recently reclaimed by João Cezar de Castro Rocha, always with an eye to Sérgio Buarque de Holanda.[37]

Interestingly, Antonio Candido recognizes "Sérgio Buarque de Holanda's eminence as a literary critic, one of the greatest in Brazil's history." Candido's own towering place on the literary criticism scene in Brazil is well-known, and his frequent praises of his friend— an effort to restore the literary critic in Buarque de Holanda—are very significant.[38] In the end, a question about the differences and similarities between the two will always hang in the air. During the same decade that found Buarque de Holanda abandoning the literary criticism he had been publishing in newspapers, Candido sought to understand the manifestations that comprised Brazilian literature at its very dawn. It would be unfair and insufficient to reduce Candido's critical contribution to his monumental and perennially productive *Formação da literatura brasileira* [Formation of Brazilian Literature] (1959), but it is quite thought provoking—at least for me—to consider that just as Candido was finishing up his research for one of the most important books in the Brazilian critical tradition, Buarque de Holanda was forsaking yet another project; in fact, he never completed a book about Brazilian literature during his lifetime. This lack of conclusion may hold the secret to an oeuvre whose commitment to Brazil may not hold up against doubts around the country's constitution, or as to the very existence of an essentially comprehensible and explicable national entity. But if Brazil as an element poses such difficulties in determining its time and place, then how to imagine its roots? Where do they come from, or what do they point to?

Perhaps Sérgio Buarque de Holanda was right back in 1950. The answer is still, eternally, in the hands of Joaquim Nabuco: Brazilian sentiment and European imagination. To loosely borrow Roberto Schwarz's turn of phrase (while suggesting that the genealogy of the expression stretches quite far back in the history of Brazilian thought), we might say that this is precisely where the country's roots lie: in a strange orbit, always slightly "misplaced."[39]

* * *

Within Latin American intellectual history as a whole, Candido remains crucial in the formation of a field of research around Brazilian modernism. In this context, Buarque de Holanda stands out precisely because the intersection between social studies and literature, as I argued above, stands at the center of his work. Interpretations of Buarque de Holanda's oeuvre, despite our attempts to flee from abrupt temporal breaks, point to a watershed in the 1996 publication of *O espírito e a letra* [The Spirit and the Letter], the two volumes of literary criticism edited by Antonio Arnoni Prado.[40] As Walnice Nogueira Galvão observed, the critical reception of Sérgio Buarque de Holanda as a literary critic has just begun.[41] We are indebted to Arnoni Prado for his research and critical annotations, which have paved the way for a more nuanced and complete vision of the intellectual trajectory of the author of *Roots of Brazil*. In terms of criticism, readers already had access to *Cobra de vidro* [Glass Snake] (1944) and *Tentativas de mitologia* [Attempts at Mythology] (1979), as well as the posthumous works *Raízes de Sérgio Buarque de Holanda* and *Capítulos de literatura colonial*. But the publication of the full corpus of his literary criticism has lent the oeuvre a new dimension.

Problems align and begin to illuminate one another when the historian's reflections are read alongside those of the literary critic. In particular, I believe that the issue of order and law, as well as the letter as the negation of life, are constants throughout his work as a whole, whether in his attempt to understand new poetics—from the vanguards of the early twentieth century to the experiments of the 1950s, without forgetting the rhetorical singularity of colonial literature in Portuguese America—or in his critique of political attempts to silence people's spontaneity. In historiographical terms, for example, his analysis of the stifling of innovative trends and of the ingrained conservatism of Brazil's political and intellectual elites all but ties together the two sides to his production; it suggests that his critique of the authoritarian interwar mentality in *Roots of Brazil* is paralleled in the investigation of the antidemocratic tradition that would be resuscitated in Brazil's various dictatorships, rooted in the imperial elites' fear of any profound social change. This is exactly the picture presented in Buarque de Holanda's 1972 *Do Império à República* [From the Empire to the Republic], a book on the dictatorial leanings of the late Brazilian Empire (1822–1889), conceived and published under Brazil's last military dictatorship (1964–1985), as has already been noted.[42]

We are dealing with different territories here, but there is still room to investigate whether there are strong ties, on an analytical level, between political conservatism and a certain aesthetic conservatism. The latter, after all, implies both shackling oneself to rigid creative norms and also, on a deeper level, the definitive taming of intelligence—and hence a love of ready-made formulas. However, as Arnoni Prado notes, Buarque de Holanda made use of "all sorts of sources to reject the idea that in poetry, invention is inferior to convention, for example, and to recognize that each period recreates works in keeping with their own, familiar frameworks of taste."[43] To wit, while "convention" and "creation" may line up, the conventional can also be explained only through a deep historical sense of differences. Recall, for example, how Buarque de Holanda's analysis of the Portuguese colonial poets of the eighteenth-century school of *arcadismo* moved to substitute the notions of free inspiration and spontaneity with those of study and effort. This led a contemporary critic to praise him for precisely his analytic sensitivity to the specificity of the Luso-Brazilian colonial literary period, which lacked Romantic ideas of a unique, irreplaceable personality, not to mention nationalistic ideals themselves—notions that would thus be foreign to a contextualized (read: historicized) analysis of literature.[44] Comprehending the text would necessarily call for an empathic exercise in understanding the mentality of another time. Here, literary criticism and historical analysis join hands, and the equilibrium between "norm" and "invention" becomes prime analytic material.

The same attention to "studies" and "effort" as poetic principles, as well as a certain equilibrium between novelty and norm, would lead Buarque de Holanda to a critical vision of the so-called 1945 Generation (a group itself posterior to the first winds of Brazilian modernism). The issue of "construction" and the complexity of literature as historically formed material would also lead him to Auerbach's *Mimesis*, as we have already seen, all the while with an eye to the importance of New Criticism, whose works Buarque de Holanda accompanied with particular care and interest.[45]

* * *

To reduce *O espírito e a letra* to an array of formulas and observations would be, however, an exercise in folly. Let me simply note that, in terms of the critical reception of his work, the publication of studies on Buarque de Holanda's literary criticism did indeed, as Galvão and Candido hoped, open up an entirely new terrain for the analysis of his thought.[46] In terms of the critical restoration of Sérgio Buarque de Holanda, however, we should also recall the importance of the commemorative works produced by disciples and colleagues, especially after his death in 1982.[47] Within the scope of these publications, but also going beyond them, we find Maria Odila Leite da Silva Dias; we might say that she, like Antonio Candido, leaves an indelible mark on the comprehension of Buarque de Holanda's oeuvre in returning to an examination of its stylistic aspects and placing it in the context of the national and international historiographical debate—which is in great part what his writings are dialoguing with.[48]

In the following chapters, I will engage with both the classic critical literature on Buarque de Holanda and the texts that emerge in its wake, or against it, with special attention to the understanding of *Roots of Brazil* as a turning point in his works. If more recent studies are any indication, this "turning point" stretches on for years and perhaps even decades, until the historian and critic finally decided—particularly after the third revised Brazilian edition of *Roots of Brazil*, in 1956—to let the text alone, leaving us, his readers, faced with aporias best expressed and sustained by the idea of exile, which will resonate throughout the book.[49]

CHAPTER 2

A Familial Tragedy (in Hegel's Shadow)

Roots of Brazil, by Sérgio Buarque de Holanda, was released in 1936, the same year that Gilberto Freyre (1900–1987) brought out *Sobrados e mucambos* [The Mansions and the Shanties], three years after the publication of *The Masters and the Slaves*.[1] Like those two books, Buarque de Holanda's essay expresses the widespread commotion before a new spectacle that, of course, cannot be seen as universally Brazilian. This was the blossoming of the city, or the mental universe of the metropolis—but also the simultaneous and arresting emergence of conflict on the urban stage, both between social classes and between the familial and the public spheres. Inasmuch as this also expressed a struggle between classes, exacerbating the exploitation and centuries-old exclusion of the poor, that conflict also bloomed in the heart of each man—each citizen, that is.

The *heart* takes on extraordinary power in the body of this essay, or rather the body of essays that is *Roots of Brazil*.[2] As an emblem of that power, the first edition of the book contained an epigraph to the chapter on the "cordial man," although it would be omitted in later editions. This was a snippet from Samuel Johnson, although attributed to Milton, with the following exclamation: "How small of all that human hart endure / That part that kings or laws can cause or cure."[3] In a poetic register, the heart is not merely a pulsating irrigator, but also the center of life itself—that is to say, the intersection of passions (in an archaic register) or emotions (in a modern sense with a Romantic air about it). However, we cannot understand Samuel Johnson's text outside the register of passion, or the pathos that dominates the mind and body of man. The cordial man, in this case.

If it is true that *Roots of Brazil* expresses the conflict between the familial and public spheres, it will be important to trace, albeit briefly, the characteristics that define the relevant types in this essay, looking to hit upon the outline that will crystallize into the cordial man in the fifth chapter. The formulation of types such as the "worker" and the "adventurer," beyond the German inspiration behind them (as will be noted below), suggests an array of sources as diverse as Paretian sociology, with its *speculatori* and *rentieri*, and a then-budding branch of North American sociology.

As for Vilfredo Pareto (1848–1923), there are notable similarities— which Buarque de Holanda himself would indicate from the essay's first edition—between the Brazilian author's formulations and the defining characteristics of several of the portraits sprung from the pen of the Italian social scientist. In conjuring up speculators and rentiers, within the complex and rich framework of "logical" and "nonlogical" actions, Pareto refers to figures he dubs "entrepreneurs," as well as "owners of savings." I will not flesh out those categories here, but I should recall that Pareto may at times remind us of a physiognomist in the style of, say, Charles Le Brun. His writings include at least one curiously zoomorphic description, when men suddenly seem like rabbits: owners of savings are "quiet, timorous souls sitting at all times with their ears cocked in apprehension, like rabbits, and hoping little and fearing much from any change." Entrepreneurs, meanwhile, are adventurers, given to movement and vast expanses.[4]

Let me close my Paretian parenthesis and open up a cleft in which North American sociology can flow: Buarque de Holanda would be an attentive reader of the extensive work of William Isaac Thomas (1863–1947) and Florian Znaniecki (1882–1958) on Polish former peasants in the city of Chicago in the 1920s, although perhaps only after the release of the first edition of *Roots of Brazil*.[5] The dimensions of time and space, essential in Buarque de Holanda's imagination, are crucially present in the framework Thomas used to establish the "four fundamental desires," to quote a simplification of his theory in a manual by Park and Burgess, which the Brazilian historian would also use to a great degree.[6] It is equally important, in this case, to recognize how the shaping of attitudes or social actions on the methodological terrain trod by Thomas and Znaniecki is guided precisely by a value-based system, thus linking actions to certain values shared by individuals. In *Roots of Brazil*, however, this method does not result in schemes born of a supposedly neutral analysis of reality—on the contrary, it spawns frameworks that are highly dependent on the author's gaze, the cultural universe from which he is examining historical sources, and the relationship between his own storytelling and the constellation of problems of his time.

Beyond underlining the typological characteristics found in the formulation of William Isaac Thomas's "four fundamental desires," which may also be found in the formulation of the types in *Roots of Brazil* after its second (1948) edition, I might recall an element that seems especially relevant in this theory born on North American soil: its empiricism. In serving as the object of Thomas's and Znaniecki's sociological work—a sort of cornerstone of the Chicago School, responsible for a unique take on Max Weber in the United States, with global consequences—the story of Polish former peasants in a city like Chicago is the experience of terror and fascination before the emerging metropolis. But this was more than the Orphic enchantment with the megalopolis, which would guide vanguard aesthetics in the 1920s;[7] this was also the fear and dread struck into immigrants' hearts. In this case, fear dwelt in the hearts of those members of the families of former peasants who, upon cutting themselves loose from the familial fabric, deepened the experience that Oswald de Andrade would dub, in his interpretation of *Roots of Brazil*, "desolidarization."[8]

In *Roots of Brazil*'s diagnosis, the symptom of this desolidarization is, more or less in line with Gilberto Freyre, a certain sense of orphanhood. Families saw the fraying of their social structure, which had retained at least some rigidity until then, while Brazilian society seemed ruled by the whims of the *pater familias* and his discretionary power. *Sobrados e mucambos* presents a somewhat less gloomy picture, however: no longer the welcoming shade of the magnificent, "democratic" trees around historic Recife, as we shall see in the next chapter, now Freyre turned to the shadow of the future to be resisted, from his vantage point on the mansion's veranda. In the case of *Roots of Brazil*, there is also a play of shadows here, although the light is not shining directly from an idealized Iberian past, nor from a sweetened vision of miscegenation. The light filters in slowly through a painstaking array of contrasts, in a prose more halting than Freyre's, as Alfredo Bosi observed.[9]

Matters of language are not secondary. Buarque de Holanda's prose, on that note, is far more discreet than Freyre's. Discreet, but dense and halting prose. Under an apparently fluid veneer, we glimpse a world of tensions, a mesh that expresses the confrontation between the spheres of the family and the city. This is no longer essayistic expressionism, or Paulo Prado's self-proclaimed "Impressionism" in his 1928 *Retrato do Brasil* [Portrait of Brazil], but the expression of conflict in the very logic of the text, through an array of oppositions, or in Antonio Candido's oft-quoted turn of phrase, an "admirable methodology of opposites."[10] Opposing types are set against one another in this game: adventure and work, city and country, Spanish and Portuguese, Jesuits and Protestants, cordiality and individuality. Opposites come into conflict, and elucidation comes in the dialectical antithesis: that what is *not* contains the secret of that which *is*.

Max Weber, in turn, provided more than a typological architecture formed in the wake of the methodological debates whose echoes Buarque de Holanda would hear *in loco*, in Germany, as we have seen. At the end of a series of reflections on the bourgeoisie, the author of *The Protestant Ethic and the Spirit of Capitalism* formulates a notion of the "market," in which people are made utterly abstract and individuals find themselves surrounded by products and things, abandoned to the nonsense of an immanent, infinite progress. Headed for where? The question pulsates here, in beautiful passages from Weber, that obstinate reader of Tolstoy.[11] The same question also lurks between the lines of *Roots of Brazil*.

It has been observed that the essay does not answer any questions; but neither is this its nature. The essay does not answer, it provokes; it does not resolve, it disputes; it does not fix, it shifts. The constant change in focus, in somewhat erratic prose, is the weapon that lays out the conflict: between the family and that which transcends it. In the chapter on the cordial man, Buarque de Holanda turns to the works of Sophocles—or, rather, to a certain reading of Greek tragedy—to identify, in the conflict between Creon and Antigone, the expression of the negation of the familial sphere, with the affirmation of an ethic that is not natural, but universal. His reference is the light that Hegel sheds on Sophocles's play: the author of *The Phenomenology of Spirit* argues that the ethical, transcending the natural order that reigns over the family, stakes out a place in the universal. The ethical is the universal in and of itself, denying the immediacy and singularity of the family. The archetypal tension around this contradiction is, in Hegel's text, the relationship between brother and sister.[12]

The brother is the side of the family that turns to the Other and passes on the consciousness of universality; he obtains effective ethicality, becoming conscious of himself, when he transcends and negates the familial sphere, as defended in the figure of the sister. I call attention to this part of Hegel's reasoning because it strikes me as extremely significant that Buarque de Holanda muddled his reference to the relationship between Creon and Antigone, calling them siblings in *Roots of Brazil*, when they are in fact uncle and niece (Creon is Jocasta's brother, not Oedipus's): "Creon incarnates the abstract, impersonal idea of the city in a struggle against the concrete and tangible reality: the family. By burying Polyneices against the orders of the state, Antigone draws the ire of her brother [sic], who acts in the name not of his personal will, but of the supposed general will of the citizens, of the city-state."[13]

The "slip" in the text is not random, as it echoes the contradiction between the force of the Law of the City (represented by Creon) and the strength of the heart—a "cordial" power—as seen in Antigone. After all, in burying Polyneices, Antigone commits a crime, knowing that her defiance of Creon's order, and by extension of the will of the collectivity, spells her death.

It may help to set Hegel aside for a moment and turn our attention to Sophocles himself.[14] The last in the so-called Theban trilogy, the play opens with a dialogue between the sisters Ismene and Antigone, just after the failed attempt at invading Thebes has culminated in the deaths of Eteocles and Polyneices—both sons and brothers of

Oedipus. As ruler of the city, Creon decrees that faithful Eteocles be buried but prohibits anyone from giving Polyneices a decent burial on pain of death, ordering that his body be thrown to the dogs. The predicament before young, bold Antigone is precisely her desire to give her brother a funeral, which would force her to disrespect Creon's ban. (This may be the most dramatic case of that which Bataille would identify as the profound complicity between the law and its violation.)[15]

Ismene, the fearful sister, tells Antigone that "a hopeless quest should not be made at all," to which Antigone responds by asking her to respect this madness of hers. ("But leave me, and the folly that is mine alone, to suffer this dread thing.") Pathos emerges as a negation of the law, and the flouting of the civic order is the flip side of a desire to respect the dead, and a brother at that—although he was not acting in accordance with the supposed collective will of the city. It becomes difficult, here, to read Sophocles while listening to Hegel. After all, in Creon's prohibition there lies not only universal ethicality, as Hegel would have it, but also the underlying arbitrary, violent nature of the laws of the City. To take this even further: let us leave Hegel for a moment to understand the darkest and, paradoxically, most luminous aspect of *Roots of Brazil*, being the irresolution of conflict:

> Indeed, the most suggestive link between Sérgio Buarque de Holanda's essay and the genre illustrated by Sophocles' *Antigone* springs from this muddying of their luminous and Apollonian aspects, to use the illustrious category somewhat loosely, when within reason there blooms contradiction, the movement in the opposite direction, the ambivalent negation of the desired thing—and when the book, seemingly a prognosis, silences any liberating solution in its examination of the frightening depths of that which it calls "roots."[16]

The absence of a programmatic ending in *Roots of Brazil* may not simply be a sign of openness to the future, as has often been hopefully proposed.[17] Rather than an opening, this irresolution is home to an ambivalent and unconfessed well of conservation. Not "conservatism" as such, but conservation, perhaps, of the irresistible force of the heart beating madly in the deleted epigraph by John Milton—Samuel Johnson, rather—in the 1936 edition. If there is indeed a conflict between the family and the city, the domestic nucleus and the state, then *Roots of Brazil* does not lead us toward the simple victory of the civic spirit. That spirit is evidently often behind the machine of legitimate violence, whenever the civilizing project is declared and put in motion. The year 1936, for that matter, was not so far from the first popular revolts that had hampered some of the Brazilian Republic's civilizing initiatives, nor too distant from the decades in which the workers' movement attained unheard-of levels of organization in the country.[18]

Even political radicalism, in the sense that Antonio Candido lends it, is eclipsed if we believe that that heart continues to beat. Although the construction of memory around the historian often conjures up the image of a bust of a serenely liberal-democratic Sérgio Buarque de Holanda, we would do well to remember that with the 1930s in full swing, totalitarianism was not quite the creature we understand it to be today, and the field of values, to borrow the rhetoric of Weber and Nietzsche, had seductive demons posted on both sides, the Right and the Left.

Candido's interpretation offers a reading that aligns Buarque de Holanda to the also "radical" Joaquim Nabuco and André Rebouças, as I have noted.[19] From his perspective, this is not, however, an attempt at a soft-focus portrait of the author of *Roots of Brazil*, although the "radicalism" attributed here ultimately presents him as an exemplary character in that lineage. The challenge in understanding Buarque de Holanda may then lie, if I am not mistaken, in the possibility of delving into just what that radicalism disguises and which may reveal itself at the points when doubt appears in the text. I should say once again that this is not to deny Antonio Candido's interpretation and see Sérgio Buarque de Holanda as seduced by the "other side," that is, totalitarianism or conservatism. We should recall that even the countless alterations to the text of *Roots of Brazil*, starting with the second edition, do not alter its air of doubt. While he denied the solutions of Order—in a subliminal dialogue with an entire authoritarian tradition, with Oliveira Vianna at its head and Catholic conservative thinking as one of its fulcrums—Buarque de Holanda is frequently seen to question the liberal option, going so far as to remind us of the fallacy in the affirmation that tyrannical expedients can produce no lasting and interesting results.[20]

The conflict between the familial sphere and public order stands as a provocative tension in *Roots of Brazil*. This is a battle of values, with no space for compassion. The conflict is expressed in the perennially insoluble clash between the heart of young Antigone and the violence of Creon, the man who is serving as the supreme guide of the state, and shall be judged as such. If we return to Sophocles, we will see that Antigone does not waver. When asked why she was driven to return her traitorous brother (Polyneices) to the earth, she responds beautifully: "It was his [Eteocle's] brother, not his slave, that perished."[21] In the very breast of the city, Polyneices and Antigone, the accursed children of Oedipus, become criminals. It is in the vast city, the megalopolis, that the foreigner becomes a stranger, just as man becomes strange to man himself.

The stranger is he who arrives from outside the city, and adventure comes from the Latin *advenire*, "to arrive." I believe this is also the "adventure" of which Buarque de Holanda speaks in *Roots of Brazil*. The Fall is not merely surrender before a welcoming piece of ground, but means more: the abandonment of a world in which spirits have not yet settled around human norms, and where laws themselves seem dictated by nature, or by the gods. A furious Creon argues that a good man cannot be equated to an evil one. Antigone replies, "Who knows but this seems blameless in the world below?" Consecration is violated by the will of the unjust laws of the City. Taking her orders from another time, one to which Creon does not belong, Antigone speaks of a universe where evil and good are unequivocal, within the sacred order of the family. Creon believes that he is speaking in name of his citizens, but in doing so he defiles the familial order, bringing death to the scattered members of an accursed line.

There can be no sturdy bridge between such far-flung works. Even so, we can see how the impossibility of a solution in the classical plot is so uncomfortable that Hegel's discourse will completely pave over that irresolution, creating a world of clear oppositions and feeding into an overarching confidence in the victory of the Spirit, which will always be on Creon's side. The violence of such a reading would only help "clarify" Buarque de Holanda's reading if we believed, making his discourse into a blank slate, that the order of the City ought to prevail over the familial order at any cost. The teleology implicit in an inexorable "revolution" is one possible reading of *Roots of Brazil*, but a mistaken one. It is true that a subterranean revolution is gnawing away at the rural pillars supporting the cordial man, as we will see, but it is no less true that the "more intimate and essential world," as we read in *Roots of Brazil*, stands, troubling, defying any and all capricious solutions in terms of politics, or even interpretations.

The order of the City breaks onto the scene, corrupting the cordial organism sustained by familial ties. Antonio Candido is precisely the person to help us here. In a classic study from the 1950s on *caipiras paulistas* (those living in the countryside of the state of São Paulo) and their ways of life, he makes reference to a reality that might serve as an illustration of the collapse of all models of family life, seen here in miniature by the empathic observer:

> But the feeling of kinship is being wiped away, as, tossed from one place to another by the vicissitudes of work, the landless *caipira* becomes detached from siblings, aunts and uncles, and parents in general. At the same time, the bonds of *compadresco* [the relationships around the act of godparenting] slacken, as in their mobility, individuals grow distant from one another, and relationships suffer as a result. To sum up this part, we might say that mobility, in its ancient and current forms, acts to dissolve kinship and *compadresco*, and leads the nuclear family to close in on itself.[22]

In a sociological line of reasoning—and, we might note, broadly supported by Buarque de Holanda's research post–*Roots of Brazil*[23]— Candido would use the image of the "atrophied *bandeirante* [frontiersman]" to speak of a regression in terms of urban patterns, with the creation of a world that emerges outside the influence of cities and which, from a sociological point of view, might be considered dangerously close to anomie: a world outside civilization, or a culture that is naturally resistant to it.

When equilibrium, even if it is an ominous one from a political point of view, is broken, tragedy is on the horizon. I think that *Roots of Brazil* may be understood as not only a drama of the formation of the public space in Brazil, but also of the tragedy that marks the ruin of an older, warm familial order. This is how we may see the narration of the shift from corporative to wage labor in the book:

> Whoever ... compares the labor system of the old corporations and craftsmen's guilds with the "wage slavery" of modern factories possesses a precious element for judging the social unrest of our days. In the old corporations, the master and his apprentices and day-workers made up a family, whose members were subject to a natural hierarchy but shared the same privations and comforts. The modern industrial system, by separating employers and employees in the manufacturing process and increasingly differentiating their functions, has suppressed the intimate atmosphere between the two and has stimulated class antagonisms. The new system made it easier, moreover, for the capitalist to exploit the labor of his employees in exchange for trifling wages.[24]

Beyond the idealization of the age of the "old corporations," we should note that this is not a wake for the ruined order of the patriarchal family only. Instead, Buarque de Holanda is emphasizing the ruin of all families in a painful process that marks a universal conflict—to wit, the fraying of the social fabric, as the complex weft and warp of traditional sociability becomes undone, when the welcoming shade of the primary nucleus becomes insufficient and can no longer give meaning to the still-precarious existence of the line. This is, in other words, a modern plot; the individual is thrown into the whirlwind of the unknown, in the enigmatic, disturbing city coming into focus in the 1920s and 1930s, which would also provide ample material for fiction and poetry both in Brazil and abroad.

If these suggestions seem reasonable, then one might imagine that *Roots of Brazil* has few or no proposals at its core. The book speaks of a world in ruins, rejecting brilliant and compensatory edifications. We may read it in this tone, not merely as the narrative of the collapse of the colonial order, but as essentially motivated by the ruin of working families in modernity. In Brazil, this period saw immigrants, former slaves, workers who were never sufficiently "free," and their descendants come together under the deceptive republican sun. A period of the loosening of bonds that seemed to keep people united, for better or for worse. An inexorable outcome ordained by the indifferent, insensible hand of the men who, expelled from time and the ancient world, set about wandering through the city, tormented and errant, seeming exiles in the land of men itself. Or, as a poet would say in another context, each of them feeling himself, in the end, "a pilgrim in his own land."[25]

CHAPTER 3

Rural Roots of the Brazilian Family

Sérgio Buarque de Holanda and Gilberto Freyre

Although *The Masters and the Slaves* may be the best-known book of Gilberto Freyre (1900–1987), *Sobrados e mucambos* [The Mansions and the Shanties], published in 1936, is a crucial reference for understanding the urbanization and decline of patriarchalism in Brazil. *Roots of Brazil*, whose first edition dates from the same year, also addresses urbanization, as well as the loss of that which Buarque de Holanda would call the "rural roots" of Brazilian society. In both cases, the second edition would come out more than ten years after the first, with substantial revisions and additions to the text, incorporating or fending off a number of critiques, which is an indication of the respective authors' intense engagement with critical literature and primary sources. Though these were works from relatively young writers (Buarque de Holanda was thirty-four years old when *Roots of Brazil* came off the presses, and Freyre was thirty-six when *Sobrados e mucambos* was published), both essays are charged with such polemical and stylistic strength that one is tempted to use them as a prism by which to understand the intellectual trajectory of the authors over the following decades.[1]

In both cases, the influence of modernism around the time of their intellectual formation is quite manifest. Note, however, that modernism in Brazil, unlike the late-nineteenth-century modernism of Hispanic America, should be considered part and parcel with the vanguards elsewhere, especially after the famous Modern

Art Week of 1922 in São Paulo, although the movement takes on an openly nationalistic tone at a number of points, especially over the course of the next decade, in the context of the political and cultural reorganization under Getúlio Vargas's first presidency (1930–1945).

In any case, back in the "heroic" years of Brazilian modernism, shortly after the *Semana de 22*, Buarque de Holanda stood out for his intransigent defense of the renewal of language, the "descoelhonetização" (dis-Coelho-Netization) of literature, as he put it at the time, in an ironic reference to the *passadista*, or "backwards-looking," poet Henrique Maximiliano Coelho Neto (1864–1934).[2] As Freyre saw it, the renewal of language would also be fundamental, not only from an aesthetic angle, but also as a scientific and literary project. That said, urges toward renewal could not smooth over latent differences and tensions, these less simply personal than regional: Buarque de Holanda spoke of the Brazilian Southeast (home to Rio de Janeiro and his native São Paulo), while Freyre tended to write about the Northeast (the region of his home state of Pernambuco). In Freyre's case, in order to understand this regionalist bent, we might simply recall the debate around his 1926 *Manifesto Regionalista* [Regionalist Manifesto], and the care he took to affirm the Northeast as an active, productive hub in the creation of a literature that was both modern and profoundly regional, tied to local language in all its variety, and which in turn would seek to denounce the grotesque side of the "pseudo-architects" of modernist literature in São Paulo, as Mário Marroquim so acidly put it.[3]

The latent friction between their visions, while present since the formative years of both, did not impede the construction of a sort of mythology around their youthful camaraderie—when, back in their intellectual Bohemia in Rio de Janeiro, they shared in the same ideas and showed off their erudition. The mystical air around these encounters has practically reached the status of a *topos* in the imagination of Brazilian modernism. In an article published shortly after Buarque de Holanda's death in 1982, Freyre referred to his old colleague as a "master of masters," in a very Freyrian recollection of the harmony of a common youth lost in time:

Bohemians, in our taste for Brazilian, Afro-Brazilian, Carioca popular music. More than once, sunup caught us [with Prudente de Moraes Neto], drinking beers in traditional Rio bars, listening to those we considered supremely Brazilian, both masters and friends of Brazilian culture, Donga, Patrício [Teixeira], and Pixinguinha. Sources, for the three of us, of an authentically popular culture that was extra-European at its base, and a good part of which was in the music that they mastered.... Back then, we three were modernists, in our own way. But nostalgic, too. Affinities between this modernism—that of *Estética*—and the radiant "regionalism" of Recife.[4]

Although he calls attention to their common liking of samba and the Rio de Janeiro nightlife in the 1920s, also referring to *Estética* magazine (inspired by T. S. Eliot's *The Criterion*), all three issues of which would be edited by Buarque de Holanda and Prudente de Moraes Neto, Freyre does not reveal in these laudatory recollections that the "modernist" ranks in which he and the future author of *Roots of Brazil* had enlisted were divergent factions, nor that they would take different approaches to the development of language and the recovery of the past.

As for Buarque de Holanda, his concern with the condition of the writer and the impasses of writing manifests itself very early—this, incidentally, being the link between the young article writer and the older scholar, who believed that the historian should always tackle the complicated mission of "reviving" specific phenomena so as to unearth their cultural and historical nexuses, a challenge that was as much narrative as methodological. In this respect, the words of a septuagenarian Sérgio Buarque de Holanda are illuminating. The opening of *Tentativas de mitologia* [Attempts at Mythology] (1979) finds him affirming that the historian, "in dealing with particular phenomena so as to revive them in their pulsations and due density, so that they fit within broader contexts, taking on new and higher dimensions and meanings, must ... turn to resources of expression besides those of a mere report or a scientific exposition. If this is not so, one will never obtain the rank of historian."[5]

The young writer, as he developed *Roots of Brazil*, may not have felt the need for such a zealous separation between science and literature. His debut book stands in a hazy zone—not only between Europe and Africa, but also between the "scientific" disciplines and art. It would hardly be a stretch to suggest that *Roots of Brazil* takes part in a long essayistic tradition begun in the nineteenth century and which would reach its peak in Brazil under modernism, in works with a frankly impressionistic tone, as in the notable case of Paulo Prado's 1928 *Retrato do Brazil* [Portrait of Brazil].[6]

It seems clear, however, that in flirting with a rigor that we can safely refer to as academic by this point, *Roots of Brazil* differentiates itself from Prado's essay. Buarque de Holanda makes use of an elaborate theoretical framework in his understanding of history. To use an image that I will return to in a later chapter, *Roots of Brazil* is the site of a battle with words. The revision of the text for the second edition, in 1948, leaves little room for doubt on this count. Beyond the ideological and typological aspects from which the author slowly seeks to unshackle himself, the attention paid to words shows us a writer oscillating between a demand for stricter objectivity and a personal tone in his expression. In this respect, as well, the "Germans" that Antonio Candido refers to may have served as an inspiration. We have only to recall the dilemmas of Max Weber and his expressed desire to someday use writing the way that a great musician used a score.[7]

We are speaking here of the desire to refer to several things at once, in a synchrony of expression that, in its very impossibility, touches off the historian's anguish. How, in using a variety of sources—the accounts of chroniclers and travelers, documents from the Crown and other parties—could one establish a discourse that might illuminate the dilemmas laid bare by urbanization, in the context of the Iberian colonial heritage? The vocabulary at the historian's disposition was not up to the task; nor was there, by the 1930s, a solid tradition of sociological or historical studies, to say nothing of a truly technical lexicon one might use. It is in this sense that the three "great" interpreters of Brazil, in Candido's view—Caio Prado Júnior, Sérgio Buarque de Holanda, and Gilberto Freyre—would be seen as pioneers, as well: the semantic universe that they dealt with overflowed the expressive capacities of the vocabulary available up to that point. The meaning of colonization escaped words. At the same time, a still-faltering, still-incipient tradition practically forced them into eclecticism. It was a necessary eclecticism, and perhaps an inevitable one, which meant an almost constant transit between literature and social sciences in this period before academic knowledge was truly institutionalized in Brazil.

Symptomatically, for example, Buarque de Holanda's first teaching experience came at the ephemeral Universidade do Distrito Federal, in Rio de Janeiro, around the time that *Roots of Brazil* was published. The Universidade de São Paulo (USP), meanwhile, although it had incorporated the old Escola de Direito do Largo de São Francisco, a law school dating from the previous century, would have its triumphal inauguration only in 1934. Buarque de Holanda would come to teach there in the late 1950s, meanwhile, having returned to the city. We might say that it is only then that he finally becomes an academic in the institutional sense of the word.[8]

Freyre, for his part, was never an academic, although he would give countless talks and teach as a visiting professor at universities across the world. In any case, the movement between literature and the sciences is even clearer in his case (as it is more programmatic for him). None who have read him would deny that the Pernambucan sociologist was a gifted writer. That being said, his beautiful sentences and colorful images may be of less interest here than the methodological implications of his turning to literature, or the resources of literature, which highlights the topic of eclecticism. In countless passages across *The Masters and the Slaves* and *Sobrados e mucambos*, Freyre openly preaches greater methodological flexibility in the attempt to apprehend an intimate history of the Brazilian family. The reader of a work like the latter is constantly faced with affirmations of the insufficiency of an exclusively sociological, exclusively anthropological, or exclusively psychological approach. *Exclusivity* is a forbidden concept in Freyre's texts.[9] Moreover, his oft-praised or -questioned ability to amalgamate disparate elements suggests an ability to make antagonisms coexist serenely, within language.

This eclecticism would become a target for many sociologists' criticisms—especially, and not by chance, those from São Paulo, as I noted in the Introduction to this book. This is not a case of a simple regional war, however, although the "region" would become a fundamental element, especially after the 1930s in Brazil, whether in addressing broad questions around the economic and social development of the country or in the battle waged over the creation of a language able to fuse the universal and the local, and thus crossing geographical and poetic borders in speaking of both economic development and the ruins and wreckage it leaves in its wake. Once again, the problem was at once scientific and literary.[10]

Eclecticism, we might as well say explicitly, is one of the mortal sins that both Buarque de Holanda and Freyre would be accused of for quite some time. Curiously, the latter maintained a lifelong fidelity to a spirit that rejected academic compartmentalization, while the former built a career in higher education that would mold him, even as he helped to mold what would come to be, at least in the context of historical studies in Brazil, the career of the historian.[11] The fact that Buarque de Holanda himself helped to found the Instituto de Estudos Brasileiros at USP in the 1960s may be read as a symptom of the search for an antidote against strict specialization, with the promotion of a transdisciplinary ideal that still remains as dear as it is difficult to realize. In one way or another, and even once he had become a respected historian, I argue that he would never fully escape the shadow that many of those at USP cast around his debut book.[12]

Returning to Freyre, I should emphasize the erratic and digressive bent to his prose, which has given rise to both stinging critiques and fervent admiration, recalling his notably "Proustian," rather than "Durkheimian," approach to his object. Proust is evoked in the "Introduction" to the second edition (1951) of *Sobrados e mucambos*:

> The point of interest in our studies of Brazil's patriarchal society is not to prove that it is possible to study this or that subject under a single criterion and by a single method—sociology, say,

or history. The point of interest is the maximum illumination of the subject: a subject in its generality, independent of time and space, and in its particularities, limited in time and space. Thus we do not shy from impressionism itself, when necessary: the [style] that, in literature, even historical literature, is like Impressionism in painting, an attempt to surprise life in movement, and thus variable, depending on the interpretative criterion with which one surprises it. We should guard against facile, irresponsible impressionism, whether journalistic or belletristic, without shunning the variety that sheds light as a direct, almost immediate vision of an event seen or reconstituted practically with the naked eye, whether confirmed or not by techniques of verification. On the past, one might borrow Proust's words on the world: it is constantly being recreated by art. And science may take after art, [in] the search for or pursuit of the complex reality lying within apparently dead events, just as in still lifes [*natureza morta*, or "dead nature" in Portuguese]: both valorized and incorporated into human knowledge by the impressionism that reveals the slippery or fleeting aspects of a reality that is ostensibly alive, or only apparently dead.[13]

This is an intentionally controversial claim: "impressionism" and "eclecticism" together, defended as fundamental elements in the reconstruction and recuperation of the vital force of past, "apparently" dead things. The reference to impressionist painting alongside the alleged Proustian link is peculiar. After all, if we look to find a difference between Proust and the impressionists, we soon find the decrepit bourgeoisie of the portrait he paints of lost time, while painting *en plein air*, as in the case of the impressionist painters, generally celebrates the fatuous joy of that very same social class, which was indeed ascending, and not only in France.

In Freyre's case, one has only to recall the tone around the reconstitution of the private world of a decadent social class—more celebratory than critical—to see that these are not chance references. The question remains as to which is his "madeleine," the poetic element that can restore the light to a lost, longed-for past, projected in a mythical dimension that is simultaneously historical and personal. Literature and history, together; or, we might say: history in literature and through it.

Walt Whitman is another writer evoked here. "Good gray Whitman," as Freyre wrote, "in his open-collared shirt, in his white nurse's smock, in his typesetter's work clothes," a symbol of "integral, pan-human, pan-democratic Americanism."[14] The list of inspirations might stretch on: from the Victorians recovered by Maria Lúcia Pallares-Burke to the Spanish of the Generation of '98, studied by Elide Rugai Bastos. In both cases, we have illuminating studies of Freyre's intellectual trajectory, with a keen eye to the literary molds that leave their mark on it.[15]

Rather than returning to the pantheon of his intellectual heroes, I would like to emphasize, in a counterpoint with Buarque de Holanda, the importance in Freyre's sociology of the full recovery of a lost time by means of poetry. Penetrating into the intimate history of the Brazilian family might be possible through an empathic, vicarious language, retrieving and reviving daily life in the Big House and the slaves' quarters, the mansion and the shanties, or the intermediate spaces that both separate and connect them. Interestingly, the relatively recent *História da vida privada no Brasil* [History of Private Life in Brazil], inspired by Philippe Ariès and Georges Duby's approach in France, does not shy away from Freyre's broad novelty, and presents *Sobrados e mucambos* as a sort of godfather figure, as we hear from Luiz Felipe de Alencastro, editor of the volume on the Empire:

> More so than *The Masters and the Slaves* (1933), a book that takes great flights in time and space, *Sobrados e mucambos* draws close to the gold standards of the great history-books: a topic defined by the knowledge of a specific circumstance (the urbanization of the rural patriarchal family), a time period befitting the theme (the Empire, the stage for the shift from the Big House to urban mansions), and, finally, sources befitting the problem and the era (diaries, correspondence, travelers' narratives, newspapers, and 19th-century university theses).[16]

Biographical elements are obviously important, as Freyre is not speaking of some foreign reality, but rather of the patriarchal past to which he is an heir. The oft-repeated accusation that he saw Brazil from the veranda of the Big House ought to be considered along with the observation that he did not limit himself to that space, although his perspective is doubtless indebted to a sensibility that he sought to both critique and defend. His point of view is that of an heir of a broader patriarchal mentality, a continuer—through his poetics—of that which was being lost in terms of economy and society. It is, in short, the perspective of a "conservative," to recall the label that he accepted as he vigorously rejected the imprecation of "reactionary."[17]

To return to convergences and differences, we might see a series of affinities, but also incompatibilities, between *Sobrados e mucambos* and *Roots of Brazil*. Both discuss the agrarian origins of Brazilian society and the weight of the familial and domestic sphere on the political culture and sociability forged out of the colony. Here lies an internal counterpoint between the works, however: each speaks of the *city* when speaking of the Brazilian agrarian past, referring broadly to the development of a new urban patriarchy, or to the dissolution of traditional patriarchal bonds. One might say that creative drive and theoretical zeal come together, in both cases, for a solution—or at least for a clarification—of urban dilemmas, each turning to the establishment of an impersonal political order and observing, albeit in different tones and from different angles, the values that guide individuals in the city, bringing to the fore the issue of the workforce, particularly after the official end of the transatlantic slave trade in 1850 and the fate of the rural and urban classes in Brazil.

If we can indeed imagine a dialogue between the two works, the reader will still not find clear and constant references in the books to one another. There is, however, a series of points of contact, moments in which they draw close or distance themselves, in clashes, assimilations, and critiques, which may be identified. The common jumping-off point is, as I suggested, urbanization—to wit, the revolution of the city, in one case, and the momentary destabilization of antagonisms, in the other. But there is one point at which the dialogue becomes more tangible, placing the authors face-to-face. This is the 1951 publication of a series of articles in Rio de Janeiro's *Diário Carioca* and in the *Folha da Manhã* in São Paulo, with an extensive review of *Sobrados e mucambos* from Sérgio Buarque de Holanda. In it the São Paulo–born historian lays out a series of laudatory references, tempered by a severe overarching critique that particularly addresses the organization of ideas in Freyre's oeuvre, especially in the announced (and never completely finished) books that would comprise the "Introduction to the History of Patriarchal Society in Brazil," *The Masters and the Slaves* and *Sobrados e mucambos* being the first volumes.

The critique becomes evident in his evaluation of the five volumes published up to that point, which constituted a "truly monumental" work, according to the author of the review, having attained a "well-defined organic unity." However, that which had seemed like a compliment at first glance actually announces a critical take on this "organic cycle" in which Brazilian patriarchal and semipatriarchal society allegedly found itself, including "birth, maturity, decline, [and] death." On this note, Buarque de Holanda exposes the harshest angle of his critique, returning to the problem of language:

> Principally as a result of that organic structure, he [Freyre] was able to ultimately master, and give form, meaning, and value to a vast array of material often incompatible with any approach founded on the resources of natural sciences. Such an approach would doubtless demand a more prolonged examination of the conditioning processes or intersections that link often-contradictory aspects of reality, more so than of the aspects themselves, presented in raw, suggestive hues. The author's process, which is fundamentally cumulative, still emphasizes those traits that, in striking a deep blow at the imagination, seem to animate the events with a life of their own, incompatible with writings that feature more rigorous discursive reasoning.[18]

In exploring the constitution of Freyre's discourse, Buarque de Holanda sharply reinforces his colleague's distance from a rigorously—or exclusively—scientific approach, and especially those approaches that feature methods of the natural sciences. So far we might read this as a simple compliment, since Buarque de Holanda's theoretical affiliations also set him resolutely apart from the hard sciences, leaning closer to the field where, in the German nomenclature of the nineteenth century, blossoms the "science of spirit."[19] This will lead, however, into a severe critique of empathetic closeness; Freyre, in his liberally strewn language, draws altogether too close to his object, becoming a sort of guardian of patriarchal values. In Buarque de Holanda's words, his

> attention[,] fixed on concrete facts, more so than abstractions and ideas, determined to penetrate into the most secret nooks and crannies, only becomes truly effective, however, when it is driven by an intense affective warmth. His is a "close vision," amorous even in repulsion; this is what makes it naturally partial and exclusivist. His so often-iterated support for the preservation of regional styles and values across Brazil is fed by a fervent—in some cases, we might say almost nostalgic—devotion to certain traditional values and styles of the area dominated in the past by a latifundiary monoculture, and above all by sugar-cane cultivation, founded on slave labor.[20]

We see here a recurring critique of Freyre's work—which, incidentally, would be joined to another reproof, this one more methodological than ideological, aimed at the fundamental way in which the organization and constitution of mentalities in colonial and imperial Brazil are presented. *Semi-feudal, patriarchal,* and *tutelary family* are terms that the author of *Sobrados e mucambos* employed to address not merely a regional phenomenon, or the localized manifestation of a certain kind of sociability, but rather the fundamental form of a sociability in place across the whole of Brazil. At the end of his lengthy Introduction to the second edition of the book, in referring to the relative continuity between the cultural traits of the masters of the plantation houses and the masters of urban mansions, Freyre recalls that they are distinct in substance, but not in their fundamental form. "As differences in form," he writes, "are the sociologically significant [ones], we shall repeat that those of substance become, from a sociological or historico-sociological perspective, negligible."

What is at stake are the rural origins of the Brazilian family, situated sociologically (or *fundamentally*, in this imagining of things) in the sugar plantation Northeast of his childhood. This clarifies critiques of the prominence he lends the Northeast, which in turn casts its shadow over the rest of the country, as if his "Pernambucanness," back around the period of the *Regionalist Manifesto*, were cropping up again in his social analysis, with a focus that, while not exclusive, does privilege the Northeast, and Pernambuco in particular. It is striking how much care Freyre takes in the prefaces to the second and third editions of *Sobrados e mucambos* to reaffirm his thesis of Brazil as a constellation of regions with its chief star in the Northeast, in the form of the antagonism between the Big House and the slaves' quarters—an antagonism softened, or allayed, by ample contact between the races, with the predominance of black cultural features, in a sort of paradoxical victory for the losers (the subjugated, rather). As if slave culture were on equal footing with European culture—Iberian and Portuguese culture, more specifically.

But here Buarque de Holanda's critique reveals itself. While strictly methodological at first, at a later point it carries a heavily political bent. The methodological criticism makes sense if we recall the date of the review of *Sobrados e mucambos*—1951, the year that the second edition came out. This is not merely the author of *Roots of Brazil* reading Gilberto Freyre; now he has written *Monções* [Monsoons] (1945) and most of the monographs that would later be published in 1957 as *Caminhos e fronteiras* [Paths and Frontiers]. The critique, then, is coming from not an essayist, but a researcher concerned with the direction being taken by historical investigation in Brazil, building off the legacy of Capistrano de Abreu and Affonso Taunay, for example, as well as more recent historiography, and who had been studying material civilization in Brazil, especially through inroads into the backlands over the Piratininga highlands, where lies the city of São Paulo.[21] That is to say, Buarque de Holanda's 1951 critique of *Sobrados e mucambos* is rooted in a concern that goes beyond the fixation of a *forma mentis*, a way of thinking, in a long temporal arc, calling for redoubled attention to the more fleeting and momentary details of material experience. To recall a celebrated,

Braudelian metaphor, attention here was being split between the surface and the deeper waters in the attempt to understand the historical phenomenon.

Care with language is also, in this sense, a way of attending to the primacy that Freyre allegedly lent the notions of "content" and "form," which he borrows from Simmel, in an appropriation whose errors seem extremely clear to the author of the review:

> The notions to which he [Freyre] is so attached, of "form" and "content," or substance, ultimately stemming from Simmel's social philosophy, draw all of their strength from their very indefiniteness. It is true that in Simmel they are no more than simple metaphors, at least theoretically. In the version of the author of *Sobrados e mucambos*, however, this deliberate nominalism seems to fall away, even in theory. What had been instruments of exposition, distinction, confrontation, and analysis become more or less empirical realities, serving to support barely-disguised value judgments. Thus, in his writings, social "forms" transform smoothly, at times into real entities, like biological organisms— and then they are practically indistinguishable from social "processes," capable of growth, maturation, and death—and at times into "ideas" with a Hegelian bent—ideas from which "material objects" themselves must mysteriously emanate.[22]

This methodological critique reaffirms the importance of language: the organic metaphor has apparently been taken too far, and Freyre, in Buarque de Holanda's view, takes a "social form"—the patriarchal family with rural origins—as a living, practically autonomous organism. As if magically granted autonomy, the phenomenon takes on a life of its own and dictates the meaning of Portuguese colonization to the researcher. This critique also suggests that, for Freyre, the patriarchal family stands as a value above all else, the chief star of that constellation of regions. The genesis of social formation, and of the forms of coexistence established across the various regions of the Brazilian territory, is called into question. Curiously enough, however, this critique returns to Buarque de Holanda's original thesis;

it is as if the historian of *Monções* were momentarily giving in to the strength of the irresistible arguments of the essayist of *Roots of Brazil*. In short, the author seems to find himself again:

> The form of Brazilian society, if we must accept a violently realist notion such as the one proposed by Gilberto Freyre—realist less in the sense of current sociology than in the sense of medieval theology—did not emerge from the sugar-cane fields, or in another specific Brazilian region; it would be more plausible to believe that it arrived in its finished form from the Old World, adapting here, for better or for worse, to the geographical, ethnic, and economic circumstances in each separate area, and taking on a different form in each. The chief star in this constellation of the clearly differentiated regions that emerged in this Portuguese America, would lie in Lusitanian and Iberian Europe, then, not in the world of the Big House and the slaves' quarters or in some other regional area of the colony.[23]

It is interesting to see the historian in 1951 replicating the initial theses of *Roots of Brazil*, published fifteen years earlier (1936) and intensely revised in a later republication (1948). Why this insistence on the Iberian origin of Brazilian colonization?

Of course, Buarque de Holanda and Freyre share in the basic idea of an "origin" in the Iberian Peninsula, linking the Brazilian experience to both Europe and Africa. In the words of *Sobrados e mucambos*: to both the West and the Orient. However, this is precisely where their analyses diverge, at the point of entry through the rural roots of the Brazilian family, a breaking point that should clarify the clash between *Roots of Brazil* and *Sobrados e mucambos*.[24]

In *Roots of Brazil*, Buarque de Holanda seeks to transfer the "chief star" in the constellation elsewhere, proposing that the patriarchal form—sociologically fundamental, in Freyre's words—stemmed from classical antiquity and would thus not be an original, uniquely Brazilian form (as it appears in *Sobrados e mucambos*). The same form, in Freyre's understanding, meanwhile, should not remain intact like an artifact in a museum but could and ought to be used as a source of motivation for the future.

In a time of collectivization via work, but also growing individualism, familial privatism must necessarily be reorganized and overcome, although Freyre would argue that one should at least hear out the patriarchal past, ultimately recognizing, in short,

> in the mansion, as well as in the Brazilian patriarchal Big House, sources of valuable suggestions for the architect who seeks to create architecture that is both collectivist and personalist, in Brazil, shaped by the lessons of the Brazilian experience; and not, either out of political passion or aesthetic sectarianism, systematically contrary to that very experience; or in a void.[25]

Were the aesthetic experiments of the São Paulo modernists born of the "void," then? One way or another, and just as at the dawn of modernism in Brazil, there emerged the selective return to cultural and artistic legacies, inevitably interrogating the "Brazilian" character of a patriarchal, familist order that was beginning to crumble and which Freyre would have preserved, although transformed, while Buarque de Holanda ultimately wished to see it overcome. Of course, I have produced quite a rigid and simplified opposition here, but it should help, for the time being, to frame the dialogue between the two authors.

This is not some remote discussion or just nitpicking over our understanding of the past. The matter of the architectural "suggestions" provided by the colonial world would continue to inform the country's imagination of the future. At the time of the review, there had emerged no new chief star on the horizon, a new center for the country, but quite soon thereafter, under the Juscelino Kubitschek administration (1956–1961), the new capital, Brasília, would rise from the Planalto Central. The discussion around the architecture of this modernist city would be shaped by those very suggestions left by the Brazilian patriarchal past, albeit resignified by an avant-garde aesthetic keen to find a local form for its sensibilities and attaching itself to an idealized colonial moment. Here I might recall a critique from Edson Nery da Fonseca of some of the architectural solutions created by Oscar Niemeyer, who along with Lúcio Costa designed Brasília. A great scholar of Gilberto Freyre, Fonseca recollects that, when he lived in Brasília, one of his pastimes

> was to show the city to visiting friends, leaving for last a residence in the area known as Park Way. This is a house surrounded by vast terraces, topped with a tiled "quatro águas" roof [a roof of four sides], like the Big Houses of the plantations in the Northeast and ranches in Minas Gerais. When asked why I considered this the greatest *boutade* in Brasília, I explained: because this is how Oscar Niemeyer, the modernist, likes to live—in a colonial-style house.[26]

Beyond the sarcastic tone taken with the architects of modernity, we should note that the discussion always takes place in an urban environment. For Freyre as much as for Buarque de Holanda, the city stood as a crucial counterpoint in their thinking. Domestic, familial sociability was made to face down the ordering, individualizing spirit of urbanization. The key date for this clash, although neither of the authors insists on chronologies, varies here. Buarque de Holanda saw 1888 as the beginning of a new era, with the foundation of the patriarchal order abolished along with slavery. For Freyre, the same order was first clearly shaken in 1808, with King D. João VI's coming to Brazil and the installation of the Portuguese court in the Brazilian colony after Napoleon's invasion of the Iberian Peninsula: a monarch suddenly come to a land as "antimonarchical" as Brazil, as he put it.[27]

The integration of new values into a traditionally privatist society, or the "re-Europeanizing" of Brazil—a sort of tropical Reconquista, including a deorientalization in the nineteenth century, in Freyre's peculiar view—apparently happened in a simultaneously harmonious and conflictive fashion, as is the case, one might add, with the events in *Sobrados e mucambos*. On one side were the *gamenhos* [dandies] who irritated Father Lopes Gama in Recife; the Anglophilia of the Viscount of Cairu at the Court; and the thirst for anything and everything English or French. On the other hand, during the same nineteenth century, as the street became a privileged space for social relations, there emerged a new equilibrium:

> A period of equilibrium between the two tendencies (the collectivist and the individualist), it saw the accentuation of some of the most charming traits of the moral physiognomy of the Brazilian. The political talent for temporizing. The judicial talent for harmonizing. The ability to imitate foreigners and assimilate the finest points of their culture, not merely the superficial ones. Broadly speaking, the typical Brazilian shed his Paulista and Pernambucan sharp edges and became a Bahianized politician, man of the city, or even courtier.[28]

Moreover, the morbidly privatist tendencies of the Big House were already moving toward an equilibrium with the civil and cooperative spirit of the *quilombos* (communities of runaway slaves). Solidarity, so weakened under patriarchalism, blossomed among the black *quilombola* residents, a sentiment born of both race and class, according to Freyre.[29] A different social configuration was emerging from the nineteenth century, as expressed in the new urban landscape. The street was now illuminated, as we read in one of the most striking passages of *Sobrados e mucambos*:

> The chief cities of the empire saw the imperial age come to an end as streets and squares were illuminated with gas lighting. This diminished the number of attacks—vagrants, thieves, or *capoeira* fighters attacking peaceable citizens—on central streets, while it also diminished the number of apparitions of tormented souls, werewolves, headless mules and demonic goats, some becoming either purely rustic phenomena (at most, surviving on the outskirts of the city), others taking refuge inside the mansions abandoned by down-at-the-heels families, some of them too large to ever be entirely well lit by gas lanterns or Belgian lamps. In churches, in cemeteries, in the ruins of old convents, there cowered the specters which had once haunted poorly lit streets.[30]

The metaphor is crystal clear: families decay, and fearsome apparitions find shelter in the increasingly scanty shadows of the city. The house and the street should ideally harmonize, although the patriarchal house of yesteryear will never return. As Freyre puts it, "the Big Houses of the interior [were] eclipsed by the mansions of the capitals."[31] The street imposes itself, and guttersnipes face down the house. An inescapable tension emerges:

> It is true that the more stimulating urban environment—the "street"—with which city urchins were in intimate contact from early on—urchins even more different from the white boys of the mansions than the boys of the sugar mills had been from the young masters of the Big Houses; it is true that the more stimulating urban environment accelerated their development in the direction of a precocious, unchanneled rebelliousness. An anti-social one, to an extent—mischief, the fruit stolen from the aristocrats' plots, the sweets and cakes swiped from street vendor women's trays and Portuguese merchants' stalls, the stones chucked through the windows of the mansions, the caricatures on fences and walls, where it was often the little mulatto, more daring than the black boy, who scrawled smut, sexual organs, obscene sketches, or swear words in charcoal or even tar. The walls of the country manors and city mansions were often left squalid by the filthy scribblings of these mulatto or black caricaturists from the shanties, whose resentment of the aristocratic houses, conscious or not, also expressed itself in the habit, common to city urchins, beggars, and vagrants, of making the thresholds of illustrious gateways, the corners of fine mansions, the shadows of patriarchal walls, into their urinals and at times even their latrines.[32]

The expression of possibly unconscious resentment through feces and urine suggests, from a sociological point of view, the field of tensions blossoming between the house and the street—but it can also lead to a reflection, from a contemporary perspective, around the narrator's awareness of the psychological mechanism behind these very basic antisocial reactions. Can we see a hidden psychoanalytical tang to Freyre's observations, as if they foreshadowed Melanie Klein?

In this game of back-and-forths, one loses an order that, in the eyes of the author of *Sobrados e mucambos*, was as morbid as it was wholesome. To continue on the metaphorical plane of light and shadow, and in a spirit of oscillating compensations, nature attenuates the excesses of the tropics: while the street was lit up at night, banishing the shadowy corners where ghosts appeared, by day those same shadows served as a salve to the harsh climate. An Oriental shade ... After all, from Freyre's point of view, "the tropics cannot be overcome without shading them, in some fashion, after the Arabs or the Orientals. Without narrow streets. Without shawls, *panos-da-Costa*, or Orientally vast parasols for walks under the sun of the hottest days. Without the shadows of great Asiatic and African trees like the mango-tree, the jackfruit tree, the gameleira."[33]

Without going on for too long about the back-and-forths in urbanization, we can see that the picture before us indicates social disequilibrium—or the alteration, whether subtle or violent, of society's equilibrium. The mechanism is a complex one, because disequilibrium seems to always call for, or set off, some sort of reaction that leads the whole toward a new equilibrium.

But how does this discussion appear in *Roots of Brazil*? While for Freyre each destabilizing tendency finds an opposite force that keeps it in check—ultimately an "equilibrium of antagonisms"—in Buarque de Holanda the situation is altogether more dramatic, if not tragic. His essay portrays the progressive loss of the "rural roots" of Brazilian society as marking a clash between two spheres of order: the urban and the rural. Or, in the terms we have been using here, a fundamental conflict between the familial and political spheres. The very constitution of public space is challenged in *Roots of Brazil*, as the autarchic nature of the familial nucleus would logically impede the existence of any sociability beyond the family, transcending it.[34] Any sort of contract, in its universalizing pretensions, would be neutralized by the arbitrary will of the master.

The market itself is thwarted, in that it (having grown beyond the market of colonial production, of course) presupposes basic rules of conduct, so as to guarantee the fulfillment of the expectations of the agents in question. In the terrain ruled by personal will, however, one can take no expectation as a rational guide; there is no conduct that can be regarded as even the slightest bit constant. *Inconstancy* is the order of the day. The norms of the market pale before the whims of the master. And whims are emphatically not a part of the rational, modern market, at least not in the Weberian form that Buarque de Holanda lends it. This inconstancy will also appear in *Sobrados e mucambos*, we might note, linked to the commercial bargains that were not always honored by the masters—and is one of the elements at work in the revolts of the cities against the countryside, the peddlers against the masters.

An interesting anecdote from *Roots of Brazil* is exemplary in this respect. Repeating an observation from Frei Vicente do Salvador, Buarque de Holanda writes that a Dominican bishop who found himself in Brazil once requested that a large chicken, four eggs, and a fish be bought. Nothing was purchased, of course, because there was no market and no slaughterhouse; but when the list was requested from a private residence, the bishop quickly got his chicken, eggs, and fish. At this, he apparently exclaimed, in words for the ages, "Truly, in this land, things are backwards, because it is not a republic; rather, each house is a republic."[35]

This is truly a fantastical alteration of principles. Brazil's society functioned in a peculiar fashion—which does not, however, in *Roots of Brazil*'s case, mean imagining it as a genuinely Brazilian creation. Here, there resurfaces the discussion around the Iberian tradition and the mark left by historical experience on the colonized terrain of America. Methodologically speaking, as I have already argued extensively, *Roots of Brazil* pins down a theoretical or typical attitude that prevailed during colonization: to wit, a set of behaviors on the part of individuals that might explain, or at least clarify, the dilemmas brought on by urbanization.[36] If the land was not a republic and each house was one in and of itself, it was because individuals—social agents—took their lead from familial norms. The *res publica* did not exist, as the will of the master and familial ties stood above all. The business-focused mentality of an industrialist like the Viscount of

Mauá, for example, would have run straight up against the uncooperativeness of the masters of the period. Over the course of the nineteenth century, bank contracts, drafts, and impersonal titles deeply bothered those individuals accustomed to the time in which a simple handshake was all the guarantee one could wish for.

Behind that mythical handshake lay the concrete reality of a personal relationship, person-to-person good faith, just as one might, ideally, trust in a relative or a sibling. The *person* stood above the *individual*, marking a tense relationship between public and private and paving the way for a long-standing reflection around the individual and the citizen, suggesting a Brazilian specificity that would be sought out not in terms of some mystical national "essence," but in the realm of social relations. It is always interesting to ask oneself whether that line of reflection favors Freyre or Buarque de Holanda. One way or another, it is in placing these two authors against each other that we find the foundations of that examination of the "person" and the "individual" in the formation of Brazilian culture.[37]

For Buarque de Holanda, this tension is not resolved in a single, composite whole, or through a balance of antagonisms. Rather, it stands throughout *Roots of Brazil* as a sort of tragic flaw in the formation of Brazil: an impersonal, bureaucratic state could never be constituted while primary, personal, and familial relationships were concretely dominant. Hence the recurrent metaphor of cordiality, and its insistence on the *coração*, the heart, as the ultimate master in these relations. "That heart," as Gilberto Freyre put it, "which, if the Portuguese were able, he would spend all his time voluptuously caressing."[38] Here we may find a characteristic indicated in *Roots of Brazil*, where it synthesizes the behavior of those who ignore all outside the familial sphere, in an attitude that breaks down the borders of civility and reverence and creates a superficial zone of confraternization. This is where Freyre and Buarque de Holanda dovetail most closely. But between a so-called racial democracy and that perennially discussed cordiality, there are several key differences, which emerge when we examine the fact that cordiality is not a value to be defended unconditionally. It was in 1948, for that matter, the year of the second edition of *Roots of Brazil*, that Buarque de Holanda declared to Cassiano

Ricardo that the cordial man was dead, eliminated by the depersonalizing force of the city, which had imposed itself not only on urban zones, but had also marked relationships in the countryside.[39]

This incompatibility would rarely be as clear as in the passages in *Roots of Brazil* where Buarque de Holanda touches on education. Turning to modern theories (we are "in" 1936, of course), the historian proposes, in step with contemporary North American pedagogy, the definitive separation of the individual from the domestic community: liberation from one's parents, and hence from all "family virtues." Looking to Knight Dunlap, the author of *Roots of Brazil* imagines that, in the modern world, where the family is no longer responsible for the education of the citizen, "'the child should be prepared to disobey in situations where his parents' predictions may be fallible.' . . . He should progressively acquire individuality, 'the only just basis of family relations.'"[40]

The infallibility of the father has been eliminated, which would evidently shock anti-liberals. The affirmation of this new pedagogy evidences a profound incompatibility with the values that Gilberto Freyre held most dear. After all, even if the author of *Sobrados e mucambos* recognizes and even analyzes the overwhelming strength of impersonal values, he looks to a society in which parental strength and power still stood for something, where the Brazilian paternalist tradition might not be cast aside altogether, and where the colonial mansion, to return to the architectural example, might still persist as part of the urban landscape, blending tradition and modernity. Opting for individuality, to the degree imagined by the American psychologist cited in *Roots of Brazil*, is unimaginable for Freyre.

Calling up Father Lopes Gama, a great observer of Recife in the nineteenth century, Freyre illustrates the tension between the power of the father, on the one hand, and the affirmation of the individual on the other, making the words of *o padre carapuceiro* ("Father Capmaker," as Lopes Gama was known) his own. Faced with contemporary boys' shamelessness, Freyre/Lopes Gama exclaim(s),

> What times are these, God in Heaven? These youths so lacking in fear, so lacking in respect for their elders and even for the

saints, for the Holy Sacrament itself? What end of the world is this? It was the decline of patriarchalism. The fall of terrible grandfathers, now softened into grandpapas. The fall of "Sir," now become simply "Father" or even "Papa." This was the boy beginning to free himself from the tyranny of the man. The student beginning to free himself from the tyranny of the master. The son turning against his father. The grandson against the grandfather. The young taking on places that had been seen as the exclusive province of the old. It was the start of that which Joaquim Nabuco would call the *neocracy*: "the abdication from fathers to sons, from maturity to adolescence. . . ." This phenomenon struck him as "exclusively [Brazilian]," but it appears to characterize, with all its procession of excesses, any transition from patriarchalism to individualism.[41]

Excess: a hallmark in Freyre's thought. An excess, however, wedded to equilibrium. But in such a delicate state of affairs, one so easily thrown off balance, how might equilibrium come about? Where, amidst the turbulence of the nineteenth century, might one look for a new point of equilibrium? This question marks the return of miscegenation, imbued with total explanatory power. It is true that the free mulatto in the city could suffer just as much as the immigrant, thrown into the antagonism between the mansion and the hovel, or the mansion and the shanty. Moreover, interracial fraternization, along the same lines of black-and-white mingling during the age of the Big House, might come to an end in the age of the city—as it did for many, in Freyre's view. Recall, however, that this was also an era of an equilibrium between individualism and collectivism, bringing out some of the Brazilian's most charming moral qualities, and hence the reappearance of the figure of the mulatto, serving once again to approximate and combine the extremes of domination. This is not only the educated mulatto, however, but the cordial mulatto.

Gilberto Freyre's "cordial man" is the mulatto: "Charm in the Brazilian fashion—the charming man we so often discuss, the man who is 'ugly, but charming,' or even 'wicked or rascally,' it's true, but very charming; the 'cordial man' that Srs. Ribeiro Couto and Sérgio

Buarque de Holanda refer to—this charm and this cordiality, flow above all from the mulatto."[42]

The mulatto is thus cordial, in this singular interpretation of cordiality. This is a take that leans closer to Cassiano Ricardo than to Sérgio Buarque de Holanda and which will have important political consequences, as I hope to suggest at greater length later on.[43]

While in *Roots of Brazil* the cordial man is indeed the expression of the personalized, familial conduct of social agents, he also affords a glimpse of the dilemmas that accompany the entry of the individual into the political arena. To reduce this all to an impoverished but correct formula, *the cordial man expresses the intersection of the traditional and the modern*—although this issue is rather more political than moral, in Buarque de Holanda's view. The confusion between the moral and the political is a common inversion, which Freyre puts forth when using the idea of cordiality, in the second edition of *Sobrados e mucambos*. Freyre's cordial mulatto is perennially smiling, affable, conciliating, a malleable victor in the field of interpersonal relations. To spell it out: he is a promise for the future. Or, if we delve fully into Freyre's argument, the mulatto, that composite creature that still "expresses" today, to many Brazilian and international eyes, a Brazilian promise for civilization as a whole, stood then as the guarantee of the continuity of an equilibrium that was slipping away.

The warmth with which Gilberto Freyre's theses may be reread in Brazil, in this time of combative discussions around affirmative action, would merit a study on its own—especially because many of the harshest critics of yesteryear are those now examining with greater care, or less rancor, the promise that may be lurking behind the ideological label of "racial democracy." The topic has sparked particular interest, of course, in contrast with the North American experience.[44] It is significant, incidentally, that Edward Telles, in his broad investigation of racism in Brazil, proposes the terms of an enigma that would have escaped many researchers of race relations in Brazil, for whom "miscegenation" was pure "ideology," serving to conceal the reality of racism even in a country where a one-drop rule never existed:

The evidence used by the current generation is based largely on official statistics that have demonstrated high levels of racial inequality. Furthermore, these academics have marshaled plenty of evidence of discrimination to support their view. But have current scholars [2004] examined race relations widely enough and asked all the right questions? Has all the proper evidence been brought to bear? For an ideology of inclusion to be so pervasively accepted for so many years would seem to require some evidence, however limited, of its existence. What is it about the Brazilian system that supported arguments about racial inclusivity? And if there is any support for them, how can inclusiveness coexist with exclusiveness? For me, this remains the enigma of Brazilian race relations.[45]

But let us return to Freyre and see how, starting with Aluísio Azevedo's novel *O mulato* (1881), he interprets the mulatto as the figure capable of "exquisite seduction," with a "typically warm Brazilian" grin, in Gilberto Amado's words. A smile, as the author of *Sobrados e mucambos* dubbed it,

> quintessentially servile, generally in relation to the master, in the slaveholding systems finely balanced by the accommodation between their various elements. Command fosters loud voices in the masters and mild, soft speech in servants, almost always accompanied by sweet smiles. For that matter, in terms of smile, speech, and gesture, the patriarchal system of slavery, long dominant in Brazil, seems to have developed in the slave—and, through the slave, in his mulatto descendent—an agreeable manner that sprang from servants' desire to insinuate themselves into the liking, if not the love, of their masters.... Here we shall simply recall that the embrace, today such a typically Brazilian ritual of friendship between men, and apparently of Oriental or Indian origin, when accompanied by the traditional slaps on the back, has taken on warmth among us, moving from an Apollonian to a Dionysian gesture, thanks to the influence of the mulatto: from the exuberance of his cordiality.[46]

The smile becomes emblematic of an approximation between individuals sans conflict. The metaphor is a powerful one: the cordial mulatto is celebratory, sociable, joyful, and festive. The formula takes on life and moves from the Apollonian to the Dionysian. One might argue that, in Buarque de Holanda as well, the cordial man is Dionysian; the Apollonian figure is the formal man, marked by civility and reverence, who fears drawing too close and respects barriers. The cordial man, meanwhile, "lives through others"; here the historian recalls Nietzsche's declaration that "Your inadequate self-love makes you a captive of isolation."[47]

In *Roots of Brazil*, cordiality is, indeed, a stumbling block to the realization of the values of a liberal democracy. The dilemma is clear: democracy would demand that the person cede to the collectivity, giving way to the citizen, a figure juridically equal to all the other citizens circulating through the polis. But if we lend an ear to the suggestions latent in Buarque de Holanda's text, there is no way to simply eradicate cordiality. This being said—while the power of the family may no longer be the same, the logical underpinnings of *Roots of Brazil* lead us to a sense of disquiet, as if there were a slim chance that, in disentangling oneself from the cordial mesh or resignifying it in the contemporary political scene, the individual might emerge as finally freed from the power of family and tradition. In Freyre's case, this liberation is neither desired nor hinted at; and as soon as the bonds of tradition begin to slacken, a new and promising equilibrium of tensions is seen to emerge in the evasive, ascendant figure of the mulatto.

Roots of Brazil is constructed under the sign of conflict: between the individual and the family, the polis and the subject, the citizen and the Father, between Creon and Antigone. *Sobrados e mucambos*, meanwhile, takes shape around conciliation, equilibrium, and accommodation. These are all political matters, but as suggested at the start of this chapter, they cannot be read independently of the dimension of language.

Sérgio Buarque de Holanda's prose is economical, almost always limpid, marked by the "terse" style identified by Alexandre Eulalio.[48] Tension is resolved in the delicate, unstable economy of opposites and contrasts, with swift and elegant digressions: tensions between types, tendencies, and values. But among other Nietzschean streaks in *Roots of Brazil*, there emerge promising, seductive demons that present themselves in instantaneous flashes, as if the placid surface of the prose were hiding a deeper unrest.

The prose of *Sobrados e mucambos*, meanwhile, flows sprawling and colloquial, investing in the power of cascading images, offered to the reader in the beautiful, monotonous rhythm of the griot. Let it be said, in homage to the author who scholars so frequently and zealously seek to differentiate from Buarque de Holanda, that Freyre ultimately enchants readers and may be the better writer. It is difficult to deny that in *Sobrados e mucambos* we are taken along the streets of Recife in the search for the signs of a future where everything fuses together, without clashes or tensions, into an ever-so-slightly sweetened form.

PART II

The Nonexistent American

CHAPTER 4

Wandering Origins
The Impertinence of Belonging

The death of interpretation is to believe that there are signs, signs that exist primarily, originally, actually, as coherent, permanent, and systematic marks.
—Michel Foucault, "Nietzsche, Freud, Marx," 1967

I will begin with a somewhat worn question: what is Brazil?

If formulated in the 1930s—when, at least in Brazil, it was not yet uncommon to write about the nature of peoples—the question might lead to a deep investigation into the characteristics of the collectivity, having us seek out or conjure up the lines tracing a collective entity, identifying that which defines and differentiates it from other national groups. However, the 1930s are long gone. If we ask "what is a country?" today, we are no longer seeking an essence, or an ossified ideological characterization of the national entity. A question possible today might operate in terms of language: What does "Brazil" mean? What does the word set off, what does it evoke, what does it reveal, and what does it conceal?

The most appropriate way to respond to this question may be to return to the idea of the *journey*, for the simple reason that it is in traveling that we understand what we have left. It is no insight to say that we should leave the place where we find ourselves to know it: I leave my country (literally or imaginarily) so that I can know it, just as I abandon my family to know myself. Only when I leave it, can I *re-cognize*, *know again* the place where I had been, marking it as a space of pertinence, or belonging.[1]

A journey necessarily lies behind any investigation into the sign of belonging, or any question about that in which the subject can still recognize him- or herself. The list of the travelers who left home so as to understand it is a long one. We can recall one of the most illustrious, Odysseus, and we will see that, from Homer to James Joyce, displacement is a condition of the narrative. There would be no stories, nor history, without the instability that displacement forces upon us. If everything were familiar, there would be no reason to narrate. "Weave, weaver of the wind," we read in the extraordinary modern Odyssey.[2]

But while it may be true that there is no story without displacement, this does not make the voyage an atemporal topos. It is not present at all times in the same form. And while there may be no novelty in relating literature to displacement, we might ask, What novelty is there in the questions posed around displacement? When we interrogate this movement, what lies deep down in our questions—the fascinations, the obsessions, the recurrences, the fears, the reproofs that guide and condition us?

To make the most of this critically, we would do well to avoid an atemporal question around voyages and literature, understanding that we are captives of the moment, hostages to a series of specters that only exist in time and through it—as most specters tend to, one might add. In less metaphorical terms, this chapter might be opened with the question: why are terms like *borders*, *limits*, *margins*, *edge-spaces*, *intermediate spaces*, *liminal*, and *threshold* all so fascinating at this point in time?

* * *

We always speak of a place and a time that are our own prisons—in other words, the place from which we are writing and thinking. Prison is a privileged space for writing, and the list of imprisoned writers would also be a long and brilliant roll. But what is my place, and which my time? It becomes impossible to avoid the shadow of the subject when such inquiries begin. If I wish to understand the space from which I am speaking, I cannot avoid weaving myself into an autobiographical mesh, which is where the subject may reveal or hide him- or herself—rather, it is the mesh through which the subject reveals and hides him- or herself at the same time.

North American academia, at a time when frontiers find themselves in crisis, is the place I am speaking of. In my case, frontiers enter into crisis in the precise moment that I begin to speak, because I do not know exactly what I am speaking about, nor where I am speaking from. Brazil? What is Brazil, in North American academia? First of all, Brazil is no longer the place I left, because that act makes it a sign operated in another universe, with its own laws of gravity: its own issues, problems, its "topics," its obsessions, and its favorite specters. The Brazil I am speaking about from the United States will never be the same one that I speak about in Brazil. For that matter, I might note that in a rich volume of essays on Brazilian culture, literature, and society, João Cezar de Castro Rocha opens by evoking two verses from Carlos Drummond de Andrade: "No Brazil exists. / And who's to say Brazilians exist?"[3]

"Brazil" becomes a problematic place, starting in the moment in which I am able to say that it no longer exists, or at least that it does not mean what it might have meant at another point. This is the crisis of a sign, or perhaps the crisis of signification itself. This idea draws us toward an entry into the world of linguistics, where the sign (conceived schematically as the space where sound and meaning come together) bears a profound ambiguity, precisely because it represents the joining of the concrete and the abstract, its functioning as a physical stage for the resolution of meaning, which is the ultimate aim of the sign—that is, to *signify*.[4]

In one of the fragments found in the notebooks of Ferdinand de Saussure (1857–1913), there is a question as to the identity of symbols, these "primeval materials" that make up legend. This is not to propose a Saussurean analysis of the symbol of the homeland; rather, we might seek out, in this fragment from the great linguist, a jumping-off point for the question about Brazil, the signification of which calls for a displacement: "Where is its identity now? In general, one responds by smiling, as if this were indeed a curiosity, disregarding its philosophical significance, which goes so far as to state that any symbol, once in general circulation—and symbols exist only *because* they are in circulation—is absolutely incapable of defining at any given instant what its identity will be at any subsequent instant."[5]

Linguists know that this discussion, although incipient in Saussure's work, heralds the possibility of an understanding of language (and discourse) as the space of the more or less conscious utilization of phonetic or graphic elements, which flows into the most peculiar investigations of anaphony, anagrams, paragrams, hypograms, and so on. This may pose somewhat of a dark forest for those who consider ourselves laypeople, but we might recall, albeit briefly, that discourse is the mobilization of those concrete, phonic, or graphic elements, which combine and, in combining, allow for words, or topic-words, to present or make present things that are not apparent, designating that which is hidden or latent.

The modern idea has it that this which *signifies* exists in a sort of edge of knowledge, which is the limit-moment at which the symbol—to return to that fragment from Saussure—cannot say what will comprise its identity in the next moment, and this is fascinating and pregnant with theoretical consequences. The very possibility of fixing one's identity, enclosing it in a perfect circle, vanishes and obliterates itself, once it assumes that signification pulls us into a space of undecidability, or profound indeterminacy.[6] Operating on another level, we might suppose that the conception of language, far before the foundation of modern linguistics, indicated a transcendence where meaning was resolved, or revealed. Think of Saint Augustine, and of Abelard himself: a meaning always conceals itself from us but opens up on the horizon of the bliss sprung of the divine, the sacred, silence in prayer and respect for transcendence. Let us see.

The famous debate over the universals, which pits Abelard (1079–1142) against the neo-Platonist conceptions that arrive in the twelfth century via Boethius's commentaries on Porphyry, develops around the question of the location of the universal, whether on the level of things (*res*) or of language (*voces*). Abelard's nominalism does not, however, question the Augustinian framework behind the dichotomy between things and language. I will indulge in a long quotation here, the importance of which will soon be clarified:

> In this passage [where Priscian suggests that genera and species, being universals, may pertain to the general and special forms of "things which were given intelligibility in the divine mind before being produced in bodies"] he views God after the fashion of an artist who first conceives in his mind a [model or] exemplar form of what he is to fashion and who works according to the likeness of this form, which form is said to be embodied when a real thing is constructed in its likeness. It may be all right to ascribe such a common conception to God, but not to man. For those works of God like a man, a soul, or a stone represent general or special states of nature, whereas those of a human artisan like a house or a sword do not. For "house" and "sword" do not pertain to nature as the other terms do. They are the names not of a substance but of something accidental and therefore they are neither genera not ultimate species. Conceptions by abstraction [of the true nature of things] may well be ascribed to the divine mind but may not be ascribed to that of man, because men, who know things only through the medium of their senses, scarcely ever arrive at such an ideal understanding and never conceive the [underlying] natures of things in their purity. But God knew all things he created for what they were and this even before they actually existed. He can discriminate between these individual states as they are in themselves; senses are no hindrance to him who alone has true understanding of things. Of those things which men have not experienced through the senses, they happen to have opinions rather than understanding, as we learn from experience. For having thought of some city before seeing it, we find on arriving there that it is quite different than we had thought.[7]

Substitute, in that last sentence, "country" for "city," and it deepens the comprehension of a space that is always imagined, after all, to be "different than we had thought." Such is the Brazil of which we are speaking. But my aim here may be summed up in the paradox examined by Abelard, in the example that would add so greatly to the fortune of Umberto Eco (1932–2016):

> We do not want to speak of there being universal *names* when the things they name have perished and they can no longer be predicated of many and are not common names of anything, as would be the case when all the roses were gone. Nevertheless, "rose" would still have meaning for the mind even though it names nothing. Otherwise, "There is no rose" would not be a proposition.[8]

The name of the rose becomes a logical problem "when all the roses [are] gone." Even so, the word retains its power of signification, because it is still possible to say that roses do not exist. While the term *rose* may have lost its power to name (after all, there are no more roses in Abelard's hypothetical world), intellection is still called in to make present that which is not, or is no longer, there.[9] From a modern point of view, the power of the word is expanded precisely in the absence of the divine link with nature that the very idea of intellection assumes. In these times, the mind is asked to imagine something of which we may legitimately ask if it ever truly existed. What is in question here, after all, is the nature of Brazil. This becomes even more interesting when we look to find, in that last sentence from Abelard, an echo of Drummond's poetic formula, taken up by Castro Rocha with an eye to Buarque de Holanda: "no Brazil exists," or, we might say, there is no Brazil.

In the present, we have learned, for better or for worse, to lose our respect for transcendence. There is no graver sin, in certain contemporary theoretical circles, than maintaining faith in transcendence, or in the final resolution of meaning. No need to look far: one may simply recall, for example, how the adjective "teleological," and even the epithet "Hegelian," when employed in particular academic contexts, become anathema, in a truly purgatory sort of conceptual auto-da-fé. We step forth and declare proudly that we are not among the ranks of those who believe in transcendence and in the final resolution of meaning and history.[10]

Let us come back down to ground, however, the ground here being the texts, and turn to the first paragraph of *Roots of Brazil*. The excerpt is from the most recent version of the text, as set in 1956, here in the English translation:

> The effort to implant European culture in an extensive stretch of territory under conditions largely foreign, if not adverse, to Europe's thousand-year tradition is the dominant fact in the origins of Brazilian society and the one that has yielded the most valuable consequences. We have brought our forms of association, our institutions, and our ideas from distant countries, and though we take pride in maintaining all of them in an often unfavorable and hostile environment, we remain exiles in our own land. We can accomplish great things, add new and unexpected features to our human nature, and forge the type of civilization that we represent—nevertheless, all the fruits of both our work and our sloth seem to belong to an evolutionary system from another climate and another landscape.[11]

The dated vocabulary here—climate, landscape, nature, roots—albeit tempered by the extremely modern opposition between work and sloth,[12] might suggest that we are dealing with a text that owes its energy to the nineteenth century, the incubator of great questions around national character and the identity of peoples, with a prevailing faith in a transcendence that, in keeping with Romantic tastes, would be tied to the spirit of a people.

Of course Buarque de Holanda, in his attention to "roots," is also a creature of the mental universe of the nineteenth century. It is equally clear that the question as to national identity is the product of a historical process to which we are all heirs, like it or not. But it may be interesting to imagine the text in question as slightly ahead of the era of the great questions around the definition of collective identity, back when the symbol was still perfect because one knew what would be revealed after it: hence the tautology of the patriotic discourse that postcolonial criticism has sought to shed, evoking (or perhaps invoking) "margins" and everything outside the narrow bounds of the national symbol.[13] In short, Buarque de Holanda's text would, from this angle, stand between the age of grand narratives of national imagination (the "foundational fictions" that Doris Sommer refers to) and another age (our own), of profound uncertainty as to what frontiers are, or ought to be.[14]

This is not to urge a simple defense of the erasure of border lines—this would lead to a simplistic apology of globalization, wherein we should simply wait placidly for the market to creep over the lines that trace uncomfortable separations between countries. Rather, we might recall the zone of instability in which we stand whenever we can envision ourselves in a meaningful relationship with symbolic frontiers. This is a very rich and productive moment, when the meaning and the sense of belonging or not belonging, being present or absent, become a problem that is both theoretical and political, where being there and not being there can coexist as possibilities. After all, there lies a keen doubt in the opening of this book, which is called, after all, *Roots of Brazil*: Has the transplanting of a European culture to American soil been a success or a failure? Does this place exist, where roots come together (if they do at all)? Or is it all a colossal "chronicle of disconnects"?[15]

The question around places, and displacement, is posed from the imprecise zone from which roots emerge, but also from where they are planted: of which Europe, and which America, is Sérgio Buarque de Holanda speaking? In the historian's imagination, Europe is the Iberian Peninsula; and, with it, there emerges the powerful fantasy of a "bridge-territory," in the terms that Freyre used back when Buarque de Holanda published *Roots of Brazil* in 1936 and which he had borrowed from nineteenth-century Portuguese historian Alexandre Herculano.[16] In other terms, ones also dear to our contemporary sensibility, the Iberian Peninsula might be seen as a contact zone between Africa and Europe beyond the Pyrenees.[17]

It is curious that the great fantasy of this pleasant proximity to Africa, of the so-often-idealized mestizo identity, the vision of a people open to the Other, should be attached to "us" Brazilians as much as to "them," the Portuguese. The pronouns here are shielded with quotation marks not out of any fear of imprecision, or any nicety of style, but because pronominal use is the greatest trap set by the symbol in its perfection, when I know *what will come after me*, when I finally recognize the figure at my side and join with him, closing the circle of *belonging*.

But who, or what, are *they*? Or are *we* all the same, Portuguese and Brazilians? Radically the same—with common roots—or radically other, after the definitive break with that which once joined us? I myself was forced to, at a given point in my academic experience, realize that the fantasy of a mixed-race, cordial identity is not an exclusively Brazilian one, but stands full-fledged in the "Portuguese soul"; and this realization was, one might say, imposed by the place where I situate myself. After all, in North American academia, one is impeded from fully endorsing the Brazilian modernist vision of a deep break, the profound difference between Brazil and Portugal, which would go so far as, in the voice of an author like Mário de Andrade (1893–1945), the proposition of a different language entirely, with the suggestion of a "gramatiquinha brasileira," a Brazilian grammar, ultimately separating "us" from the deleterious, backwards-looking Portuguese influence.[18]

In the North American academy, Brazilians coexist with the "other side" (the Portuguese) in a twofold sense. Geographically, the field of a specialist in "Brazilian literature" is already invaded by the Other that is Portugal, despite the subject's attempts to find refuge in the Brazilianist corners of professional associations and preach the greater popularity of the Brazilian variant of the language among American students, or perhaps bitterly critique the imperialist doings of the Instituto Camões, invariably casting it as the equally undesirable twin (from a "Latin Americanist" point of view that seeks to shield itself from the "Peninsularists," in the complex geopolitics of departments of Spanish and Portuguese) of Spain's Instituto Cervantes. A Brazilian in North American academia finds spaces mingled and frontiers redrawn. The map of the world is not divided by the avid hands of the Empire into specific sectors, out of sync with the "actual" geography of foreign nations; rather, spaces blend together because, once subjected to the forces of North American administration and curiosity (both extremely powerful), one's very gaze, and the place from which the discourse is enunciated, are altered considerably.[19] The Other is drawn closer, so close that even I can recognize myself as Other. Rimbaud's noun phrase, "I is an other," takes on incredible urgency here.[20]

Displacement, or that original sin of the conscience that winds up leaving Brazil by the wayside, makes it imperative that the subject be displaced once again, and again, until whatever he or she has abandoned becomes a new, unknown territory: "strange and familiar," in Freudian terms. From a psychoanalytic angle, for that matter, anguish can bring us back to precisely the fact that not only are we lacking a referent, but also that we *feel a lack* of that familiar lack, in the moment when the terrain of lacking is suddenly invaded, and the subject is driven to anguish because the absent place where he ought to find his home produces a lack, as we see with Lacan.[21] Anguish emerges precisely when I can no longer locate my lack: in feeling *saudades*, I do not know precisely what I am missing, or what I should miss, because the desired space has been erased, perhaps permanently. The *rose* has gone, and the name Brazil is floating in the void of its own signification.

Let us return, however, to the fantasy of the bridge-territory or contact zone as the origin of it all: the Iberian Peninsula. In *Roots of Brazil*, the Iberian world appears as a whole in the first chapter, although it is set up as a duo of opposites (Spain and Portugal) over the course of the book, and even more so over the course of Buarque de Holanda's career, especially in his investigation into the search for paradise on earth in colonial America, in the 1958 magnum opus *Visão do paraíso* [Vision of Paradise].[22]

The Iberian Peninsula is the bridge-territory where the mixture seems to begin.[23] All the Brazilian modernist idealizations around the bloodless meeting in the tropics—of the very possibility of a cannibalistic reversal, with the Brazilian I devouring the European Other, the Indians lounging in the beds on Pedro Álvares Cabral's ship, as we read in Pero Vaz de Caminha's letter to the king in 1500[24]—the idea of an encounter that refuses to be stained by blood is already present, albeit incipient, in the territory that generously opens itself up to the Other in keeping with a long-held fantasy around the recovery of a Europe allegedly muddied with Africanisms. A less Europeanized Europe, in the end. To put it yet another way, the fantastic edge of Europe (the Iberian Peninsula, and Portugal in particular) appears as the "reserve of dreams" that Eduardo Lourenço evokes in a text that, not by chance, references Wim Wenders's marvelous film *Lisbon Story* (1994), and explores Portugal's reintegration into Europe, postulating the entry of an "other" Europe (south of the Pyrenees) into that Europe (north of them) which advanced and now seeks to return to its past Other, to incorporate it harmoniously into a touching—but perhaps deceptive—civilizational promise.[25]

Politically, this may be the most interesting aspect of the fantasy around difference, postulated out of the original "mixture" forged in the Iberian "bridge-territory," which is Portugal as well. We are familiar, however, with the dangers around the fable of Lusitanian difference. I am referring to the specter of the dictatorship of António de Oliveira Salazar (1932–1968), which stretched across more than a third of the twentieth century in Portugal, and which was most perfectly expressed in the declarations of his minister Marcelo Caetano, who stated that "relations between Europeans and indigenous peoples in Portuguese colonies [were] the best in the world" shortly after the end of World War II, when the map of Africa, redrawn by European imperialist greed from the late nineteenth century, was being disputed one more time. Here lies the utopian desire to reshape history "as a relationship without power or conflict," as Miguel Vale de Almeida puts it.[26] In any case, the idealization of the bridge-territory gives rise to the fantasy around difference and another Europe, which in turn would bring forth another America.

In the critical return to the fantastical geography of Shakespeare's *The Tempest*, there also comes the postulation of difference in relation to that European Other—a swerve away from that space to the north of the Pyrenees on the Old Continent. In short, in coming from "central" Europe and crossing the Pyrenees, the observer is apparently made privy to another history entirely, in a tense, mirrored relationship with the United States of America, as I plan to suggest and elaborate on over the chapters that follow. History as it shaped Brazil would, in this vision, be the outcome of that framework developed south of the Pyrenees, marked by other, not so exclusively "European" narratives. Through these idealizing lenses, Brazil emerges as the offshoot of another Europe, this one more open and porous—differently from the emergence of the United States, whose roots ought to be found in "another" Europe.

It is curious to reflect that, ever since the colonial period, the possibility of voluntary exile (an initiatory experience for the bureaucratic and intellectual elite of the Portuguese colony in America) was linked to a displacement to that very same peninsular Europe. The sons of the colonial elite in Brazil—which, unlike the Spanish colonies, boasted not a single university—do not go to France mainly, or to the "rest" of Europe, but rather, and above all, to Coimbra. Later on, at the start of the twentieth century, the modernist generation would "rediscover" the country, the green-and-yellow homeland, and the tropical charm of its birdsong, while looking back from France.[27] But before the modernists and Romantics, Portugal is the primary space of this displacement, the reunion with and rediscovery of the land left behind, which a Romantic or modernist reading will cast as perennially Brazilian, as if from the very moment that the first Portuguese set foot in America, Brazil was already there, fresh and enchanting.

Buarque de Holanda occupies a special place in Brazilian modernism. Himself a literary critic, historian, and traveler from an early age, his nontautological explanation of Brazil begins, in a book suggestively entitled *Roots of Brazil*, with a piercing question that—we have learned through criticism—is not a static query, but an interrogation that morphs over time. That time is the shifting of editions and revisions, in the moment when the author is still a reader of himself, who feels out an initial hypothesis (the success of the transplant) before turning to the cruelest uncertainty of all, expressed in the question: to what extent do we represent that which we have left behind? This is the opening question of *Roots of Brazil*, in its "definitive" version.[28]

There is a palpitating horizon to this peculiar Europe, which is both the Peninsula as a whole and Portugal in particular, comprising the "European Frontiers" that provide the title for the first chapter of *Roots of Brazil*. This is an idealized Finisterra that spreads beyond itself, be it in the imperial dream of Luís de Camões (1524–1580), the prophetic delirium of Father Vieira (1608–1697), the flights of the poetic–Portuguese Soul of Fernando Pessoa (1888–1935) in *Message*, or even the tatters of the imperial standard fluttering in the ruined dream of *The Return of the Caravels*, by Lobo Antunes (b. 1942).[29] Nevertheless, if we look deeply into the tradition that we ("we" Brazilians) set ourselves apart from, the specter of the Other emerges: the bridge-territory shifts and gives chase, with its chain of alterities. We know, for that matter, that this contact zone of a territory is always on the verge of breaking off from the land beyond the Pyrenees, which José Saramago (1922–2010) ironically referred to as "nearby Europe" in *The Stone Raft*.[30]

But the enchantment with difference and the blood, now finally American, running in Brazilian veins, still fuels the dream of many modernists—a dream shared, to an extent, by Sérgio Buarque de Holanda. However, in *Roots of Brazil*, a book published in a time when the heroic phase of Brazilian modernism had already passed, the certainty of difference and an unshakable symbolic identity was already taking on water. In the 1930s, in Buarque de Holanda's vision, we can no longer speak of a single "Brazil." The search for such an identity is a doomed undertaking. Finding an origin means also recognizing an Other that I repudiate, but which is within me, and will be so ever more deeply the more I try to disentangle myself from it. Much like a specter, for that matter.

* * *

The specificity of writing would thus be intimately bound to the absence of the father.
—Jacques Derrida, "Plato's Pharmacy," 1968

It is tempting to reconstruct a genealogy of exile in Brazilian literature: from Gonçalves Dias (1823–1864) to Sérgio Buarque de Holanda, including, of course, Euclides da Cunha (1866–1909). When one speaks of the homeland, a displacement is inevitable.[31] But this exercise might include yet another interesting stop. I would like to bring in "The Third Bank of the River," the story by João Guimarães Rosa (1908–1967), a text that is also an adventure in recognition, where belonging and unbelonging come together in the problematic attempt to draw close to the father.

What happens in the story? The plot is simple and profound, like almost everything in Guimarães Rosa: one day, a father decides to build a canoe and abandon his family, albeit never actually leaving. The canoe remains aimlessly between the banks of the river, the father perennially rowing around, haunting his family with the unfulfilled promise of his disappearance. But one day, much later, he responds to his son's calls and reappears before him, inviting him to embark. And the son, who is the closest of all the family to his father, refuses.

Precisely when the father decides to abandon his family, he is threatened by the mother (feminine figures are central in Guimarães Rosa's world), who says: "Go or stay; but if you go, don't you ever come back!" The father's answer is left hanging, however: "Father left his answer in suspense."[32] The sentiments of the guilty, tormented son, called to take his father's place, are unsayable, unnameable. The impossibility of embarking in the canoe is the result of the inability to close the circle of a father-sign, sustaining the importance of the father figure. But there is yet another level of ineffability here, tied to the existential geography of Rosa's works.[33] The reader may sense something of Dante in Guimarães Rosa's journeys. We know that "the sertão [backlands] is the world," and that the *sertanejo* inhabiting it is the subject abandoned between the forces of good and evil. However, there is a fundamental difference from Dante's tale: Rosa's cosmology cuts loose the metaphysical, transcendent ballast of the *Divine Comedy*.[34]

Dante, as the walking subject of the text (and in the text), travels through a world shaped by medieval hierarchies, as Buarque de Holanda himself suggests in *Roots of Brazil*.[35] However, the wanderer in Guimarães Rosa moves through a universe where God, in a modern fashion, hides from view (a *Deus absconditus*, to recall Blaise Pascal's formula), and the key to understanding the human condition is the man abandoned to himself.[36] The man—whether the son, the backcountry bandit, or the child becoming an adult—must grapple with a geography of abandonment, of eternal exile, as there is no heaven or hell to head toward. Both hell and heaven can be found in the world down here, a mark of the exile from the universe ruled, in the medieval mentality, by faith in the transcendence of places. On that regard, one could say that medieval mentality had faith in the places of signification as well.

The modern subject is robbed of paradise, hell, and meaning, and transcendence is no longer a possibility. Transcendence is spectral, and the father, as a sign of origin and belonging—"our father," in the story, being a sign of character as well—loses himself, dimly visible between the banks of signification. But it is interesting that he is, in Guimarães Rosa's story, a stubborn figure: the incomprehensible insistence on remaining between banks, in the shadows of an intermediary space, suggests the space of signification itself. The fluvial matter, meanwhile, evokes the flux and the damming up of a narrative that, being modern, is not hale. This matter is in constant dilution, to stick to the metaphorical field at hand.

But questions cannot be limited to the sign. One must interrogate the subject, because he is the one who is facing down the sign in a battle of life and death. The boy-narrator, who is in fact an adult-narrator attempting to understand the moment in which his childhood was abandoned (yet another clearly Rosian theme), is constituted before a father who stands as an Other, in which the "I" recognizes itself and within which it runs the risk of losing itself. The possibility of becoming that Other stems from a fascination with the journey through a space that, to return to the psychoanalytic imaginary, is at once familiar and strange. In the very possibility of abandoning oneself wholly to the Other that is the sign of belonging (the father, here), there lies the risk of going insane, a risk that arises at the crucial moment in which madness breaks into the fabric of the story as a malignant, uncomfortably close potential. In classificatory terms, and if one accepts a certain mapping of the human psyche, turning oneself absolutely over to the Other might recall a psychotic structure, marked by substitution—that is, something beyond a simple rejection of reality.

After one of his many syntheses of psychoanalytic knowledge produced during the 1920s, Freud returned to the thorny question of the differences between neurosis and psychosis:

> Now, one might expect that when a psychosis breaks out something analogous to the process in a neurosis happens, though of course between different institutions in the mind; that is, that two steps may be visible in a psychosis also, the first of which tears the ego away from reality, while the second tries to make good the damage done and re-establish the relationship to reality at the expense of the *id*. And something of the kind can really be observed in a psychosis; there are indeed two stages in it, the second of which bears the character of a reparation—but then the analogy gives way to a far more extensive similarity in the two processes. The second step in a psychosis is also an attempt to make good the loss of reality, not, however, at the expense of a restriction laid on the *id*—as in neurosis at the expense of the relation with reality—but in another, a more lordly manner, *by creating a new reality which is no longer open to objections like that which has been forsaken.* The second step, therefore, in both neurosis and psychosis, is induced by the same tendencies. . . . Neurosis and psychosis . . . are far more distinguishable from each other in the reaction at the outbreak than in the attempt at reparation which follows it. The difference at the beginning comes to expression at the end in this way: in neurosis *a part of reality is avoided by a sort of flight, but in psychosis it is remodelled.* Or one may say that in psychosis flight at the beginning is succeeded by an active phase of reconstruction, while *in neurosis obedience at the beginning is followed by a subsequent attempt at flight.* Or, to express it in yet another way, neurosis does not deny the existence of reality, it merely tries to ignore it; psychosis denies it and tries to substitute something else for it. A reaction which combines features of both of these is the one we call normal or "healthy"; it denies reality as little as neurosis, but then, like a psychosis, is concerned with effecting a change in it. This expedient normal attitude leads naturally to some active achievement in the outer

world and is not content, like a psychosis, with establishing the alteration within itself [emphases added].[37]

To return to Guimarães Rosa—the loss of the boundaries that separate the subject from the unreal (the phantasmatic father) would seem to ultimately mark his own ruin. In terms of signification, and taking the father as a sign of origin and belonging, the possibility of the subject's falling apart would be figured in the inability to halt the perfect circle that will transform me once again into that father, thus confirming that I am not an Other, that "I" is not an "Other." The whole of the drama is there, poetically, in the refusal to embark.[38]

Look to the penultimate paragraph of the story, when the father responds to his son's call, and the sign finally offers itself:

> He heard me. He got to his feet. He dipped the paddle in the water, the bow pointed toward me; he had agreed. And suddenly I shuddered deeply, because he lifted his arm and gestured a greeting—the first, after so many years. And I could not.... Panic-stricken, my hair standing on end, I ran, I fled, I left the place behind me in a mad headlong rush. For he seemed to be coming from the hereafter. And I am pleading, pleading, pleading for forgiveness.[39]

What is there behind the guilt that calls for an eternal pardon—marked, to return to Freud's terms, by a repeatedly delayed escape? With the father taken as a sign of belonging and origin, the guilt reveals the prohibition of hesitation. The subject is not authorized to hesitate; but hesitation and refusal before the sign in which he ought to recognize himself are what constitute him as a subject. Even having refused, however, as we know, the subject will never free himself from the specter of the father.[40]

It is extremely interesting that the father seems to come "from the hereafter." The very notion of transcendence is at play here. The hereafter is no longer a place one can choose to inhabit, nor a space outside the subject. Transcendence, in short, is no longer the beyond that Thomistic cosmology attempted to map out in the medieval mind. A slippery inner space, the hereafter is the *sertão* within the subject, the subject-river unable to find the banks of his own definition, perhaps because the sign of origin can no longer complete itself before him. "I am what never was—the unspeakable," says the narrator, standing on the bank.[41]

Trying to weave together the threads cast throughout this chapter, although without any hope of tying up the boat on the bank (if you'll forgive the mixed metaphor)—the *impertinence of belonging* may suggest that the tautology of the national sign (Brazil, which is Brazil because it is Brazil) falls apart only when I dare to throw myself into the oscillation of signification. After all, the sign is itself the impetuous flow that is the stuff of literature, which no one can check in the end. National discourse, however, is no more than a framework, or a machine for producing symbols that are eternally equal to themselves, frozen in a constant and insipid reshaping of the same. But if we pay attention to signification, the symbol, when examined in terms of the functioning of language, is incapable of saying what will come next. If we believe Saussure, it is incapable of fixing identity in the moment to come.

What does it mean to "be Brazilian," then? What answer is reserved for those who interrogate the Brazil-sign and are drawn into the fruitless search for its ontology? The question will never be resolved, as we can never escape the slippage of the sign; it slides away just as the subject moves to grasp it. It is fascinating that guilt should spring from the impossibility of completely apprehending the sign; that guilt should ultimately be the result of the refusal to surrender to the perfect circle of signification and put an end to oscillation, once and for all. The national discourse, as we know, is an avowed enemy of oscillation, as it is no more than a perverse factory, a *dispositif* of symbols that are always the same.

What remains is the subject's desire to seek out some calm—the wish to put an end to oscillation and wipe clean one's debts with one's origin. It is significant that this desire may find a shape in the form of the death drive: at the end of Guimarães Rosa's story, I wish to become the father again, to be put into a canoe, so that I can float "down the river, away from the river, into the river—the river."[42] In reflecting on displacement, symbolic belonging is a constant challenge; but a conclusive reply to the sign and the comfort of immediate recognition of the sign of origin are the path to the death of the subject. This may be what literature is always saying. Perhaps Sérgio Buarque de Holanda found this same discomfort when he grappled with roots and discovered the Portuguese as a spectral Other and the nonplace that is Brazil. We should recall that, for Buarque de Holanda, the idea of the "frontier" is omnipresent, not only because he addresses it explicitly in works after *Roots of Brazil*, but also because, from *Roots of Brazil* onward, the interrogation of the sign leads inexorably to the frontier.

Here I might recall Ettore Finazzi-Agrò's conclusion to an essay in which he attempts to clarify the meaning of the "trivial" experience of the *sertanejo*—the character who inhabits the (spatial, cultural, temporal) frontier that the author of *Caminhos e fronteiras* [Paths and Frontiers] had sought out when he investigated the westward push in Portuguese America:

> Placed between *Roots of Brazil* and *Visão do paraíso*, *Caminhos e fronteiras* is that which its title prescribes: a labyrinthine walk down thorny paths, the snarls of a cultural territory situated between multiplying barriers; an inexhaustible search for that which emerges spontaneously between experience and fantasy, between the roots of the present and visions of the past, which only a stubborn, nostalgic memory can save from oblivion. Because it is precisely here, at these symbolic crossroads, erased by time and shaped by power, that we may surprise and be surprised by a third, contingent meaning, a banished and abandoned knowledge, a "trivial" truth, calling our certainties into question and ultimately showing the forbidden [*interdito*] that is constantly spoken [*dito entre*] in the spaces between social and ideological oppositions, racial frontiers, and any sort of cultural delimitation.[43]

Beyond the history of *sertanejos*, émigrés, or ordinary travelers, the possibility of inhabiting the frontier and finding shelter there is reserved for those who accept the burden of the guilt left by the abandonment of their origin, casting themselves into a territory (that of language) in which belonging is transmuted into unbelonging, because the house to which the subject ought to return ceased to exist at the moment in which it was left—the moment in which all things, Rosa and roses among them, were left behind. What is left can be nothing more than a paradoxical presentification of absence, when the subject is called upon to articulate an entirely irreparable loss.

The power of signification in *Roots of Brazil* lies coded, as strange as it may seem, in the impotence of the national discourse that the book reveals. *Roots of Brazil*, we might say, is the portrait of a territory about to lose itself. Because we learn, in the end, that we cannot speak of any land, be it mine, or ours, or theirs, without undergoing exile—which is the place from which one inevitably speaks.

CHAPTER 5

Seeking America
The Impasses of Liberalism (1)

> *Does it make sense, to think of disenchantment as the entrance into a world full of meaning? For Weber, it does. If we fail to understand this, it is because we still have not understood how Weber sees the disenchantment of the world.*
> —Antônio Flávio Pierucci, O desencantamento do mundo: Todos os passos do conceito em Max Weber, 2003

At times in *Roots of Brazil*, the reader's imagination is led along by the pull of the investigative dive. In addressing the starting point of the Iberian origins of Brazilian culture, the book—from its very title, from its first paragraph—is a call for slow progression and far-reaching exploration, as if the process of examining the civilizational and cultural experience meant necessarily reviving the marine metaphors that often aid historians in understanding the long survival of forms of socializing and traditional values in times and places of constant transformation. Using the metaphorical field in question, we might say that movements on the surface do little more than dissemble the drive below, whose foundations and irresistible power frustrate many of men's efforts and gestures. This imagining proposes a profound, slow story of the Americas, which the essay unveils in tracing a sort of submarine cartography—or, to return to the original metaphor, a subterranean map that, once unfolded, would reveal the broad strokes of a culture in the Iberian model.[1]

Sérgio Buarque de Holanda's Romantic influences have already been identified and studied, both in *Roots of Brazil* as well as his masterpiece, *Visão do paraíso* [Vision of Paradise] (1958).[2] Indeed, the pull of the investigative dive—if that suggestion holds water—recalls the sublime experience of the surrender, "body and soul," to the earth and its secrets. Buarque de Holanda himself emphasized, in one of his few autobiographical texts, the "darker" side to German culture as he experienced it during his time in Berlin (1929–1930), when in the twilight of the Weimar Republic, he became acquainted with "mystical and irrationalist philosophies," as he describes his first contact with Ludwig Klages.[3]

I do not wish to discuss the "Romantic" Sérgio Buarque de Holanda. I shall simply recall that his German stay also brought him to Sombart, Simmel, and Weber, all of whom may thus be placed at the conception, or at least in the development, of *Roots of Brazil*. There is an important turn here. The Weberian method, for example, is indebted to the "method dispute" that shook the field of human sciences (or the sciences "of spirit") in the latter half of the nineteenth century, founding the comprehension of history on the observation and cataloguing of *action*, and thus attenuating that which, restricted to the level of the individual, would be reserved for psychology. The conception of culture that emerges here is founded on *ethics*—the prevailing actions of individuals who, guiding themselves by certain values and bowing to a certain vision of the world, reshape society on a daily basis, although not out of any personal whim. Powerful forces govern the world of men and women, and social theory sets itself out to understand them. In confirming or imagining the existence of those powerful, extra-individual forces, we are once again left with the feeling that we are being dragged along by a deep current, without knowing exactly how or why.[4]

The issue might be boiled down to an understanding of this thrust, or irresistible subterranean force. Seeing it as an irreducible telluric force disdainful of human invention is one path among many. To read *Roots of Brazil* this way, however, would be to retreat in our understanding, returning the essay to Romantic frameworks that, while perhaps shaping the imagination of a young Buarque de Holanda, may not be sufficient to understand the scope of his debut book.[5] It is true that the vocabulary and the imaginary of *Roots of Brazil*, from the first edition to the "definitive" version, may lead to the conclusion that history is governed by irrational principles, or by those "specific needs" of society that, while somewhat inexplicable, come together in the form of the "more intimate and essential world" referred to in the book's final paragraph. We should recall, however, that here we are facing a charged metaphorical field.[6]

Undoubtedly, organic and essentialist metaphors bear the weight of traditions of thought dating back to at least the nineteenth century. It can be no accident, for that matter, that these same references appear in the chapters whose "essence," if we trust in Buarque de Holanda's memory, was brought over from Germany as part of a pretentious "Teoria da América" [Theory of America].[7] However, the composition of *Roots of Brazil* may also point in the opposite direction, shaping a perception of history not exclusively founded on irreducible, conclusive principles of "national character." Rather, we might be seeing the subtle revelation of certain cultural constants that, in the Ibero-American realm, condense—once again, metaphorically—into a cartographical image: the "European Frontiers."[8]

The difference is an important one. If we take the metaphors literally, then "roots" and "essences" are seen to operate as primordial forces in a deterministic explanation, in which the "tropical and sub-tropical" environment, as one reads in the first edition of *Roots of Brazil*, sets the pace for subsequent transformations—or simply a telluric interpretation, where the rhythm or "ebb and flow" of society stems from the mysterious emanations of the land. In the history of Brazilian social thought, the inescapable precedent of a mesological and telluric reading of the nation's history dates from the turn of the twentieth century; although, in the illustrious case of *Rebellion in the Backlands* (1902), by Euclides da Cunha, we should recall that the forces of the land are at once the natural elements governing men and the dramatic figuration of a political and human tragedy.[9]

The reference is not a casual one; it is hard to imagine that a discussion of Iberian roots in the 1930s could possibly ignore the *forma mentis* that cast the physical environment as the great theater of the Brazilian civilizational adventure. Not only does the phrase "exiles in our own land" recall the eloquent and torturous prose of Euclides da Cunha, but the imaginary constructed in *Roots of Brazil* also transforms that adventure into a drama set against the landscape.[10] Nevertheless, while the first chapter of Buarque de Holanda's essay unfolds from a geographical image, let us respect rhetoric as such: an understanding of the historical problem comes through the mobilization of recognizable images that may illuminate the constellation of contemporary problems for the reader. Hence we have the then-current conception of the Iberian Peninsula as a European "bridge-territory," in keeping with Gilberto Freyre's earlier proposition in *The Masters and the Slaves*.[11] A Europe that reaches beyond itself, in the image that today's readers will recognize in the fictional plane of their own time.[12]

The Pyrenees are the geographical limit of this symbolic order. The space between the mountains and Gibraltar apparently gave rise to something apart from the major lines of European history. The "cult of the personality" is the defining characteristic in one of Buarque de Holanda's main characters: the Iberian man. To brutally simplify it, we might say that the atrophy of the public sphere is the logical result of an inflated personality: in a land of endless barons, the political pact is reduced to relationships of loyalty or hate. To follow the clearly organicist-inspired metaphors, "anarchical elements" blossom, while "active intentions" are lost in a world of imperious individual passions. Here emerge the characteristics of an imagined other America, tied to a different civilizational paradigm, hostile to the origins of liberalism and resisting the erasure or curbing of individual passions. In Buarque de Holanda's plausibly Weberian take, among Iberian peoples the surrender to the world never came through the nullification or sublimation of the powers and appetites of the individual. There was never any surrender to the dimension (originally religious, posteriorly secularized) in which the individual dives fully into the world of work—the point at which asceticism left the monastery, in Max Weber's famous image.[13]

As we know, the conception of capitalism that springs from this vision has post–Reformation Europe as a reference but also constantly alludes to the "America" that had haunted Weber himself and that appears as an oblique, not always fully revealed reference in *Roots of Brazil*. The United States, one might argue, provides the uncomfortable mirrored image of a supposedly successful experiment, relegating Brazilians to seeing themselves as the reflection or development of another reality, of another Europe: another Europe, another America.[14]

Here we find ourselves before the imaginary formation of two worlds, or two ethics: *work* and *adventure*. Given the contrast between them, one can formulate the question that hangs over the reader of *Roots of Brazil*: what pact may be struck around the ethics of exploiting the land to the maximum, extreme mobility among people, and the exaltation of the immediate strength of the individual? What political community would emerge from such a foundation? Here we may have found the point where Buarque de Holanda's analysis ventures into a different interpretation, in a deliberately economic register; the problem is also related to accumulation and the formation of a national community able to manage what it produces. I am referring to a classical explanation for Brazilian "backwardness" and its colonial Iberian roots, its origins going back to historian Caio Prado Júnior (1907–1990) and stretching through the work of economist Celso Furtado (1920–2004).[15] The central issue is that the organizing principle of society falls short of satisfying its own "active intentions," which sink into an unsettling disorder.

As a possible answer to *disorder*—a paradoxical, but logical one—there is the individual's unconditional surrender to a superior force that he fears. Without an ethic founded on the unifying frameworks of constant, methodical work (as in the "Protestant" world formulated by Max Weber), the only conceivable discipline lies in absolute obedience to an order outside mankind. Hence the "extraordinary rationalization" of the Jesuit missions during the colonial period, as the author remarks in the first chapter of *Roots of Brazil*. Hence the Counter-Reformist shadow looming over the Iberian political experience.

"Disorder," *lato sensu*, is the key element that, in traditional political imaginings, triggers the need for ordering forces. The social body, it seems, can remain whole only if the seeds of dissolution are kept under tight control. This is precisely the conservative framework that Buarque de Holanda's investigation is challenging. By 1936, if we believe the historian, "simple obedience" had been exhausted as a principle of discipline; at the same time, however, that sclerotic foundation of blind obedience was giving rise to the vilest authoritarian ideologies, with the justification of "overcom[ing] the effects of our restless and disorderly nature" at all costs.[16]

A detailed analysis of *Roots of Brazil* may reveal its dialogues with the ideological currents of its time. At the end of the book, Buarque de Holanda brandishes an energetic pen against the "incipient Brazilian 'Mussolinism'" of the integralists, while he also, and more subtly, registers his discontent with any and all order-imposing philosophies that target the "restless and disorderly," the "more intimate and essential world," "our own spontaneous rhythm"—which, read out of context, may come off as altogether too mysterious, or perhaps simply irrational. What rhythm; what essential world?[17] To better understand this move, one must turn to literature and the "modernist" movement, where the author's aesthetic and ideological projects intersect.[18]

Roots of Brazil opens up to a discussion of burning impasses in a society experiencing the clash between liberal values and totalitarian inspirations at a time when new forms of political and labor associations were stamping out previous experiments, feeding into the personalist vein of Latin American political history. In this sense, the book mulls over the present and interrogates the future. At the same time, *Roots of Brazil* is written with an eye on the past, erecting a bridge between the young critic and the present writer. While some of the early visions of the modernist movement had already fallen by the wayside, they had not been obliterated completely in spirit—in Buarque de Holanda's case, at least, the literary critic of the previous decade, the 1920s, had not been completely wiped away.[19]

To put it extremely concisely and schematically, one might say that "O lado oposto e outros lados" [The Opposite Side and Other Sides], an article published in 1926 in *Revista do Brasil*, is a watershed in Buarque de Holanda's early career, where he introduces some of the ideas that would appear ten years later, mediated by his German experience, in *Roots of Brazil*. In less-than-cordial fashion, young Buarque de Holanda tosses diplomacy to the wind and sets down a harsh critique of the academicizing modernists who, believing themselves to be mastering a uniquely "national expression," were simply imposing their hierarchy onto the world of art in an updated version of the very sort of pretentious, lettered attitude that Brazilian modernism had sought to topple. I will not enter into a detailed discussion of the complex network of dialogues that emerges in the article; the reader should simply recall that, in addition to the article's apparent targets, Ronald de Carvalho (1893–1935) and Guilherme de Almeida (1890–1969), we should look to Catholic thinker Alceu Amoroso Lima (1893–1983) and the still-imposing, uncomfortable shadow of the venerable lettered patriarch José Pereira da Graça Aranha (1868–1931).[20]

Buarque de Holanda summoned up these specters in order to exorcize them. "O lado oposto e outros lados" is a splendid discussion of the advocates of "order," on one side, and those who, positioning themselves on "other sides," distrusted order in any form and pinned their hopes on spontaneity, conceived of as the "freedom" that could stave off authoritarian tendencies. Interestingly enough, the same spontaneity that the young modernist defended in 1926 would later reappear in *Roots of Brazil* as the element thwarting the authoritarian plans of those seeking to "organize our disorder," as we read in the book's last paragraph.

There are important points of convergence between *Roots of Brazil* and this article. Let us lend an ear to the young, polemical author's extended diatribe in "O lado oposto e outros lados" against the partisans of order, those

> well-intentioned people ... who may in any case be on the verge of imposing on us a hierarchy, an order, [and] a system that will once and for all stamp out our heedlessness, that of a people abundant in youth and lacking in judgment. We lack for an art, a literature, a school of thought, they say, that might translate any sort of constructive urge. And they insist on this abominable

panacea of *construction*. Because as they see it, for the moment, we are writhing around in chaos and delighting in disorder. [But] what is disorderly? This question is essential, as the order that is disturbed here is undoubtedly not, nor can it be, *our order*; it must be a fictitious, foreign thing, a dead law, which we have imported—if not from another world, then at least from the Old World. We send for these corsets so that we can learn to make ourselves presentable and attractive to others' eyes. Their error lies in their wishing to spirit away our freedom, which is, at least for the moment, our most considerable asset, in favor of a detestable abstraction, entirely inopportune and empty of meaning.[21]

Compare the "heedlessness, that of a people abundant in youth and lacking in judgment," from the pen of the twenty-four-year-old, with the "restless and disordered nature" in his debut book, written ten years later. In both cases, he is vindicating and defending a rhythm, or a pulse, set against the idealizing raptures of political architects (in *Roots of Brazil*, in 1936) or the framers of Brazilian art (in the 1926 article). In both cases, the so-called reform proposed by the partisans of order is ultimately nothing more than a reaction, or a "subtle counter-reform[ation]," as Buarque de Holanda ironically suggests, in referring to the possibility of fascism's finding a foothold in Brazil.

Still within the ambit of Iberian origins, as discussed in the first chapter of *Roots of Brazil*, it seems that the impasse—which is at once aesthetic and ideological—springs from the two extremes that a cult of personality leads to, since the "desire to command and the propensity to carry out orders are equally peculiar to [Iberian peoples]. Dictatorships and the Holy Office seem to be aspects as typical of their character as the inclination to anarchy and disorder. Their outlook includes no kind of well-conceived discipline other than that based on [the] excessive centralization of power and on obedience."[22]

The drive to obey and command is at play here, always in terms of the (aesthetic or ideological) values that, mirrored in a heaven of certainties, stretch out like a sort of immutable slate that is eternally identical to itself. The Scholastic imaginary is very much present, from the first chapter of *Roots of Brazil*:

The Middle Ages were hardly aware of conscious aspirations to reform civil society. The world was organized on the basis of eternal and unquestionable iron laws, imposed from another world by the supreme organizer of all things. By a singular paradox, society's formative principle was, in its clearest expression, an enemy to the world and life. All the work of medieval thinkers, of the great builders of systems, meant nothing more than the effort to disguise, to the utmost extent possible, the antagonism between Spirit and Life (*Gratia naturam non tollit sed perficit* [Grace does not destroy nature but improves it]). This is, in a certain sense, a fertile and venerable task, but one whose essential meaning our era does not wish to comprehend. The enthusiasm that this grandiose hierarchical concept can inspire today, as it was known in the Middle Ages, is in reality a passion of professors.[23]

Between the "supreme organizer" of the world and the "professors" enchanted by the perfection of their own concepts, there is a key difference: in the medieval mentality, the static nature of values was an unequivocal and, in the final balance, a productive fact. This is how we may understand the "modern" nature of the Council of Trent (1545–1563), as a Counter-Reformist reaction to the world flourishing farther to the north in the wake of the Protestant Reformation, which was establishing an entirely different conception of individualism.

Thomist principles would suggest that the distance from that ideal heaven would not impede but rather pave the way for perfecting the natural world through the light of revelation. Buarque de Holanda's discomfort comes at the (contemporary) point when overweening social engineering becomes the unquestionable model for achieving political perfection. In Thomist terms, sacred doctrine is not up for discussion; this would make it a product of reason or authority, robbing it of dignity in the process. But as we read in response to such an objection in the *Summa Theologica* (the source of the quotation in *Roots of Brazil*), sacred doctrine may well be based on the arguments of authority. After all, it is ultimately imperative that we believe in the *authority of those to whom the revelation was made*. Reducing that authority to an anachronistic, ridiculous "passion of professors" is, precisely, the essayist's very contemporary aim.[24]

A deep examination of Buarque de Holanda's discussion here also requires that we understand this: one of the great villains of Counter-Reformist thinking is the reader who frees himself from the shackles of orthodoxy. Within the imaginary of these two worlds (and here we would have to discuss the case of France, wracked by religious wars), there opens up, in Reformist Europe, a new horizon of interpretation through the possibility of an individualized reading of the Scriptures, returning to the mystical experience of epiphany—the revelation of meaning—in its radically intimate sense. For an imagination marked by readings of Weber and a broad understanding of Reformist mentalities, the meaning of the world can only be revealed, and precariously at that, in the space that connects text and reader, without the mediation of authority. The truth of men's designs remains the province of the "other world"—although, for a modern mentality (a Weberian modernity), the hereafter has been almost completely obliterated. All that is left to the individual is the fervent, patient dedication to secular tasks, among which are the reading and interpretation of the world.

In the Ibero-American context, a belated Thomist reaction would be possible, as "professors" still see themselves as the bearers of a lifeline for the community—which, given over to its own impulses (or its own interpretations of the world), would inevitably stray and be lost. We might say that, in the world of the Protestant Reformation, intimacy shields subjects who know themselves to be autonomous in interpreting the world, while the Counter-Reformist mentality leans on the acceptance of tradition, mediated by a strict policing of the *doxa* (a generally accepted opinion) by those who, possessed of unquestionable knowledge, serve to guide the consciences of the rest. In both cases, the hereafter hangs over the world; but within a Reformist mentality, that hereafter is infinitely distant and does not make its way directly into daily life, nor does it allow for figures to dub themselves the arbiters of the revealed word, as if it lay dormant in the Scriptures awaiting an exceptional reading that might revitalize it. This is, in short, a complex problem of interpretation and the search for meaning. The foundational paradox of modernity in its

Protestant form would thus be this: armed with the knowledge of one's infinite distance from the divine realm, the individual is given an even more peremptory role, turned over entirely to edifying work, tragically imprisoned in the world, seeing free will as nothing more than an illusion, with no other path but work to grow closer to God. Any deviation from the work ethic is a mortal blow, as well as the proof of the arrogance of the individual who fails to give in entirely to the task of constructing the community of the Elect.

In restoring the importance of the polemics around free will, which take center stage in the religious and political debates of the modern era, Buarque de Holanda recalls that "the Spanish and Portuguese always looked with distrust and opposition on theories denying free will." With personality being the supreme value for Iberians, "spontaneous organization" becomes difficult, and now we see that this difficulty does not stem solely from an excess of "barons." The root problem is the difficulty of individuals in moderating their gestures and fitting themselves to a pact with the community, ultimately accepting that hierarchies are not, and cannot be, definitively consummated in this world. In short, for this figure of the Buarquian imagination—the Iberian man—individual surrender is not a methodical capitulation to the constancy of everyday work. Rather, it comes through the spectacular gesture of prostrating oneself before a higher truth, which, incarnate in a given idea or person, may reveal itself on the plane in which we live, offering definitive solutions to all our ills. In the Iberian context, for this other America, salvation is a political project led by an exceptional creature.[25]

Roots of Brazil contains a clear aporia, with vast consequences. On the one hand, modernist criticism (as updated in this book) apparently seeks to pour all its ammunition into those who defend the "dead law," seeking out order in the "other world," which is also the "Old World," to recall the 1926 article. On the other hand, there is a "common soul" linking Brazilians to their Iberian lineage, the source of the "present form of our culture," and which, if well understood, would draw us closer to what we are. And what we are is also the other world, then, and the Old World. In simpler terms, here we have a dual, incongruous defense: of spontaneity and originality on the one hand, and a shared identity with the antecessor on the other. This is a clearly modernist imbroglio, and it is only natural that the twenty-four-year-old, in 1926, should have leaned toward a passionate vindication of irreverent authenticity, while the more mature writer, in 1936, finds himself before a chain of impasses, believing at once in originality and its opposite.[26]

There is a logical flow in *Roots of Brazil*, leading the imagination to the extreme point of proposing an "original contribution" to the world through the realization of a singular collective entity. But the original creature itself succumbs to its author's prophecy: once the historical conditions that gave rise to him have fallen away, the "cordial man" will vanish.[27] Cordiality is an evanescent category that nevertheless persists in remaining, as if it were a remnant that one might not shed, or forget.[28]

Beyond these contradictions, it may be possible to glimpse a sort of modernist attitude, especially in Brazilian modernism's "cannibalistic" mode: as we reveal ourselves to the world, we are called upon to draw closer to a nucleus that is more "our own," deviant from the European norm and resistant to permanent lineages, apt to pervert them even as it assimilates them. No matter that this nucleus may be unreal; all the stuff of imagination is necessarily so. I should call our attention, however, to that which emerges in *Roots of Brazil* as a "spontaneous rhythm," or the "more intimate and essential world," disdaining human inventions and threatening even the most elaborate political architecture. I believe that this is a point of entry to be explored. Why is such a high value placed on this deviance and the active intentions that scorn ideal solutions?

To return to the metaphorical field where we began this chapter, it seems that the problem lies in finding a singular "ebb and flow" that does not merely stir the surface, but churns up the seabed as well. The transformation of this potential deviance and supposed singularity into a constructive force is an intricate logical problem, finding easier solutions in the poetic realm than in political terms. The Latin American imagination harbors a powerful desire, at least a century old, to vindicate the autochthonous forces that might sever America's colonial or postcolonial condition at the root. But there always remains the agonizing question as to what would be left after that profound destruction, after the uprooting had been definitively consummated. There is a nagging sensation of the vagueness and mystery around the possibilities contained in these "active intentions," always ready to resist the specious engineering of traditional politics. It would be tempting to read this element as the "people" and identify in the 1936 Sérgio Buarque de Holanda all the radicalism that Antonio Candido lends him.[29] But one may also, and without contradicting the former, imagine that the author of *Roots of Brazil* is laying out dilemmas that we, eighty years later, can respond to with a serenity that would have been improbable at the time.

There remains to emerge a careful examination of the concerns that the debate over liberal and totalitarian principles sparked in Buarque de Holanda while he wrote *Roots of Brazil*. The latest editions of the book offer mitigating comments as to the "fraudulent" nature (as it read in 1936) of the "liberal mythology," according to which "tyrannical expedients could bring about nothing lasting." This is not, it should be emphasized, any attempt to identify an early fascination with authoritarian regimes; I insist that that would be an error.[30] Rather, one should simply acknowledge that before the Estado Novo (1937–1945) and World War II (1939–1945), a critique of liberal principles (particularly, as Buarque de Holanda writes in a 1935 article on Carl Schmitt, the idea that "the State tends to be a mere servant of a neutral society, or a new sort of society"[31]) was already present in the thesis that the Iberian experience in America had constituted an alternative concept of politics that the posterior success of the liberal world would bury for quite a while (or forever, from the eschatological perspective of a neoliberal imagination).

Finding a conclusive answer and affirming that Buarque de Holanda was really on this or that side would not be satisfying. Significantly enough, near the end of his life, when an editor asked him to write an essay "updating his ideas" for the French edition of *Roots of Brazil*, he tried and failed to do so—as he would say more than once in interviews.[32] The failure of the rewriting may have to do with dated vocabulary, the bad graces that grand essays found themselves in by the seventies in Brazil, or simply the impossibility of rewriting the same book. But it might also stem from his suspicion that the *organic* nature and the revelation of those "active intentions" might point toward the potential failure of the liberal pact, bringing forth the need for "recovery of historical design or mission," as Richard McGee Morse (1922–2001) valiantly put it—he being the author who may have taken the rewriting of *Roots of Brazil* the farthest, although his *Prospero's Mirror* (1982, in Spanish; 1988, in Portuguese) does not allude once to Sérgio Buarque de Holanda.

If we discount Morse's acrimony, which springs from his disenchantment with the North American liberal conscience as well as from an Adornian scorn of the United States, we will see that *Prospero's Mirror* may well serve as a mirror to *Roots of Brazil*. This mirror deforms and extends that which in Buarque de Holanda's essay had remained implicit or simply unnoticed. In seeking to understand, map, and evaluate the intellectual choices that, in the prehistory of modern mentalities, would have given rise to the crossroads of European political thought, the American historian does not hide his profound sympathy for the "Iberian option." It is as if the "successful attempt" at transplanting European culture, as we read in the first edition of *Roots of Brazil*, had been rescued by Morse; he, in turn, deepens and expands upon the consequences of a civilization that took a different path from that blazed by the "Protestant peoples," England in particular. In his concise, provocative formulation, "For two centuries a North American mirror has been held aggressively to the South, with unsettling consequences. The time has perhaps come to turn the reflecting surface around."[33]

In short, Morse's enchantment with the Iberian way comes from the possibility of making out, in the medieval Scholastics (and in the branches that will blossom into neo-Thomism, illustrious among Iberian thinkers), a sensitivity to the role of *conjecture* and *hypothesis* in the construction of thought, against the grain of "modern" science's desire to demonstrate an "ultimate certainty, to lay bare reality itself."[34] We may be drawing very close to Buarque de Holanda's observation in *Roots of Brazil* that "Scholasticism was creative in the Middle Ages because it was current." To bolster the arguments here, we are now very much aware of how much can be learned from medieval intellectual history, and how much the "pre-modern" world and its premises enrich and lend density to the perception of a universe governed by modern scientific paradigms—which, in our time, constantly feed back into our belief in science's unlimited capacities of revelation, restricting the field of possibilities to the area bound by a single circle. To recall that the world governed by modern science has its own "premises" and assumptions, without which science itself is stripped of meaning and validity, may remind us that there are other, equally legitimizable worlds, certainly deserving of respect. The quarrel over the "various possible worlds," then, emerges in all its longevity, a discussion that is at once "current and uncurrent," to recall categories dear to Buarque de Holanda.

The seduction of the Iberian route invites the scholar to broaden, in both space and time, those conceptions—of the individual, the national interest, or a possible mission of the people—forged and developed in a bygone era. This is, to an extent, where *Roots of Brazil* and *Prospero's Mirror* meet: in the recognition that a history of the Americas must necessarily dialogue with a remote European history. A faith in the Iberians and their allegedly more porous universalism, open to diversity and the variety of the human race, evidently finds an extreme supporter in Morse, while Buarque de Holanda, eighty years ago, seems more reserved. But it is plausible that in both cases, distrust of the liberal model may be the driving force, the primary cause of their writing. At the heart of it all is the suspicion of the erasure of the individual, the abstraction of his singularity, and the unconditional surrender to the progress of the material world.

In keeping with Morse's literary intuition, the problem is patent in the counterpoint between the poets T. S. Eliot and Mário de Andrade, between J. Alfred Prufrock, with his "irreparably damaged self," and Andrade's harlequin poet, who shouts and sobs (impotently, we should always recall) in the hallucinated metropolis. The "generalized Western city" in Eliot meets itself and finds itself impoverished before the mirror of Mário de Andrade's still-enchanted São Paulo. Morse's interpretation heralds an unswerving sympathy for the other side of the mirror, taken in all its Latin American or Ibero-American breadth: Colonel Aureliano Buendía against Colonel Thomas Sutpen, García Márquez's Macondo against Faulkner's Yoknapatawpha County. In this clear and candid vision, a "split between aesthetic and scientific sensibilities, which in Mariátegui were united, has shifted to Ibero-American novelists, poets, and artists the burden of responsibility for rendering their world as center and not periphery."[35] For Morse, the poetic realm prophesies and shelters the solutions that never really came to fruition on the political plane.

The matter is revisited in Morse's response to the stinging critiques he received from Simon Schwartzman (to which I will return in the next chapter), when in the essayistic spirit that he fully embraced, the North American historian confessed himself "drawn to the playful exploration of the human consciousness," presenting in his defense a line of authors whom he cast as preserving "the function of the *homo ludens*, whose vitality Huizinga considered the fundamental ingredient in art, culture, and social improvisation, and which, he declared in 1944, was declining rapidly in Europe."[36] This observation becomes even more interesting when, in a later article on Freyre and Buarque de Holanda, Morse compares both authors to Huizinga, although he sees in the latter a "classical" tendency, as opposed to the "baroque" mentality of the former:

> If Gilberto Freyre suggests one of Huizinga's medieval chroniclers, his contemporary, Sérgio Buarque de Holanda, takes the path of Huizinga himself. Both pursue the secret of Brazil, but Gilberto evokes its image while Sérgio inserts the nation into Western historical process and prescribes for its extrication from traditional politics. One, in an American spirit of anthropological pluralism, celebrates his discovery of Brazilian patriarchal culture; the other uses his European training to explore the tension between inherited patriarchalism and the encroachment of Western liberalism. In the categories of art historian Heinrich Wölfflin, Freyre's was a baroque or painterly mentality that explored variations on a central theme while Sérgio Buarque followed a classical or linear search for tectonic strength.[37]

As a final problem—long ardent, but especially provocative in 1936—there remained the relationship between the individual and the state, or the very nature of the state. This is not to put on the dusty record that still often echoes in our ears, discussing "greater" or "smaller" state presence in the life of its citizens. To return to Buarque de Holanda's concerns when discussing Carl Schmitt, this is much more a question of daring to see the state not as a neutral creature, but as one intimately bestowed with a mission, incarnating what Morse, then speaking of the "Catholic monarchs," identifies as the "responsibility for choosing common objectives," which in England had been "withdrawn from the state and assigned, in an Ockhamite spirit of pluralism, to a presumptively 'free' marketplace of private ideas and prescriptions, now treated as 'commodities.'"[38] To indulge in a bit of metaphorical exaggeration, I believe that here we have hit the muddy ground that the reader of *Roots of Brazil* tends to avoid.

The political history of the twentieth century has amply revealed the disastrous potential of the state as the incarnation of a mission. In the Latin American sphere, our expertise in dictatorships may authorize us to prudently retreat from any attempts at investing the state with a seamless organicity that would logically make it the bearer of a collective mission, at the moment in which—to remain faithful to our organic imaginary—the state apparatus reveals itself to be the congenital form of society's active intentions, a sovereign protector of the potentially good sociological order of the land, as might well be suggested by a conservative thinker such as Francisco José de Oliveira Vianna (1883–1951).[39]

Drinking from a Hegelian fount, Buarque de Holanda saw the state as a "creature of the mind" that "is opposed to and transcends the natural order." The challenge lies precisely in defining the bounds of the social body, its intrinsic needs—or, to return to Morse's terms, its "designs." In Buarque de Holanda's defense, we must recall that these "higher forms [or *exterior* forms, as we read in the first edition of *Roots of Brazil*] of society" are not conceived of as an "order" finally attained and revealed. On the contrary, and in the best young-modernist spirit, these higher forms of society "continually emerge from its specific needs, and never from capricious choices."[40] There is something lively and restive in these never sufficiently explained "specific necessities." The intertextual fabric of *Roots of Brazil* does not authorize us to advance as far as Antonio Gramsci (1891–1937), although its complex web of "specific necessities" might open up to a discussion of hegemony, which Morse will take from Raymond Williams's formulations (hegemony as a "lived social process," organized by dominant, but not exclusive, meanings and values), and which we might conceive of nowadays in terms of reflections around Brazil's "passive revolution."[41]

But in the end, a dedicated and stubborn reader of Max Weber might ask—given the redemptive mission of the Ibero-American peoples, as defended by Richard Morse, and given Sérgio Buarque de Holanda's uneasiness over the future of societies of Iberian descent—mightn't the reaction to the depersonalization of the individual stem from an inability to take the path of the modern world to its ultimate consequences? Doesn't the struggle against disenchantment essentially hide the desire to seek out meaning where it has already crumbled? And couldn't this desperate search for meaning blaze the path, in turn, for a new, almost religious intellectualization, with new ends and new means? Doesn't the refutation of the "modern" path, as in Richard Morse's case, bear the risk of forging yet another rigid rationalization, simply sacralizing another ethic? What meaning can we take, ultimately, from the confident refusal of the agonistic vision of a world in which the individual is stripped of all character, becoming yet another cog in the proverbial running machine?

If indeed there is such a refusal of the individual's agony in the modern world, we cannot simply investigate its consequences; its very meaning must be sought out as well. And on the way, we may wish to keep on responding to winds from the North with beautiful windmills. The reenchantment of the world is an imaginary path that *Roots of Brazil* does not propose, but which interested readers, such as Morse and perhaps ourselves, may perfectly well blaze.

CHAPTER 6

"El hombre cordial" and Specular Poetics

The Impasses of Liberalism (2)

Even for our grandparents a "house," a "well," a familiar tower, their very clothes, their coat: were infinitely more, infinitely more intimate; almost everything a vessel in which they found the human and added to the store of the human. Now, from America, empty indifferent things are pouring across, sham things, dummy life. . . . A house, in the American sense, an American apple or grapevine over there, has nothing in common with the house, the fruit, or the grape into which went the hopes and reflections of our forefathers. . . . Live things, things lived and conscient of us, are running out and can no longer be replaced. We are perhaps the last still to have known such things.
    —Letters *of Rainer Maria Rilke,* in Giorgio Agamben,
    Stanzas: Word and Phantasm in Western Culture, *1977*

In a brief portrait of Edgar Allan Poe, Nicaraguan poet Rubén Darío (1867–1916) recalls the day he arrived for the first time in the United States, docking in New York Harbor. The landscape is marvelous and mist-shrouded ("It was a cold, damp morning when I arrived for the first time in the immense nation of the United States"), inviting the reader to embark on the discovery of a terrain replete with meanings: the metropolis that emerges between isles and the country that spreads out before the beholder, brooking no resistance. Pressed between the vastness of Long Island and the silhouette of Staten Island, even before the iron landscape of Manhattan revealed itself, the poet felt that its beauty called out to his "pencil, if not, due to lack of sun, the photographer's camera."[1]

Here we have a good jumping-off point for "Americanist" lines of inquiry that may suggest a specular poetics. America discovers itself before America, finally finding, in the crushing grandiosity of the North, its double—desired and feared, repudiated (as is clear in part of Darío's poetry and prose), but also admired. These considerations blossom, in this initial scene, amidst the hubbub of "barking Yankee slang," when the pencil, not the camera, is called in to draw that which only the poet is given to see. Instead of a simple mechanical record of light—a strict, restrictive definition of photography—the pencil facilitates free, formative strokes. These are the lines that we should attempt to decipher.

What do poets and essayists see when they make out this other America? What seductive, terrible mirror is this? How do they imagine or intuit *another* America, at times supposing it single, nearly always configuring it as resistant? How does the imagination delineate a territory that reacts with pride (and fear) before that other (North) America, which Darío's ingenuity picks out in cyclopean New York, "the irresistible capital of Capital"? What brings together such disparate intellectuals around a difference that, once postulated, practically transforms them into demiurgic agents of national and regional discourse, invested with the power to reveal the secrets of the collectivity?

In the provocative tones of the poet who ventures into enemy territory, we can make out, as if in foreshadowing, the echoes of all the *arielismos* that would so deeply mark the Latin American imagination. That imagination—the intellectual fantasy (or intellectuals' fantasy) around Latin America, or Ibero-America, was introduced by Darío even before José Enrique Rodó (1872–1917), when in his 1894 study on Poe, the Nicaraguan poet suggested that on the other side of the mirror, Caliban was king:

"Those cyclops ... ," says Groussac; "those fierce Calibans ... ," writes Péladan. Was Péladan right when he called these men of North America by those names? Caliban does reign on the island of Manhattan, and in San Francisco, Boston, Washington, as well—indeed, throughout the land. He has managed to institute the empire of *Matter*, from its mysterious state with Edison to its apotheosis in the hog, in that awe-inspiring city of Chicago. Caliban saturates himself with whiskey, as in Shakespeare's play he does with wine; he grows and prospers, and, slave to no Prospero, martyred by no genius of the air, he grows fat and multiplies—his name is Legion. By the will of God there rises up amidst those powerful monsters some being of superior nature, who spreads his wings before the eternal Miranda of the ideal. At that, Caliban mobilizes Sycorax against him, and banishes him or kills him. The world has seen this with Edgar Allan Poe, that ill-starred swan who best knew the world of dreams, and death.[2]

From the entrails of the monster, the fabric saturated with vices, the land ruled over by vile matter, there blooms a morbid flower—one of the "misfits" who so enchant Darío. In invoking them, he finds a shelter for himself beneath the resplendent arc of the symbolists and the decadent, eccentric lovers of the spirit in its most refined form, which bourgeois society threatened to destroy with its impious parade of identical, reproducible goods. The commodity, whose name struck fear into the hearts of true poets, was then the great enemy. And its name was Legion.

The Poe that emerges from Darío's readings, we should recall, is quite peculiar and supremely Baudelairean.[3] But we should also turn to the sociological currents that, with the proper approach, may shed light on the eccentric spirit that barely disguises its profound belief in social difference, in the exception that both separates intellectuals from the rest and, paradoxically, bestows on them the power to represent that which they are separating themselves from.

That said, my aim here is another altogether: I would like to examine how the parameters may be drawn for a discourse around the American territory that, in proposing a Europe divided by the Pyrenees, ends up casting the Americas as split along another fault line. The questions raised around Ibero-American unity, and which ultimately summon up Shakespearean characters to speak of a New World, do not speak exclusively to a present difference. In investigating the here and now, we can make out a question as to the future— nothing less than the future of peoples themselves—posed just as the gaze of the South dives into the imaginary territory that, if we take the poet at his word, may be circumscribed only by an unfettered and exceptional pencil.

* * *

The Shakespearean reference here has its own history, we should recall. In an illuminating study, Chantal Zabus traces the "Calibanic genealogy" that leads to the critical and poetic rediscovery of the savage, allowing us to imagine a fundamentally important inversion of values (Caliban supplanting Ariel and, most importantly, subverting Prospero's power). The author of *Tempests after Shakespeare* associates this shift with the postcolonial imagination that allowed Aimé Césaire, for example, in *Une tempête* (1969), to reread Shakespeare in the shadow of nearly a century of Calibanic recovery, the unequivocal origin of which being Renan's 1878 "drame philosophique," *Caliban, suite de La Tempête*.[4]

Before Prospero fell from grace, however, and Caliban became a sort of postcolonial hero (so sweet on the palate of the theory currently dominating North American academia), it was Ariel, of course, who garnered the interest and admiration of intellectuals on the margins—to wit, those looking from South to North, in a strange interplay of enchantment and disenchantment. The strangeness here is that, in denying North America its seductive power and affirming the exclusive enchantment of the promises sprung from the South, one is, essentially, highlighting the promises that the North gives off. In the arithmetic of attraction and repulsion, the affirmation of disenchantment may be covering up some moment of awe—ultimately compensating for the fear of falling for that which a good conscience would teach us to spurn. In the end, we can only ask just how much enchantment is hiding behind the postulation of a disenchanted world that, I insist, a good conscience leads us to associate with the Other, not ourselves. An Other that, in this case, is the giant growing spitefully to the North, awakening the specters of domination one by one.

The fear of an overwhelming enemy force calls out for the imagination of another space. In this vein, and taking a long view of social thought, we should turn, before Ibero-America, to a "Latin" America. Spreading from the south of the United States (or that which would become the territory of the United States of America), this region would allow many intellectuals to dream, in varying degrees of vagueness, of a glorious, superlative Roman lineage. The likely imperialist, French origins of the concept of "Latin America" have been amply discussed, and we should recall that many intellectuals joyfully postulate the unity of the Latin American subcontinent; rather, to respect the nineteenth-century metaphorical field, they happily speak in terms of a "race" all its own (and, though the rest of the world may not know it, a superior one).[5] At least this is often how a creole consciousness reacts to a certain brand of elitist Europeanism and how Latin America ends up with a taste for the local—that, to update the Romantic fable and strip it of some of its exoticism, would result, in the specific case of Brazil, in the modernist vein and the many nationalist branches that it sprouted after 1922 (year of the Week of Modern Art in São Paulo, as discussed in a previous chapter), stretching both Right and Left.

Let us linger, however, on Brazilian modernism's predecessors. To remain in the Hispanic-American realm, in his preface to the Cátedra edition of *Ariel* (1900), by José Enrique Rodó, Belén Castro proposes a framework for understanding the Latin American sentiment born of the previous century:

> This nineteenth-century Latin Americanism rests on three factors that greatly affected the mentality of the period: the Romantic vision of the "spirit of nations," coded in the inheritance of race, language, and religion; the raciological and eugenicist theories of the era; and the growing vigor of the United States, which

had occupied part of Mexico around 1840 and harbored ambitions of conquering new spaces in Central America and Panama. Faced with the Anglo-Saxons who disembarked from the *Mayflower*, [these Latin Americans] brandish a cultural and spiritual genealogy that goes back to Romulus and Remus—here begins the development of a different relationship with the Spanish metropolis, now stripped of its last American possessions. The oppressive "stepmother" of another age, now economically ruined and politically defanged, will be cast as the source of a humanist treasure trove (its language, art, and literature) revitalizing the ancestral lines of classical and Christian Latinity, and using them to bolster the threatened identity of Hispanic American *criollos*.[6]

Faced with this revitalization of the "ancestral lines of classical Latinity," a Brazilian reader may feel especially drawn, or perhaps authorized, to cast an ironic gaze on this glorious lineage to which "we Brazilians" apparently also belong. This is ultimately a genealogy, and as the readers of Machado de Assis are well aware, the establishment of a definite lineage invariably involves a bit of chicanery (just look to the case of Brás Cubas and the family's fraudulent noble credentials).[7] One way or another, no matter the degree of wariness with which we approach the matter, we are now at the heart of the *hispanismo* that Arcadio Díaz-Quiñones once associated, in a broad recontextualization of the fin-de-siècle period, with the notion of war and its "silent referent" in the form of the United States. Behind the search for these mythical parents, meant to compensate for the threat of invasion, the critic identifies a Freudian "family romance," with the parents substituted by "more grandiose personages."[8] And it is with Rodó, in the 1913 collection *El mirador de Próspero* [Prospero's Observatory], that we may see the shrinking of the concept and the definitive inclusion of Brazil into the continent's mental horizons:

> We South Americans, when it comes to bolstering this racial unity, do not need to speak of a Latin America; we do not need to call ourselves Latin Americans, to lend ourselves a general name that may embrace all of us, as we may call ourselves something

that signifies a larger unit, far more intimate and concrete: we may call ourselves "Iberoamericans," grandchildren of the heroic and civilizing race that has only been split into two European nations in the political realm; and we might go farther and say that the same name, *hispanoamericanos*, [also] serves for those native to Brazil.[9]

The line of thinkers given to imagining this single race (in more or less cosmic terms) is a long one, and in the Brazilian sphere it would include heavyweights such as Joaquim Nabuco (1849–1910) and Manoel Bonfim (1868–1932), to say nothing of the essayists of the 1930s or the broad anti-Americanism that would long mold the imagination of the Brazilian intellectual class, and which dissenting voices such as Monteiro Lobato (1882–1948) would, paradoxically, only reinforce. Nor is this the place for a list of the countless Hispanic-American authors who have, with varying degrees of solemnity, idealized a *Latin* or, more specifically, *Iberian* America. Rather, I am interested by the idea of a deep sentiment, the "*unidad íntima*" spoken of by Rodó and which a reader of Buarque de Holanda will immediately associate with his cutting declaration in *Roots of Brazil*: "inside, we are still not American."[10]

The lack of a double referent—an America of our *own*, and *Americans* themselves—gives rise to a passionate but doomed search, shot through as it is by the ambiguity of the refutation of an Other that is also the object of unconscious admiration. In the literary field alone, we should look to the marvelous ambivalence, the simultaneous love and hate for the United States that are the articles by José Martí (1853–1895) written for *La Nación* in Buenos Aires, especially those on the cyclopean city of New York.[11]

* * *

The invention of a genealogy, we may say, without delving into philosophical minutiae, involves a certain fascination with a radiant center, ultimately leaning toward that which Foucault called "the death of interpretation"—to wit, the absolute belief that "there are signs,

signs that exist primarily, originally, actually, as coherent, permanent, and systematic marks."[12] Strictly speaking, this belief in an original sign would lead to the stagnation of thought, but perhaps this very point—where interpretation approaches its own "death"—may give rise to the literary richness of the search, doomed to failure as it may be. Or, rather, the poetic result of an impossible search for identity bears within it extremely important questions, with social consequences: Who is included in the sign of the collectivity? Who is the author of the collective saga? Which voices are authorized to speak in the name of the community? Who is at the margin, and who at the center of the sign? What lies outside it? And if it does lie outside, why must it always be invoked alongside the "race" itself?

As for this belief in an American *race*—this race that Sérgio Buarque de Holanda, following the path of Martí's readers, must have contemplated before declaring that there was still no fully formed American entity[13]—it poses a very "Latin American" paradox, in the postulation of a collective identity ultimately based on the impurity of mixture and mingling. Enthusiastic readers will see in this a paean to hybridism, such fertile ground for imagination, and which "we" Brazilians know so well. After all, Brazilians may have been fortunate enough to see it forged, starting in the 1930s, by none other than Gilberto Freyre, as already discussed here. We might wonder, however, what is left *outside* the construction of this identity, of a gleefully "mestizo" people. In other words, one is forced to forget the violence and ill-fated encounters that are sublimated when praising the encounter of cultures and in proposing a "mestizo" American civilization.[14]

Let us recall the final words from Prospero-Rodó in *Ariel* (1900)— exemplary words, in many respects:

> I want you to remember my words, but even more, I beseech you to cherish the indelible memory of my statue of Ariel. I want the airy and graceful image of this bronze to be imprinted forever in the innermost recesses of your mind. I remember that once while enjoying a coin collection in a museum, my attention was captured by the legend on an ancient coin: the word *Hope*, nearly effaced from the faded gold. As I gazed at that worn inscription, I pondered what its influence might have been. Who knows

"*El hombre cordial*" and Specular Poetics 125

what noble and active role in forming the character and affecting the lives of human generations we could attribute to that simple theme's working its insistent suggestion on those who held it in their hands? Who knows, as it circulated from hand to hand, how much fading joy was renewed, how many generous plans brought to fruition, how many evil proposals thwarted, when men's gaze fell upon the inspiring word incised, like a graphic cry, on the metallic disc. May this image of Ariel—imprinted upon your hearts—play the same imperceptible but decisive role in your own lives. In darkest hours of discouragement, may it revive in your consciousness an enthusiasm for the wavering ideal and restore to your heart the ardor of lost hope. Once affirmed in the bastion of your inner being, Ariel will go forth in the conquest of souls. I see him, far in the future, smiling upon you with gratitude from above as your spirit fades into the shadows. I have faith in your will, in your strength, even as I have faith in the will and strength of those to whom you will give life, to whom you will transmit your work. Often I am transported by the dream that one day may be a reality: that the Andes, soaring high above our America, may be carved to form the pedestal for this statue, the immutable altar for its veneration.[15]

Once again, *intimidad* plays an important role here. The final scene of Rodó's *Ariel* is an eloquent one: a master awakes hope supreme in his disciples and then withdraws. This retreat enshrines the "conquest of souls," which is cast as a challenge for a spiritual elite, meant to civilize the New World. The aestheticizing side to this gesture did not pass even Unamuno by.[16] But the appeal of the passage and the gesture would also touch a seventeen-year-old who, in 1920, wrote an article titled "Originalidade literária" [Literary Originality] and had it published in the *Correio Paulistano*, thanks to the help of his mentor, Affonso Taunay. In his first text published in the press, Buarque de Holanda argued for an "intellectual emancipation" that, as he then saw it, was independent of political emancipation—as the case of the French writer of the Occitan language Frédéric Mistral (1830–1914) would prove. One of the first names evoked off the bat by the young writer is the Peruvian author Francisco García Calderón, a first-class *arielista*, dedicated, as the very young Buarque de Holanda tells us, to the "complete spiritual emancipation of the New World, especially the part where the language of Cervantes holds sway."[17]

A later text from Buarque de Holanda (now at the ripe old age of eighteen), published in the *Revista do Brasil* in May 1920, is a review of *Ariel*, doubling as an obituary for Rodó, who had passed away a few years earlier.[18] The article is nothing less than a cry against the decadence of nations that, since ancient times, had knelt before the grandeur and progress of other nations, populated by exotic "races." This evocation of the past serves to trace the target of the author, who enthusiastically shares Rodó's diffuse distrust of North America. "Yankee utilitarianism" is the villain here, and the young Brazilian goes so far as to connect it with the republican nature of the United States, showing his monarchist colors in the process.[19]

In the teenager's review, Rodó's patent elitism takes on a new scale:

Switzerland is intellectually dependent on Germany, as the United States are on England. The great Germanic philosopher [Emil Strauss] once noted that his compatriots see those republics [as] endowed with a crude realism and a cold, prosaic empiricism, and that, upon being transported to that other soil, they feel the lack of the delicate atmosphere that they had breathed in their homeland. In the United States, moreover, there hangs a putrid air of corruption, exhaled by the governing classes, which one rarely finds in Europe. Utilitarianism and a preoccupation with earning money, *auri sacra fames* [accursed hunger for gold], have conquered North Americans to the detriment of their intellectual spirit, political morality, and even individual liberty. This led Schopenhauer to describe them as the proletarians of humanity. Their very character, he says, is vulgarity in all its forms: moral, intellectual, [and] aesthetic, a vulgarity that is patent not only in private life, but in public life as well. The author of *Die Welt als Wille* attributed this vulgarity in part to the republican Constitution of the United States and in part to its origin, having been originally a penal colony, and having among its ancestors "men who had reason to flee from Europe."[20]

It would be an error to associate these words, and the elitist tone, with the critique of authoritarian thought that Buarque de Holanda would draw up sixteen years later in his debut book. But we would do well to note the strong impression that the Latin American cause and Rodó's aristocratism left on the eighteen-year-old article writer, if only as a contrast. North America's "cold, prosaic empiricism" will reappear in *Roots of Brazil*, although mitigated by the Weberian theses that apparently provide the foundation for Buarque de Holanda's argument. Moreover, in the famous chapter on the "cordial man," he returns to the "contribution to the world" proposed by Ribeiro Couto in his indirect dialogue with Mexican diplomat and essayist Alfonso Reyes (1889–1959).[21]

It is in a letter from poet Rui Ribeiro Couto (1898–1963), sent to Alfonso Reyes from Marseilles in 1931, where the expression appears, apparently for the first time in Portuguese. The letter would finally be published in *Monterrey*, the literary diary that Reyes published as Mexican ambassador in Brazil from 1930 to 1936: "It is from the fusion of the Iberian man with this new land and its primitive races that an (Latin) 'American sensibility' may emerge, a new race, product of a culture and a pure intuition, the cordial man. This, as I see it, is what our America is giving to the world: the cordial man."[22]

The genealogy of the expression "cordial man," however, stretches on quite a bit farther. It is in Rubén Darío's text "The Triumph of Caliban," as already referenced, written in the heat of the intervention by the United States in the Caribbean, that the poet of *Azul* refers to a night in Buenos Aires when Roque Sáenz Peña (1851–1914), at a talk at the La Victoria theater, sponsored by the Club Español, referred to the Spanish-American War:

> In his speech at this gathering, the ever-cordial [*varón cordial*] Sáenz Peña stood and spoke as a statesman. He repeated what he has always spoken of—his conception of the peril presented by those boa constrictor jaws, ready to swallow still more, even after the enormous dinner it made of Texas; the greed of the Anglo-Saxon, the appetite the Yankee has shown, the political infamy of the government of the North; and how useful, how necessary it

is for the Hispanic nationalities of the Americas to be prepared for the boa constrictor's next strike. Only one soul has been as farsighted in this matter, as farsighted and persistent, as Sáenz Peña, and that soul was—time's strange irony!—the father of free Cuba, José Martí. Martí never ceased urging the nations of his blood that they be careful with those men of prey, that they not be lured into those pan-American schemes, but rather look to the Yankee businessmen's traps and snares. What would Martí say today when he saw that under the colors of aid to the troubled Pearl the monster was swallowing it, oyster and all? In the speech I have referred to, I have said that the man of cordiality [*el hombre cordial*] and the statesman were arm-in-arm. That Sáenz Peña is both things is attested to by his entire life. Such a man should appear in defense of the noblest of nations, fallen into the bootysack of those Yankees [*caída al bote de esos yangüeses*], in defense of the unarmed gentleman who accepts the duel with the dynamite-carrying, mechanic-overall-wearing Goliath.[23]

The boa constrictor's jaws stand in for North American imperialist greed, which the mask of benevolent Pan-Americanism fails to hide, at least to the eyes of those looking to reveal the monster of the North, threatening to fetter the liberty of the world huddled together south of the Rio Grande. Here, in defense of the unarmed *caballero*, in a reference to a passage from *Don Quijote*, there stands Sáenz Peña (not yet president of Argentina), who like Martí seems to have seen the great Yankee trap being sprung.[24] But the statesman, in his defense of the Spanish homeland and its Latin progeny, goes hand in hand with "*el hombre cordial.*"

Hard to say if this is the precise genealogy of the famous expression, but it is peculiar that the reaction to the specter of the North should spark the vision of a statesman wreathed in cordiality—a characteristic that, again, points toward the legacy that Ribeiro Couto would later celebrate, with Sérgio Buarque de Holanda then turning the expression into a powerful metaphor (or a social type, some would say) for understanding the political relationships established between Latin Americans—or, more specifically, between Brazilians.

Between Hispanic-Americans and Brazilians, however, there rises the figure of Mexican thinker José Vasconcelos (1882–1959). In his renowned 1925 take on Latin American exceptionalism, *The Cosmic Race*, we find "a thousand bridges ... for the sincere and cordial fusion of all races" as well as a "sensitive and ample heart ... that embraces and contains everything and is moved with sympathy, but, full of vigor, imposes new laws upon the world." This "cosmic" Latin American formation heralds a civilizational "scherzo" in which all come together and mingle, a far cry from the "allegro" of the Anglo-Saxon march, a ceaseless and vigorous melody, more likely to steamroller the Other before having time to assimilate it.[25]

This is not to draw a direct line from Buarque de Holanda to Darío via Ribeiro Couto and Reyes—by way of the ideological tang of Vasconcelos's writings, where the word *cordial* is thrown around, with specific references to Brazil. That said, while nothing is direct here, we may lend greater depth to the understanding of "cordiality" as a characteristic of a sociability set against an alleged North American iciness (somewhat in the vein of Japanese politeness, a reader of *Roots of Brazil* might think), in returning to the broader Latin American spectrum (which we might now call Latin Americanist), which embraces the rich debates around *arielismo*. As we have seen, these discussions are not contained in Rodó's *Ariel* (1900) but lead us back to Rubén Darío, and finally, as Carlos Jáuregui has aptly shown, from Darío to the French occultist and founder of the Rosicrucian order, Joséphin Péladan (1858–1918). There is still much to be explored here in the little-explored terrain of this archaeology of Latin American exception. A careful investigation would lead, at the very least, to Spiritism and French occultism, which lend their characteristic flavor to the fin-de-siècle decadentism and exceptionalism so dear to a poet like Darío.[26]

It should have become clear that *modernism* is a term that demands careful conceptualization, especially when dealing with an entity as imprecise as "Latin American modernism." To trace one of those broad interpretations that function on a didactic level but fall apart when one tries to analyze specific cases, the profoundly nationalistic bent of Brazilian modernism finds no counterpart in

Hispanic-American modernism, whose affirmations of identity are less related to a telluric discourse unveiling the marvels or enigmas of the nation and more tied to a reaction to the disenchantment with the modern world. This is what makes Hispanic-American modernism so singular, then—its allure is the excellence of the spirit against the massification framing modern life and practices, now drained of all vital force and charm. This is why, incidentally, the chronological and thematic parallel is generally drawn between Brazilian modernism and the Hispanic-American "vanguards."[27]

We should understand, in any case, that the United States may function as a vortex of issues and as the example of an involution to be avoided. In the "Latin" context, after all, the soul could still delight at the creative leisure of elevated spirits; elevated and misunderstood, in keeping with the late Romantic tastes of that fin de siècle, haunted both in Europe and beyond by the specters of regression, as the name of Oswald Spengler (1880–1936) finally emerged in suggesting the paths that led to the West's decline.

If we turn our gaze to the wider context, we will see that even debates around identity in Brazil—often studied in a vein that hews eternally toward domestic concerns in a sort of obsessive self-referencing—are connected to an ongoing discussion over Latin America's place as an element of resistance to the disenchanted world or as a place devoted to safeguarding the secret of that which the modern world (read: particularly in the United States) was rapidly losing. In the Hispanic-American case, the "modernism" that springs forth here is thus framed by this discomfort, and by questions as to that which is vanishing, and hence not as interested in what was then emerging on the modern horizon. This is a modernism with its eyes fixed on the world falling apart, not the world being erected from its ruins.

In Rodó we find a summary of the problem in the longing for a world where Thomas Carlyle's heroes might not fade away:

> Great civilizations, great nations, in the historical sense, are those that, once their time has passed, leave vibrating throughout eternity the harmony of their spirit and imprint their heritage upon posterity—as Carlyle said of his heroes—like a new and divine

proportion in the sum of things. In Goethe's *Faust*, when Helena, called from the realm of night, again descends into the shadow of Hades, she leaves Faust her tunic and her veil. These vestments are not the goddess herself but, as she has worn them, they are imbued with her supreme divinity and have the virtue of elevating whoever possesses them above all vulgarity.[28]

While it would be unfair to reduce all of Rodó's thought to the erudite—elitist and aestheticizing—gesture of *Ariel*,[29] we should recall that it bears something utterly seductive for an eighteen-year-old like Sérgio Buarque de Holanda in 1920 (the year of his review of *Ariel*). This is not only a world of *misfits*, but also of a vanishing universe, the recovery of which, at least in spirit, was the task set to a new generation.[30] The scene in which old Prospero-Rodó retires, leaving the attentive youths before the murmuring of the blind crowd, is extremely significant. With this in mind, it seems fair to ask—although with all due delicacy—what Rodó meant for Buarque de Holanda in the end, far before the emergence of a solid work with anti-authoritarian leanings like *Roots of Brazil*.[31]

We should recall that in 1936 the Brazilian author had the case of Uruguayan president José Batlle y Ordóñez (1856–1929) as a clear example of what might be called *liberal excess*. Rationalism "went beyond its limits," as Buarque de Holanda put it in *Roots of Brazil*, "when, in the process of establishing the supremacy of ... rules, it rigidly set them apart from real life," thus creating "a logical homogenous, but unhistoric system." This was precisely what had happened in Batlle's Uruguay, where "democratic depersonalization" had been taken to its limit. The historian takes the opportunity to argue that *caudillismo* belongs to the same family of ideas as liberalism, standing as its inverse.[32] Here creeps the shadow of the interwar period:

> Thus, Rousseau, the father of the social contract, belongs to the family of Hobbes, the father of the Leviathan state; both came from the same nest. The negation of liberalism, which was unconscious in a Rosas, a Melgarejo, or a Porfirio Díaz, is affirmed today as a body of doctrine in European fascism, which

is nothing more than a critique of liberalism in its parliamentary form erected on a positive political system. The victory of democratic doctrine will only really be possible when its antithesis, liberalism-caudillismo, is overcome.[33]

In one form or another, Carl Schmitt will crop up after this, in the 1936 edition of *Roots of Brazil*, following a series of observations about Hispanic-American political history. Curiously enough, the reference to the "illustrious professor of Public Law at the University of Bonn" would disappear in more recent editions of the book, when Schmitt's name had become associated with the Third Reich. But the problem still hung there: where to find the political principle on which to found the construction of the collectivity?[34]

* * *

A fundamental triangulation marks the imagination of the *latinoamericano*, or that which, from Sérgio Buarque de Holanda to Richard Morse, would be dubbed, more precisely, "*iberoamericano.*" Within Hispanism, the imaginary reconstruction of Iberian roots provides an important counterweight to national pride wounded by the war in the Caribbean and the North American occupation of territories once "Hispanic," even as far as the Pacific and the Philippines, in 1898. To go even farther back, the imaginary reconstruction of Iberian roots serves as a sort of antidote to the imperialist nature of the Monroe Doctrine. Brazil, conceived of in this broader American context, has its own part in the affirmation of an identity that reinforces the division of the Americas into two parts. To put it another way, there is no conceptualization or poetic imagination of roots, or even the possibility of a fantasy of a definitive severing of those roots, without the postulation of a third angle from which the United States emerges, opening up in an opposite vertex, posing a constant threat to the integrity of the world convulsing south of the Rio Grande.

Later in 1920, in a stinging bit of invective published in *A Cigarra* and directed at the United States, young Buarque de Holanda would react violently to the "chimera of Monroeism," which had led many of his compatriots to find, in the shadow of North America, a beneficent antidote to "all attempts at colonization that the European powers may well undertake in the New World." Curiously enough, however, the beardless polemicist starts out by invoking the mechanisms of desire, constructed between attraction and negation. At the close of his article, his tone is somewhat at odds with his apparently unshakable anti-Yankee sentiment: "One should always recall that Monroe's doctrine is quite like the lady who inspired Maciel Monteiro to pen those immortal verses: Who can but see you without loving you? / Who may love you without dying of it? [*Quem pode ver-te sem querer amar-te? / Quem pode amar-te sem morrer de amores?*]"[35]

The reference to these sensual, Romantic lines encompasses the interplay I have been trying to explore: the mixture of horror and attraction when encountering the North American Other. Beyond the topos of terrible beauty or the Medusan imaginary that Romantic sensibility itself recreated, there lies the profound temptation that all monsters inspire. Here, the eighteen-year-old seems to cling to his anti-Yankeeism, but he also—if inadvertently—reveals the enchantment that the other side exerts over him. A *mortal* enchantment, which brings us back to the projection of the monstrous, whether on the Other to the North or the Other to the South.

Arielismo has a complex and broad-ranging story that I have barely touched on here. Let us add Sérgio Buarque de Holanda's name, however, to the lineage of the readers of Shakespeare who often seem to swallow whole the horrifying characterization of the "savage and deformed slave"—this damned creature that North American utilitarianism reveals. The investigation of *arielismo* and its critical reception would also allow for a careful examination of the inversion of signs here, just as sympathies slide to Caliban's side. This is the case with the "Caliban," ideologizing tang aside, created later by Cuban poet and essayist Roberto Fernández Retamar (b. 1930).[36] It is always when faced with the "monster," to recall Darío and Martí, that we may make out a long tradition of the idealization of the Latin American difference.

In terms of the history of social thought in Latin America (where we can and should include the traditions of the French Caribbean), the imagination of difference is often sprung from a century-old Shakespearean geography, as I have suggested. In this sense, we might return once again to the "Calibanic genealogy" so deeply connected to fierce critique of the United States. This critique appears in various forms, blossoming from the pencils of authors like Darío and Rodó, and survives long enough for the Shakespearean canon to be rewritten "from Caliban's perspective." From the inescapable 1960s, there emerges a political need to rewrite *The Tempest* as an emblem of the postcolonial condition, with reflections such as those of Fernández Retamar, Aimé Césaire (1913–2008), or Frantz Fanon (1925–1961) flowing into ongoing discussions in ethnopsychiatry, where Dominique-Octave Mannoni (1899–1989) had famously introduced the "Prospero complex." Mannoni, who had taught Aimé Césaire in Martinique, would go on to teach Fanon.[37]

But the inversion of the signs linking *Iberoamérica* to first the spiritual powers of Ariel and then a Caliban resignified by postcolonial struggles can do little to hide the fact that, in both cases, the "antidote to Anglo-materialism," as José Guilherme Merquior put it, serves the same function. This brought the liberal critic to imagine, in the heat of a multifaceted debate around Richard Morse's *Prospero's Mirror* in Brazil, that "Morse's Calibanism is avenging Rodó's Arielism, eighty years later."[38] We must delve deeper into this inversion, understanding how, beneath the surface, there roils silently a programmatic enchantment with the "other" side, the creature of the South that Prospero's malice condemned, but which other readers, of other books and from other times, may rediscover, carrying forth not only its cause, but its redemptive message as well.

* * *

The European specter hanging over the "American" consciousness corresponds to the fantasy of a less intensely European "America," one more dedicated to the product of the encounter of different cultures on the new continent. From atop the twenty-first century, past the valorization of the local that moved to place "our" mixed culture against "their" culture—supposedly more homogenous, in the North

American case—there remains a sort of rare heritage, the evaluation of which is still subject to powerful words that made history over the past century, especially across the peripheries of the world: *miscegenation, hybridism,* and *creolization.*

Of these three terms, the first is already fairly settled in Brazilian imagination, or rather in common imaginings of Brazil. In this word—*miscegenation*—one can make out the valorization I referred to above: while the racist specter of the nineteenth century, and with it the theorization of races amidst the debates around abolition in Brazil, reemerge in the first decades of the twentieth century, the mixture once feared and detested by a legion of intellectuals is eventually valorized by another legion, often spurred on by the modernist movement.[39] But once again, this is a broad movement, not limited to Brazil. The "propitious convergence of cosmopolitism and rooted localism" guiding local vanguards suggests a true "Latin American and Afro-Antillean Renaissance,"[40] once the threat of the degeneration of the species gives way to the promise of a successful experiment of tropical ethnic mixture. This, in Brazil, would finally become normalized in the works of Gilberto Freyre and in their various rereadings, in varying degrees of politicization and official status.[41]

The conversion of excess (or tropical *hybris*) into civilizational triumph is an invention whose genealogy and long shadow still occupy a privileged place in Latin American thought. A detailed examination of the topic would demand, as a possible path for investigation, connecting works of Brazilian modernism to Hispanic-American counterparts. Think, for example, of the valorization of *hybris*, and—to look to the Caribbean—"hurricanes" in the sociology of Fernando Ortiz (1881–1969) or the fiction of Alejo Carpentier (1904–1980). Or, in another context, but still in the Cuban arena, we might look to the "barbarous style" of Juan Francisco Manzano (1797–1854), which Enrico Mario Santí refers to as he frames Ortiz's most renowned work, *Cuban Counterpoint: Tobacco and Sugar,* within the grand tradition of the Hispanic-American neobaroque, which might well be understood through the critical sensibility of Carpentier himself in his suggestion that "all symbiosis, all *mestizaje*, engenders a baroque." Or even, to follow in Santí's footsteps and look to the variety that unfolds here, we might turn to Severo Sarduy (1937–1993), invoking José Lezama Lima (1910–1976) and his neobaroque phrase, "*sintácticamente incorrecta a fuerza de recibir incompatibles elementos alógenos*" [syntactically incorrect by virtue of receiving incompatible allogenic elements], which Sarduy casts as revealing, in poetic terms, a fertile, desired "*pérdida de la concordancia*" [loss of concordance].[42]

The "loss of concordance" may be read more broadly, inside and outside the scope of the text, as a modern fascination in peripheral countries, engendering characters who set themselves against the European agenda, winnowing away at it or simply corrupting it. Back to the Francophone Caribbean—I recall Martinican poet and essayist Édouard Glissant (1928–2011) and his vision of the American landscape. Faced with the "*très réglé*" [strictly ruled] aspect of European landscapes, he decides to coin a word: *irrué*. The invented adjective might be translated as "irruptive," meaning both something that "bursts forth" and "jumps" or makes a din and rushes ahead. A small focus of distraction, we might say. This invention allows Glissant to imagine the insular landscape of the Caribbean as a "preface to the [American] continent."[43] The irruptive force wracking the metropolitan landscape is the harbinger of a new civilizational adventure.

We might go on almost indefinitely, but my aim here is simply to suggest that our understanding of Buarque de Holanda may be greatly enriched by a broad view of modern Latin American essayism.[44] And no other work may be as clear of an invitation to think such essayism than *Prospero's Mirror*, by Richard Morse.

* * *

The debate between Richard Morse and social scientist Simon Schwartzman in the late 1980s, just after the publication of *Prospero's Mirror* in Portuguese, has already been analyzed at length.[45] I feel I should summarize it, nevertheless; barbs aside, the discussion touches on some sore points in Morse's arguments, perhaps exposing some of the girders holding up *Roots of Brazil* as well.

Schwartzman sees, in the "profoundly incorrect" *Prospero's Mirror*, a "nostalgia for totality and transcendence," as if the book hid a vicious "Sorelian millenarism." Here, the focus is on the mythical aspect of the return to that which, from Schwartzman's perspective, is an idealized "lost millenary essence."[46] It is quite significant that, in response to the biting article "O espelho de Morse" [Morse's Mirror], the North American historian (in a reply published in July 1989, amidst the electoral race in which Luiz Inácio Lula da Silva of the Workers' Party first emerged as a strong presidential candidate), does not hide a certain prophetic hope in the full realization of the course of history.[47] Morse's abundant use of the future tense is striking ("there must inevitably occur," "there will necessarily come," and so on), as is his aggressive faith in what still lies ahead: "The Brazilian people as a whole, vitality intact, are taking the reins into their own hands."[48] But before labeling this as a simple populist flair, let us reflect on what is being debated here.

In the wake of the publication of *Prospero's Mirror* in Brazil, Mexican historian Mauricio Tenorio provocatively suggested that Morse might be considered "a *flamboyant* of North American historiography on Latin America," and in doing so precisely sketched out a possible ideological and theoretical context for the controversial book:

> When Morse writes of a "different tradition," of the need to recognize in Latin America a "new ideology," he is simply adding his voice (and quite a fine one at that) to the chorus running from Lévi-Strauss and Eliade to Marcuse, Adorno, Foucault, and Dumont. And one of the fundamental functions of these echoes lies in the renewed value placed on the mythic, a factor that takes on the status of a form of knowledge and life, standing abreast with scientific knowledge.[49]

Behind all this, he proposes, lies the "revalorization of the traditional," or a "critique of modernity," from some wings of social sciences and historiography sprung from the United States, especially so in the 1970s. The idea of a "return" may be too simplistic to take in the breadth of the light that Morse has shed on Iberian intellectual history in the longue durée. But here, beyond the provocations being flung back and forth, we may glimpse the perception of a singular relationship that Morse's thought establishes with religion. His is a personal hermeneutics, one that has a unique relationship to tradition, to echo the keen reading of anthropologist Otávio Velho.[50] Supporting his interpretation on Metz, Velho notes that secularization and the consequent desacralization of the world are ways of ultimately separating ourselves from the transcendent sphere that we always project somewhere beyond us and which stays put there. That sphere, nonetheless, insistently threatens to return. In terms dear to Morse's lexicon, with a whiff of Louis Dumont and a preview of his reflections post–*Prospero's Mirror*, this is holism counterbalancing individualism.[51]

In a different key, looking at the long-range history of Latin American social sciences—which Morse is also addressing—we should recall that in the 1950s, and particularly through the 1960s, there emerged a profound critique of modernization or, more precisely, of its destructive effects, which the periphery, more than any other space, would be best positioned to detect and comprehend. That is, the midcentury period inaugurates a turn in scholarship, a brusque swerve in direction for the analyses that casted contemporary Latin America as stubbornly resisting modernization. To reaffirm the Latin Americanist imaginary, the continent was giving itself over to the thrill of an alternative project, or the dream of an autochthonous modernity. In the epic footsteps of revolutionaries or in the humble yet vigorous zeal of reformists, modernity shone in all its forms, despite and even prior to Cuba's execution of the fantasy of a radical turn.

Moreover, the possibility that the periphery might gain the status of a creative center meets up squarely with previous proposals, which point toward the most deeply rooted modernist desires. In them— that is, in this intellectual tradition that Richard Morse was probing, and which he received with critical delight and poetic liberty (think of the jocoserious tone of his brilliant and hilarious "McLuhanaíma, The Solid Gold Hero; or, o Herói com Bastante Caráter, uma fuga"[52]), there was already a sort of vision of a radical reversion of the relationship of *dependence*—a word that did not attain such prestige in the region by chance.

Morse's most potent metaphor, the belief that the "mirror" ought to be turned around (an inverse teleology), may find its origin here, in the somewhat daring and inevitably a bit quixotic faith in the model and proposals of a society that supposedly strayed from the traditional pacts of Western modernity. Another West, another America, another Europe, another geography, tracing an alternative future based on the belief and faith in a singular past, leading the historian's magnificent imagination to formulate the paradox of a promising past.

It is time to bring *Roots of Brazil* back to center stage. Of course, Buarque de Holanda's essay is not *Prospero's Mirror*, although confidence in the universal future of Latin America may have found ample justification in Brazil among the modernists, including young Buarque de Holanda, who just a few pages ago was reacting violently to the "cold, prosaic empiricism" of North America. I believe that this contrast I have set up may help us to understand that secularization is still a central issue for all of us, Latin Americans or not. The issue is that the "demythologizing of the world" transforms literature, and with it the grand essays of national and regional interpretation, into a constant reconstruction of the enigma that secularization itself has promised to strip of its mystery and eliminate altogether. Here, I might recall Jorge Brioso, who with Rubén Darío in mind declares his intention to "study the different backgrounds from which Latin American modernist texts, texts that embrace their profane and disenchanted condition, incorporate enigma, revelation, and the meaning of the sacred."[53] How, then, to explain *Roots of Brazil*? How and where to situate Buarque de Holanda's essay on the spectrum that stretches from utter secularization to a wholehearted embrace of the myth?

We have already seen how *Roots of Brazil* inspires vastly different reactions and a range of extreme readings. While it may be seen as a true "preface to modernity" (as Antonio Candido once commented to me), on the other hand, I might ask, after contrasting it with the ruminations of Richard Morse, if we mightn't say that *Roots of Brazil* doesn't open up its own doors for a reenchanted vision of the world. Can't we at least say that, in examining secularization, Buarque de Holanda's book paradoxically ends up elevating Latin America to the category of *enigma*? It is as if, in Weberian fashion, disenchantment were to become the impossible search for meaning, more harrowing and urgent than ever.

Uruguayan critic Ángel Rama (1926–1983) may have a satisfactory answer for us, which is less of an answer, incidentally, and more of a research proposal. In the prologue to Biblioteca Ayacucho's edition of Rubén Darío's poetry and prose, he suggests that the poet, "on one hand, continues to believe in the 'cult of sacred Nature, a great and universal God, a mysterious law reigning over all'; on the other, he recognizes the failure of [his] project in its Romantic terms." It is then, Rama reminds us, that Darío finds in Wagner a solution for this conflict: "There might be another way of preserving the jungle, without being held hostage to a portrait of 'nature' itself. This would be a secondary reading, which would reconstruct it ... by establishing, not images, but values, that might [serve as] interpretive rationalizations capable of being expressed in cultural signs."[54]

Does *Roots of Brazil* bear something of this move toward substitution, dressing up the enigma in the rationalizing garb of grand "interpretation" and "cultural signs"? Or is it that its methodically sketched-out types ultimately serve only the task of corroborating "our" (Latin America's, or Brazil's) mysterious "contribution to the world"? Does this discourse woven into rational arguments serve simply to remind us that the enigma is being preserved for some future point, the hour and time of which only the poet knows? But how to read Buarque de Holanda's fatal prophecy for the "cordial man"? What will become of this "hero" who resists, and whose pain "only God" and the poet may feel?[55]

I hope that the contrast between *Prospero's Mirror* and *Roots of Brazil* may be of some use in this recollection of the not-always-"Apollonian" bent of Buarque de Holanda's book.[56] In his Latin Americanist passion, the historian's North American peer expands the framework of *Roots* to reveal it in its full dimensions, finally having dived unabashedly into the continental truth of poets and novelists. It may be time to revisit *Roots of Brazil*, no longer to emphasize its internal coherence or delicate architecture, but to sound out the dark depths that this luminous essay continues to disguise.

PART III

Words and Time

CHAPTER 7

Cordiality and Power
The President and Politics between Film and Essay

A Brief History

Like all the stuff of imagination, texts' origins tend to be controversial. We are used to thinking of *Roots of Brazil* as a book born of the experience of voluntary exile, when Sérgio Buarque de Holanda worked and studied in Germany from 1929 to 1930. Critical works on the author have delved further into this, exploring and feeling out the analytical reach of a gaze that may turn Brazil into a problematic space "over there," refusing a "here" satisfied in its easy self-referentialism. To accept the organic metaphor that the title offers us, we might suppose that the investigation into roots demands a previous act of uprooting, as if exile were a precondition for being able to inquire into the nation.[1]

But even prior to his departure for Germany, and just before writing "O lado oposto e outros lados" [The Opposite Side and Other Sides] (1926)—the acidic, illuminating article in which we can glimpse a few of the key ideas of *Roots of Brazil*, as we saw earlier—Buarque de Holanda had devised a "Theory of America," which he would continue to elaborate for a number of years. Back in Brazil in 1931, part of the "sheaf of 400 pages" would give rise, according to the author, not to the broad "Theory," but to the essay "Corpo e alma do Brasil" [Body and Soul of Brazil], which would be published in 1935. In it, we can find a fundamental part of that which would appear the next year as chapters 5 ("The Cordial Man") and 7 ("Our Revolution") of *Roots of Brazil*.[2] It is quite probable, however, that Buarque de Holanda's memory failed him on this count, and that the pages he salvaged from his "Theory of America" may have been used in the first chapter of *Roots of Brazil*. As it so happens, the political events alluded to in "Corpo e alma do Brasil," and even Ribeiro Couto's expression "cordial man," date from the period following his return to Brazil. Even so, the "Theory of America" exerts a powerful fascination over those who study *Roots of Brazil*; the tendency is to see in it the aborted plans of the author, his original interpretation of Brazil and its Iberian roots. In short, the reference to a portentous "Theory of America" lost to the ages sparks scholars' imaginations, as if a coherent, original sign had been left by the wayside, the author having forgotten or erased it. In a 1981 interview, referred to earlier, an elderly Buarque de Holanda recalled that some of the "less awful" parts of the work had been published by a "German commercial magazine, of varieties," while he was living in Berlin.[3]

Be that as it may, we should not forget that the text of *Roots of Brazil* currently in circulation is the result of countless revisions: over the course of decades, the author would continue to rewrite his essay. Compared to the latest edition, the first version of the book (1936) may seem less even, putting forth propositions that would later soften and lose a bit of their hard edges and controversial flair, as I suggested in previous chapters. In this sense, the first edition falls less easily on our contemporary palate but is livelier than those that followed. It still bears the marks of an organicist imagination, the projection of monarchical values, and connections to irrationalist and Romantic ways of thinking.[4]

Beyond this irrationalist side and the dilemmas that remain in the book over its many editions and revisions, it is by no means settled whether the "historian" Sérgio Buarque de Holanda, author of *Monções* [Monsoons] (1945) and *Caminhos e fronteiras* [Paths and Frontiers] (1957), does indeed clash with the "sociologist" who had proposed a grand synthesis of Brazil, in fine 1930s form in *Roots of Brazil*. However, nearly two decades ago, Evaldo Cabral de Mello's interpretation established the idea of a break between one and the other. Nevertheless, Robert Wegner has called attention to the continuities in the author's work, suggesting that *Roots of Brazil* never "became a 'dead book' for its author."[5]

It is interesting to note that Buarque de Holanda would long be haunted by *Roots of Brazil*, called upon to react to the aftereffects sparked by his interpretation of the nation. This was the case with the controversy around the cordial man, for example. Setting himself against Cassiano Ricardo, the historian would propose in 1948 that arguments around Brazilian cordiality be reconsidered; Ricardo had associated it (wrongly, to Buarque de Holanda's eye) with a "technique of goodness."[6] One would also do well to recall that interpretations of *Roots of Brazil* make their mark over the years on the understanding of the essay and mold the imaginations of past and future readers. On the one hand, as I have already noted, the comprehension and discussion of the book are now inconceivable without the 1967 preface by Antonio Candido, to which a postscript was added in 1986. On the other hand, severe critiques of Buarquian typology formed the reaction to that which would be identified—amidst the unrest of the second half of the last century, in Brazil—as a generalizing view of the nation's culture, stripped of class dynamics. The first to delve deeply into this sore spot was likely social psychologist Dante Moreira Leite in the 1950s, blazing a path for the ferocious critiques of historian Carlos Guilherme Mota, and then the more cautious objections of critic Alfredo Bosi.[7]

In short, *Roots of Brazil* was not incubated in Germany alone. Being the classic that Antonio Candido identifies it as, it is also a book in a constant state of rewriting and resignification, formed by the layers of reading and interest, praise and rejection, sympathy and antipathy, that tend to mark the most important works. The book has already been weathered by the ways in which its concepts are updated in projections and inquiries into the cultural and political landscape of eras alien to it. To use terms dear to its author's heart, it is both *current* and *uncurrent*. With this in mind, and if this is the case, we should sound out a few contemporary reflections to see where *Roots of Brazil* is now: where it resounds, where it nettles, and how some of its most famous concepts have managed to reinvent themselves in today's world.

Cordiality

Before tackling contemporary issues, we might imagine a brief genealogy for cordiality, set apart from the history I laid out in the last chapter. Now we will situate it within a long tradition of thought about Brazil. Schematically, we might say that cordiality is an ingenious formula for understanding Brazilian political and social formation: an intellectual tool, a fiction that reminds us how the republican present in Brazil has not completely shed the ties binding it to the colonial past. To run the risk of caricature, and to play with a certain foundational mythology of the nation, we might imagine the beginnings of cordiality in the letter that Pero Vaz de Caminha wrote to the Portuguese king when Pedro Álvares Cabral landed on the western edge of the Atlantic in 1500. There we have nothing like the accounts of brutal encounters with the natives of the New World that would become so famous in the Spanish Black Legend. What flows from the scrivener's pen is a sort of gentle encounter, as if comprehension had won out over incomprehension, blazing the way for the utopic projection of a bloodless society. The Encounter is never stained, in Caminha's text, with native blood. Invited to spend the night on Pedro Álvares Cabral's ship, the Indians sleep on beds "with a mattress and sheets" and sprawl there, lying in a splendid cradle, lulled by the sound of the waves and the light of a deep tropical sky. The Indian sleeps at the feet of the Portuguese in the letter describing how Brazil was found.[8]

Over four centuries later, with Brazilian modernism in full swing, Oswald de Andrade would take a playful look at the country's colonial heritage and produce a modern take on Caminha, projecting onto the text an enchantment with the tropics with inexorable modernity as its backdrop. His "Manifesto of Pau-Brasil Poetry" (1924), a composite image of skyscrapers and jungle, features the "hospitality, slightly sensual, affectionate," of our "barbarous, credulous, picturesque, and tender" natives.[9] In the modernist cipher later recreated in the songs of Tropicalists like Caetano Veloso, in the 1960s and 1970s, Brazilians are the "sweet barbarians" who offer themselves to the world, enchanting and peaceful, subversively human.

But cordiality would take on its best-known form when, borrowing the expression from Ribeiro Couto, Buarque de Holanda reinvented the "cordial man" in 1935 in "Corpo e alma do Brasil" and then in *Roots of Brazil* in the following year. Whether as a metaphor or a concept, the cordial man complicates the notion of the relative absence of violence in the encounter between native peoples and the European, allowing for a synthesis of the importance of personal relations in the shaping of public space in Brazil. In a hasty summary, he argues that Brazilians are set apart by the personalized, apparently amicable mode of their relations. A clap on the back stands in for political conflict; godfathers become protectors, looking after their electors as they would their godsons; family values invade the public arena, making it into a private space; state affairs become personal score settling; citizens are "my people"; intellectual debates give way to a war of personal interests; and, finally, the easy, spontaneous smile soothes the sting of clashing ideologies.

We should revisit Buarque de Holanda's masterful definition of cordiality in the first edition of *Roots of Brazil* in 1936:

> The affability in relationships, hospitality, generosity, and virtues extolled by visiting foreigners are indeed well-defined traits of the Brazilian character. It would be a mistake to think that those virtues can mean "good manners," or civility. Above all they are legitimate expressions of an extremely rich and overflowing emotional base. There is something coercive in civility—it can be expressed in commands and judgments.... No person is further from this ritualistic notion of life than the Brazilian. Our ordinary form of social relations is fundamentally the opposite of politeness.[10]

The cordial man, in Buarque de Holanda's fable, shies away from "politeness" out of an inability to understand the ritualized forms of social interaction. Instead of keeping his distance from others, protecting himself behind his mask, he throws himself out into the world, with arms and countenance open. The public stage is, for him, a celebration of the proximity between men; and in this, there is certainly something drawing us into the world of Latin American politics. Or, to choose a finer focus, there is something here that may allow us to understand the contemporary political scene in Brazil. It is as if the specter of cordiality, despite Buarque de Holanda's prophecies of its demise, were still haunting Brazilians, reconstituting itself in forms that may spring from other arts, beyond the written word.

Lula, Cordial?

This is the case with cinema. In this sense, we may observe the reconfiguration of cordiality—a powerful framework for understanding the Brazilian political experience—in a documentary produced in the last decade in Brazil. *Intermissions* finds João Moreira Salles (b. 1962) filming the days leading up to Lula's victory in the 2002 presidential campaign, just before the former steelworker from the poverty-stricken Northeast became president of the Republic. The film, released in 2004, ought to be understood as the complement to another documentary, *Metalworkers*, by Eduardo Coutinho (1933–2014), released in the same year and shown in Brazilian movie theaters alongside *Intermissions*, in alternating showings.[11]

Metalworkers, co-produced by Salles, takes as its jumping-off point a crucial moment in Brazil's political history, in the late 1970s, when strikes in the São Paulo metropolitan area marked one of the last violent clashes between the military government and organized civil society. From then on the dictatorship would steadily lose strength, finally expiring in the long, agonizing whimper that was the reaction to the campaign for direct presidential elections in 1984.[12] *Metalworkers* is based, in classic Coutinho fashion, on the threads of memory that are teased out slowly, before the camera lens, in the fascinating testimonies that interviewees construct in the present. The film is the fable of those who were left by the wayside; some toiling in factories, others in unions, many now retired, all left somewhere between enchantment and disenchantment. One particularly touching scene is that of the return of the retired steelworker who, upon retracing the route from São Paulo to his native Northeast, discovers that there is no more place for him, neither here nor there; he has become an "exile in his own land," to use the phrase from *Roots of Brazil* somewhat freely.

The abyss that opens up between origin and present day is framed, as in *Roots of Brazil*, by the experience of the metropolis and its power to dilute traditional, familial bonds, as we have seen. With its gaze on São Paulo's outskirts, Coutinho's film recreates the drama of those who have lost their origins and spent their lives feeding the industry of the great metropolitan area, a space both desired and feared in which new relations are to be established, in which sociability redefines itself and individuals must find themselves again, in all forms and at every turn. The films are complementary, but the stories they tell are quite different. Salles's documentary, in a thrilling move, captures the private moments of a journey on the way to the public sphere: Lula is the man whose day-to-day life we follow in the weeks that separate him from his elevation to president of the Republic. Coutinho's film, meanwhile, takes nearly the opposite path: starting out with a moment of maximum exposition in the public arena—the strikes around São Paulo, as seen in archival images—we return to the private space of the modest houses of the present, where the director seeks out the vox populi, the voice of those who have withdrawn, and for whom the public arena is a past that lives on in narrative. In *Intermissions*, the private sphere is where we behold the public man; in *Metalworkers*, that same private space is the humble stage on which those men who once took to the streets now take refuge in the stories of their parts in history.

In this interplay of private and public, we may make out the debates around cordiality. The Lula of *Intermissions* inhabits both poles simultaneously, each vital for him. However, his privacy is invaded by the public space from the start: the circulation of advisers, the swarming of the press, and the insane to-and-fro of the electoral campaign. It is no less curious that this same space is at times protected, if not always efficiently, by his circle of friends and relatives (in the film, there is Lula's birthday, the prayer from his friend Frei Betto, and so on).

When asked about his documentary at a discussion in Princeton, Salles laid out an interesting hypothesis. As he saw it, the "pragmatism" of the Lula of 2002 contained a return to the idea and practice of negotiated solutions, which in one way or another had defined the "original" Lula, the union leader of the late 1970s—the same figure who had gained the attention and sympathy of Sérgio Buarque de Holanda, by then elderly and infirm. If we take the filmmaker's lead, then, the Lula in both films, *Metalworkers* and *Intermissions*, is the man of negotiations for whom the immediate results of contact and tête-à-tête persuasion outweigh the great abstractions of political projects. (Both films, evidently, predate the suspicions of corruption that would rock the federal government in the form of the scandal that would become known as the *mensalão* [the "big monthly payment" scam], the results of which are still evident today in the pain of those individuals punished by way of example.)[13]

Concerned with the revision of the political meaning of Lula's experience between those two extremes (the 1989 Lula more "radical" and politicized than the Lula who would be elected in 2002), I asked João Moreira Salles if his hypothesis didn't run the risk of idealizing an "essential" Lula, one focused solely on commitments between people, more concerned with the concrete possibilities of the here and now than broad-ranging political projects. Is this the "true" Lula that *Intermissions* shows us? In his answer, the director reaffirmed and defended the complexity of the narrative, negating the idea of a character who, having flourished in the late 1970s, blooms again, intact, in the first decade of the twenty-first century. There were, of course, differences and nuances. However, the hypothesis (which the film seems to transform into thesis) remains firm: the 2002 Lula had returned, for some reason, to his original style of politicking—negotiation, that is, whenever possible, and a confrontational tack only when pushed to an extreme. The later retreats of the strikers' movement in the late stages of the dictatorship might be read not only as strategic (as part of a broader, openly revolutionary game plan), but also as more or less immediate answers to the possibilities open in the moment. Behind all this, we might imagine the will to negotiate, to establish contact through nonviolent means, substituting the silence of absolute conflict with the eloquence of the encounter. Deep down we can make out the desire for a fraternal rapprochement, breaking down the anguish-inducing distance of the political game.

Hearing this, I couldn't help myself: was the Lula onscreen more cordial? Speaking before an audience composed mainly of foreigners, the director suggested that one of the frameworks for understanding his film could be, indeed, Sérgio Buarque de Holanda in *Roots of Brazil*. This was no simple matter of marking the presence of the cordial man in the making of *Intermissions*, of course. The documentary goes a ways further, suggesting that behind-the-scenes interactions in private spaces may reveal that which later appears in the public sphere.[14] But it seems undeniable that, in one way or another, the way that we understand the cordial man, with his lack of aptitude for the abstractions of politics, has provided the model that allows us to understand the recent history of Brazil and may perhaps allow us to understand Lula himself better in the portraits that Salles has put forth. If I am correct, *Intermissions* is a fundamental piece in the long lineage of interpretations of Brazilian political culture, with its narrative experiments reinforcing the trend in contemporary documentary to blur the lines between public and private, between personal and collective history.[15]

In his political fable, Buarque de Holanda takes his jumping-off point from a unique vision of Sophocles's *Antigone*, which he reads, as suggested in previous chapters, through a Hegelian lens. Antigone still represents the familial sphere, blood ties (whether real or imaginary), and loyalty to those we know and with whom we share our lives, while Creon represents the "abstract, impersonal idea of the city in a struggle against the concrete and tangible reality: the family," as we read in *Roots of Brazil*.[16] The definition of "cordial" springs precisely from Antigone's victory over Creon: the bonds established in the realm of the home and family win out over abstract notions of City and polis.

But let us set this story aside to contemplate instead scenes of contemporary politics. What does it mean that, just after the start of his first term, Lula chose to start hosting *churrascos* [barbecues] at the presidential palace (a source of many comments at the time) as a possible zone for political negotiation? What Brazilian will forget the images of a roguish Lula enchanting all present with his "spontaneity," bringing together friends and enemies alike—the two poles with which politics is made, according to Carl Schmitt—in the backyard of his house, putting them all together to chat and celebrate, transforming the political scene into a huge, festive barbecue?[17] We don't need a sociology of the Brazilian barbecue to understand the symbolic importance of this shift, which was far from the only one brought about by Lula. Indeed, *Intermissions* helps shed light on some of these shifts (slips, sometimes) between the private and public spaces, with the president situating himself always somewhere between them, neither here nor there. In one key scene, Lula declares just how irritating he finds the idea of having to put up with "those military men" if he were elected, behind him, watching over him, perennially uniformed. While a leftist imagination may want to locate a remnant of resistance and the memory of oppression, the meaning here seems perfectly clear to me: what bothers him is not the military men in the past, but their uniforms in the present. What irritates him is the etiquette, the politeness, the masks of the political game, the forms that separate men instead of bringing them closer together.

That is why this imaginary draws the public space closer to home—specifically, to the backyard where all wear shirtsleeves and celebrate a proximity that can break through the distance of protocol, if only in the realm of the imagination. Nor is it coincidence that the presidents' advisers were long concerned mainly with the possibility that Lula might improvise in his speeches, himself less willing to obey protocol, with a thinly veiled desire to do away with uniforms and masks—as Antigone once did before the laws of the City, in going to bury her brother, who truly merited her care. It would be tempting, easy, and incorrect to see a streak of "populism" here. In any case, the idea of a populist as a sort of demagogue is not complex enough to explain a phenomenon such as this. When reading *Roots of Brazil* and attempting to understand Lula, it is useful to note that populism is quite often seen by theorists as an answer to a lack of stability in the traditional political order:

Populist practices emerge out of the failure of existing social and political institutions to confine and regulate political subjects into a relatively stable social order. It is the language of politics when there can be no politics as usual: a mode of identification characteristic of times of unsettlement and de-alignment, involving the radical redrawing of social borders along lines other than those that had previously structured society. It is a political appeal that seeks to change the terms of political discourse, articulate new social relations, redefine political frontiers and constitute new identities.[18]

Lula seems to have been able to find this new language of politics, for better or for worse, bringing about true rapprochement and creating, in these moments of political shift, when the censure of the public space gives way to a sort of spontaneity, the sense that distances and barriers have been overcome. But in these moments, his own humble past and his "worker's" values, his credentials being absolutely authentic on this score, allow for a sort of identification that no populism could ever bring about. The caudillo is always a father figure. Lula is "one of ours," a brother. Hence the importance of the great return to the Northeast in the film by Coutinho, and the importance of Lula's intelligent tirades in the film by Salles.

Let us recall a few scenes. Before the barber's mirror, we hear a strange utterance in the voice of power, when the decorum of a suit and tie sparks the playful observation, "If my mother could see me this way, she'd say '*eta baianinho jeitoso*' [what a handsome feller]!"[19] Or the moment when the popular imaginary literally invades the presidential palace: "Let's put up some goalposts on that lawn. . . . The palace is a sad place because [outgoing president] Fernando Henrique Cardoso never played soccer, he doesn't dance, he doesn't drink a drop. . . . I'm going to bring my goats over to graze there." Or what must be one of the most touching scenes in the film (and perhaps in recent Brazilian political history—why not?), Lula, just having found out that he has been elected, goes out and promptly gets lost in the hallways of the five-star hotel in which he had been tucked away, only finding his way and getting his bearings when he runs into two hotel employees stationed before the elevator, and the subsequent embrace brings forth the incredible reaction from the employee ("I hope we'll be looked after!" ["*que nós sejamos privilegiados depois,*" literally, "may we be privileged in the future"]), sealing an alliance that, despite all the critiques one can imagine, is absolutely real. The myth is always real, some way or another, at some point.

There is a darker side here, however. The value placed on the private sphere, for the cordial man, may be a way of shying away from the public arena, escaping the abstract commitments that it imposes.[20] In other words, the cordial man luxuriates in the comfortable proximity with his own, leaving the impersonal space of politics in the shadows and believing that social redemption ultimately hinges on the strengths of the individual and the bonds that he manages to forge around himself. After all, a certain streak of salvationism, with a millenarist tinge, began showing itself in Lula's discourse at the start of his first term in 2003. In fine cordial style, the political burden becomes personal: "I cannot make mistakes." It is true that Lula's assertion—"I cannot make mistakes"—would merit study on its own. Here we have a profound revelation of Brazil's political mechanisms, comprised of layers and layers of prejudice: how could a former factory worker missing a finger from lower-class origins in the poor Northeast, an uncultured man ("uncultured," of course, from a perspective that privileges "high culture" and does not question its self-attributed pretensions of universality)—how could such a creature be so insolent as to err? And what of the promise in the hotel corridor?

The specter of the loss of privacy may also reflect a fear of facing a space in which the limits of action are beyond the control of the individual. In the political sphere, nobody is irreplaceable, all can make mistakes, and the bonds that *I-as-a-politician* establish stretch far beyond the home, obliging me to tread on territory where compromise and conflict are ideally sprung from motives broader than individual possibilities, and rather speaking to a game of ideas that I can win only if I am able to use the proper masks, wearing them with conviction and veneration. In these negotiations, the individual is important but is not the center of the universe.

The first few years of his tenure, in particular, were haunted by a few questions hanging in the air, from both the Right and the Left: Was the Lula administration's "pragmatism," so evident in the compromises struck in the private sphere, now just a symptom of the lack of a political project? Wasn't the lack of a political project the abandonment of ideological parameters in name of governability, which would ultimately make his government similar to so many others? Wouldn't that similarity lie in the fact that many privileges (at all levels, for a variety of elites) remained intact in the end? How to leave the backyard of negotiations and move into a public dimension? For the figure standing in the house, which windows open onto the polis?

Captivating and Captive

There is one last detail here, more disturbing still. In the discussion in Princeton in question, João Moreira Salles declared that he was intrigued and concerned by what he saw as a relative lack of introspection in the future president, whom he filmed precisely between the rallies and speeches, the appearances of the public man. Indeed, to gaze through the lens of the documentary, there is something paradoxical in this Lula who believes so deeply in himself: it is almost impossible to see him on his own in a reflective moment.

This paradox, I believe, has once again been sketched out masterfully in *Roots of Brazil* when Buarque de Holanda brings in another German philosopher to help him decipher the dilemma of cordiality. In the "cordial man," he says,

> social life is, to some extent, a true liberation from the panic that he feels from living with himself and from depending on himself under all the circumstances of existence. His way of revealing himself to others continually reduces the individual to the social and peripheral part of life, which, for the Brazilian—like a good American—tends to matter most. More than anything, he lives through others. Nietzsche addressed this type of human being

when he wrote: "Your inadequate self-love makes you a captive of isolation."[21]

Unable to venture out into the public space alone, the cordial man "lives through others"—that is to say, he mirrors his own joy in others, living in a small, unfragmented world that is ideally characterized by the first stages of the individual's existence, in the welcoming space of the family. But in stepping back and avoiding the shock of differences, postponing the moment in which he finds himself disappointed with the image he has created of himself, the cordial man refuses to step out onto the grand stage of the world, into which all individuals ought to venture so as to eventually discover themselves different from the person who first left home. In Buarque de Holanda's fable, the cordial man is an individual who never grew up into the world of politics and never left home. He would wish to preserve intact the beautiful image harbored by those close to him or the self-image that he projects on the people around him, always turning, as a psychoanalyst once suggested, "to the comfort of collective solutions."[22] The cordial man is shackled to a familial phantasm, unable to strike out beyond the comforting circle of those near and dear. He cannot find the window that looks out onto the city street or onto the political stage.

To claim that there exists a cohesive bloc (the "true Workers' Party supporter," as another psychoanalyst once provocatively suggested[23]) takes us back to a cordial logic, as it is thus that the subject may find the comfort of group acceptance. Here, "betrayal" and "loyalty" start to function as fundamental political principles, ultimately wiping out subjectivity, which is left imprisoned somewhere in the depths of conscience, only to be freed with some sort of sensational gesture: Antigone, in other words.

Let us come back to Lula, while recalling that this is not a matter of personal qualities. His having been forced to go out into the world early, and the fact that his father is practically absent from his biography (in the film, his father is referred to just once, in the image in his memory of the poor, elegant laborer who left home in a suit and tie),[24] does nothing to dilute the interpretive possibilities opened up by cordiality. It doesn't matter, in the end, if Lula's intentions are good. The problem was being, or having been, the bearer of a hope that transcended the bounds of the agreements struck in the larger Brazilian political family, which we might say, never grew up. Or, if it did, it forgot to bring the country along with it.[25]

It matters very little if Lula understood or easily swallowed the rituals of protocol, linguistic elements included—in any case, protocols are often the inventions of the elite, linguistic ones in particular. What is interesting is that behind the respect for the masks of the public space may lie the discovery that politics ought to be constructed as a true representation. The political issue would thus be summed up in the dilemma as to which mask to wear. And a vision of growth in politics would lie—to extend the conceit—in the possibility of forging a true mask, one representative of what is actually going on behind it. The substance behind the mask, in Lula's case, would be quite different from that which had been going on in Brazilian politics for years, or even centuries. "It's something so far outside of sociology! The books never said that I could get as far as I did, or that someone like me could get as far as I did," says the future president, moved by his own words.

But there is a specter circling this "man of the people" who is meant to break with the oligarchical tradition once he arrives on the other side: the trench between rich and poor still stands, like a devilish sociological constant. It is also suggestive that cordiality as the promise of a more fraternal world, present in so many readings of Buarque de Holanda's oeuvre, should not be immune to Brazilian elites' perennial lack of commitment to the poor, or to the "excess of social distance" that sets off "old pleasures"—that is, the pleasure of confounding and taking possession of the body of the Other, as suggested by Contardo Calligaris.[26] This pleasure not only invokes the ghosts of slaveholding society, but also lends fuel and form to the spiral of violence that shapes the Brazilian social experience. Today, we are left with the challenge of examining the meaning of the fresh prominence of these dispossessed classes, which apparently can now possess things as well. It is as if their emergence gave rise to a world in which that macabre constant may well crumble.[27]

A few years ago, it would have been easy to watch *Intermissions* and then ask if Lula's personal traits are a true prison for the man in whom so much hope was placed. As in Nietzsche, invoked by Buarque de Holanda, "living through others" is nothing more than the dread of living with oneself. For the cordial man, proximity is an inescapable necessity, as well as an illusion that barely disguises the chasm between individuals. But indeed, the emergence of a new mass of consumers in Brazil is the answer, in many ways, to the pact sealed in that mythic moment when, in the corridors of that upper-class hotel, that employee called upon Lula to make it so that they might be "privileged" as well.

A vast paradox opens up here, when the circle of cordiality seems not to want to break—while at the same time it may already have broken, as Buarque de Holanda argued. The septuagenarian historian's sympathy with young Lula, his signing of the document officially founding the Workers' Party in 1980, and a later, "radicalizing" reading of his work all act to force an answer to this question: What became of the cordial man? Where is the fear of living with oneself now?

It may not be hyperbole to imagine the cordial man as a sort of hero, returning just as we supposed him dead:

I saw that my picture of myself is exactly like
the character I believed I would always look on
with total disdain
but that's not how it is with me,

in the poetic prediction of Caetano Veloso, for whom the cordial man remains the sinuous promise of another civilization.[28] Veloso is examining the issue of race. But if we look to the state, and the ethics of representation implied there, we may also ask, given what is unveiled in the intermissions of Brazilian political history, what such a nonconflictive approach could ultimately produce, for better or for worse. What issues remain intact, and which have progressed? What can writing or film do in the attempt to encroach on the circle of the individual consciousness? Or will introspection always remain a slippery, unattainable dimension?

Whether directly or indirectly inspired by Sérgio Buarque de Holanda, João Moreira Salles's lens was trained on the man, at a moment when his political or social project had not yet been revealed. When that time comes, however, it is no longer a man like any other who is speaking, but an Other, having moved away from the rest, in a solitude as surprising as it is necessary, in the attempt to forge the figure of the president.

CHAPTER 8

Sérgio Buarque de Holanda and Words, or Evoking Wittgenstein

Cum enim loquimur, signa facimus, de quo dictum est significare.
—Saint Augustine, *De Magistro*, 389 AD

Just over twenty years ago, Umberto Eco noted that his *The Open Work*, written in the 1960s, had inspired interpretations that privileged a free reading, to the detriment of one hewing closer to the text itself. The "rights of the interpreters," he said, were being placed above the "rights of texts."[1] In short, the semiotician was calling for due attention to the dialectic between text and author. While preaching the openness of the text, the author scolded his readers for failing to properly interpret it.

My intention is not to revive old specters, nor unearth quarrels that have already had their time and place. New generations of historians, social scientists, and literary theorists should turn their gaze precisely to that which lies beneath the polemics of the past. This is my aim when I look to revive texts forgotten in personal collections. The reader of this chapter may wonder if the topic at hand isn't excessive. Setting out to write about "Sérgio Buarque de Holanda and words" is to embark on a formidable enterprise. There may be some disconnect between what the title promises and what the text offers. There may be a considerable gap between the name of the chapter and the expectations it may create. In that case, a void will stand between the name and the things that one wishes to speak about.

Here we have a fascinating problem of language. The distance from the name to the thing, or from the name to what which it seeks to express, leads us to the birth of words themselves. After all, the word designates, or seeks to signify, that which is not necessarily present, but which I may make out even in its absence, as I may intuit. This problem grows even more important when we see that it is *in words* and what they allow us to imagine—in the text, that is—that we find much of the value that the author of *Roots of Brazil* may offer us. Of course, in suggesting that Buarque de Holanda's contribution comes from the field of language, I by no means wish to relegate the content of his reflections to a secondary plane; nor is this a return to the old schism between content and form. Rather, we should see that for the writer, *what* is said is intimately tied to *how* it is said. The word is not crystalline, nor does it function on a single plane. It does not portray things, nor does it say exactly what *is there*. Instead, the word can shed light, as it can be unpacked in meanings, speaking to a greater or lesser extent to the condition of man in history. To follow a hermeneutic inspiration, history cannot be understood except in words and through words.

The adventure of language in the works of Buarque de Holanda may of course recall Michel de Montaigne (1533–1592), who concerned himself above all with the way in which something is discussed more than that which is chosen for discussion. "No attention should be paid to the matter, only to the shape that I give it," as we read in the chapter "On Books," in his *Essays*.[2] This all may seem a simple rhetorical game. But the meaning of that game is key. To linger over the "shape" of the subject is to dive into its very signification. If we follow Montaigne's suggestion, it may lead us into the challenge of tracing the movement of the text, which is in turn inseparable from the movements of author and reader. To linger over form, in this case, is to seek out the reasons why readers are drawn in by words, arguments, and concepts. Ultimately, it may be to try and understand how they allow themselves to be seduced by words, convinced by arguments, and enlightened by concepts.

While concern with language may take on special importance in analyzing the works of Buarque de Holanda, we must guard against the enchantments of the text. Any novice scholar, for example, setting out to read an essay like *Roots of Brazil*, will see that analysis and fruition are inseparable in the appreciation of the text. While the reading is pleasant, the prose surrounds and seduces in a game in which readers are invited to let their critical guard down and delight in the words and the images they create. The images in *Roots of Brazil*, on that note, are truly striking.

Invention is a fundamental element in historians' writing, as they bring certain sources close and dialogue with them, *conversing* with the documents. Put this way, the historians' craft may seem tame and almost prosaic: a simple conversation with the sources, with other texts. However, here we see less an amicable encounter and more a full-blown battle. A dialogue, indeed. To recall the etymology of the word, dialogue seeks to tear through the *logos* itself. Here what emerges is a tension between two poles: on the one side, the text that one wishes to interpret and dialogue with; on the other, the text by the writers themselves (the historians, in this case). The text one is working with, meanwhile—a chronicle from the colonial period, say—seeks to faithfully narrate or describe what was seen. Inevitably, in faithfully narrating what they saw, chroniclers will give an authentic testimony of not so much what was seen, but *how* it was seen, and will ultimately provide us with a document of a sensibility frozen in time. Unless one believes in the description of a "pure fact," or the superstition of the "pure fact," it is impossible to imagine that the historian can provide the reader with a neutral, impartial text. This is an obvious condition when dealing with markedly antipositivist authors, as was Buarque de Holanda.[3]

The testimony of chroniclers—to keep to the example at hand—is not a neutral source, evidently. The zone in which the words of these colonial writers operate, being the terrain of language in the colonial chronicle, is already a battlefield itself. This is not the territory of pure description, nor is it a space where names correspond precisely to things, to return again to that old problem. The issue of signification is a fundamental one if the historian wishes to delve into the terrain of the witness to the past, working to decipher the documents at hand. There are no isolated facts—or "discrete variables," in mathematical parlance—to be found here. The text is signification itself, constantly ongoing, as it is also drawing on a stock of nonneutral words with multiple meanings. There is no unambiguity to the terms, just as there is no unambiguous "scientific" language. When historians delve into the realm of words that are not their own, they are obliged to find *connections of meaning* (to fall back on another Weberian turn of phrase) that may shed light on them.[4] Finding or unearthing connections of meaning is a semiotic challenge to which all who frequent the archives are fated to attempt.

Here I will return to an interesting polemic that began in the early 1970s in Brazil and involved historians Carlos Guilherme Mota, Giselda Mota, and Sérgio Buarque de Holanda himself.[5] I will focus on the reflections of the latter, as it was on this occasion that the topic of words came up in particularly explicit fashion in his work. His personal documentation, stored today at the Universidade Estadual de Campinas, is quite revealing in this respect.[6] It all seems to begin, at least publicly, with a stinging critique by the author of *Roots of Brazil* of a text by Carlos Guilherme Mota. In referring to eighteenth-century chronicler Luís dos Santos Vilhena—coiner of the famous formula of *viver em colônias* [living in colonies]—Mota had written that Vilhena seemed to lack a "clear vision of the broader phenomenon of the development of militarism in the Colony."[7] This aside, the historian casts Vilhena as a keen observer of the development of militarism in Bahia in the late eighteenth century. He corroborates this stance with a brief quotation, where Vilhena refers to the many "*policiada*" people in Salvador at the time. This term in particular (*policiada*) sparks a reply from Buarque de Holanda, who sees it as an error to give the word a contemporary meaning, reading *policiada* as referring to the "police" in the military, corporative sense of the term.[8]

If we go along with him, we will conclude that Mota did no more than most of us would today, associating the term *policiada* to a militarized guard. But, as the readers of older texts are aware, and as the author of *Roots of Brazil* would duly point out, in the eighteenth century, the word had much more of a sense of "civilized," "cultivated," or "refined," as opposed to the military meaning that Carlos Guilherme Mota attributes to it. This is the trap of "diachronic multivocities," in the bombastic turn of phrase that Buarque de Holanda employs, not without some irony. But the very word *civilization*, to which the historian refers in questioning Mota's reading, would only take off after the success of the French Revolution, having been introduced in Brazil by José da Silva Lisboa, the future Viscount of Cairu, back in 1798, and settling into the local vocabulary a few years later.

The issue is that if we wish to untangle the multiple, mutable meanings of words so as to pin down the semantic field of expressions such as these, we will find interminable and often torturous paths before us. Just as human history is alive, being both movement and process, so too is the history of words. If history is not forged solely by those who control official policy, then the history of words cannot lie solely in the hands of those who control institutionalized letters. Strictly speaking, words are owned by no one.

Buarque de Holanda seemed to see a "petrification" of the word in Carlos Guilherme Mota's text or in his stance when faced with certain terms. Not by chance, Mota's severe critiques of those who "explain" Brazil would focus particularly on the eclectic nature of their terminology, supposedly a sign of a generalizing view of Brazilian culture, disconnected from the social dynamics of class.[9]

To follow Buarque de Holanda's reasoning and add my words to his, an excess of zeal for "unambiguous" language would wind up immobilizing terms, suffocating their latent meanings. It's as if a vastly turbulent sea in which meanings construct each other, conflict, and contradict one another were subjected to tyrannical domination so that one might reach the safe harbor of some imagined scientificism. To believe absolutely in words would be to give oneself over to the unambiguous, unquestionable content of a single meaning; a fear of lexical imprecision would ultimately sterilize both thought and imagination. Scientific language may be a prison if there is an unconditional belief in the label of something as "scientific"; if historians believe in only that which is permitted through an objective lens, they will shut themselves into a semantic universe that is severely limited because it is definitively established.

The relationship between men and words is a tense one. Writing well is never a completely pleasurable or tame activity, of course. It is a war with words themselves, a polemic in the broad sense. Here we see a familiar crossroads: the problem here, as with modernists in the 1920s, is language. Recall the words of young Buarque de Holanda, at age twenty-two, writing in *Estética* magazine, which he had founded with his friend Prudente de Moraes Neto, inspired by T.S. Eliot's *Criterion*: "Words placed such confidence in the credulous spirit of men that the latter turned their back on them."[10] The tension between the world and its expression, from which all art is born (and, why not, all sciences as well), is ultimately elided if men believe themselves the masters of words or their meanings. But what does it mean to turn one's back on words? The image may suggest that, if we believe that the meaning of words is already established, then that is a sort of surrender. There is nothing to discuss, no battle to be waged. And the modernists, as we know, were determined to spark that war: in the "battle" with words, the historian, the literary critic, and the militant modernist come together.

In the 1973 article that seems to have begun the tussle with Carlos Guilherme Mota, titled "Sobre uma doença infantil da historiografia" [On an Infantile Disease in Historiography], Buarque de Holanda compares an absurd, unconditional belief in words (the condition for turning one's back on them) to such a belief in facts. This faith, he wrote, had shaped and continued to shape the work of many historians:

> It cannot be denied that the superstition of the fact, pure fact, before which a historian must shrink and elide himself as much as possible, sprang from a laudable but fallacious yen for objectivity. Precisely the same may be said of the sort of historiography that, in a similar fashion, seeks to fill the lacuna broadened by the decline of merely factual history. The difference between one and the other is vast: the old superstition of the fact has been substituted by the new superstition of the pure word, perfectly unequivocal, petrified, and valid for all time. Result: in place of those collections of facts and dates rigorously obtained via critical methods, led on to ultimate perfection, we would gaze on the explosion of a torrential

bout of dysentery of cleansed words and keywords, fit to mark the flow of events. As with all simplifiers, the vassals of these criteria place in them an impregnable trust and turn against those more skeptic with self-confidence and glorious acrimony, a relative of that ugly woman's tartness of which Dr. Johnson spoke, if I am not mistaken, around two centuries ago.[11]

A tartness rightly restored to its origin, as the critique is itself a torrent of caustic words. Unlike "cleansed words and keywords," however, the historian's terms were bent on exorcizing the magic of the "pure word." A fascinating move: the lexicon is called upon to exorcize the lexicon itself.

Exorcisms were a task that fell to the historian, as Buarque de Holanda saw it. His critique of Giselda Mota, which accompanied his criticisms of Carlos Guilherme Mota, went along the same lines, suggesting the necessity of exorcising words, sapping them of any magical substance. Hence the harsh, venomous words directed at the former, who had prepared with a commentary a "Critical Bibliography" of Brazilian independence, in the book *1822: Dimensões* [1822: Dimensions], edited by Carlos Guilherme Mota.[12] If we take Buarque de Holanda at his word, the very use of the word *fatal* in a sentence in a work of his and in a few other texts was enough for Giselda Mota to sniff out a certain, inevitable "fatality" in the analysis of history. The personal papers of the author of *Roots of Brazil* contain a long letter sent to Carlos Guilherme Mota, which would later be drawn upon for the article published in *O Estado de S. Paulo* in 1973 ("Sobre uma doença infantil da historiografia"), as well as an essay on Leopold von Ranke, published the following year.[13] The letter has a sarcastic tone to it that remains, albeit in a milder form, in the article. For example, on the use of the word "fatal," the historian suggests that

in G.M. [Giselda Mota]'s aversion to the word "fatal," an aversion that she does not display towards countless others that might be understood even more arbitrarily ... it is possible that she was thinking of the Latin *fatum*, which, despite [having] many acceptable meanings in a scientific proposition, harbors many other mysterious, naturally reprehensible ones. Those who wish to use only perfectly "neutral" and "unambiguous" terms, calling on etymology in their quest, would wind up unable to advance or retreat in their work. Retreating [*recuar*] would hardly be permitted, in the realm of immaculate decorum, since *recuar*, in its origins, might be indecent, and only explicable by way of a dirty word. And what of "*palavrão*" [dirty word]? Here we have an augmentative in a word [*palavra*], which comes from parable [*parábola*], and scientists cannot speak in parables, lest they fall into literature.[14]

Interestingly, this game with words, in a casual and calculatedly slighting tone, may reveal a fundamental problem in the philosophy of language. Retreating to the origin of words may mean re-forging some of those chains that linguists seek in order to illuminate the constant displacements between signified and signifier. The retreat, in this case, is an attempt to trace the path of signification itself, reencountering history in the history of language.

To recall a philosopher dear to Buarque de Holanda, we may suppose that this deliberate "game" with words revives the original meaning of language itself, and the playful side to speaking and communicating. Let us retreat to Ludwig Wittgenstein (1889–1951), then, to use his *Philosophical Investigations* in clarifying the meaning of what he refers to as "language-games." According to the Viennese philosopher,

> In the practice of the use of language ... one party calls out the words, the other acts on them. But in instruction in language the following process will occur: the learner *names* the objects....
>
> We can also think of the whole process of using words ... as one of those games by means of which children learn their native language. I will call these games "language-games" and will sometimes speak of a primitive language as a language-game.
>
> And the processes of naming the stones and of repeating words after someone might also be called language-games. Think of much of the use of words in games like ring-a-ring-a-roses.
>
> I shall also call the whole, consisting of language and the actions into which it is woven, a "language-game."[15]

The proposition of the game is fundamental. But where does the game take place, and what does it stand on? How do we set the rules, the reach, and the limits of this language game, through which word-signs move? Leaning on Wittgenstein here, Buarque de Holanda would say that the sign only takes on meaning in its *use*.

Let us return to the part of the *Philosophical Investigations* that the historian evokes in his letter, but examining a longer quotation. In referring to the party who acts in accordance with the rules that someone dictates, the philosopher writes:

"There is a gulf between an order and its execution. It has to be filled by the act of understanding."

"Only the act of understanding can mean that we are to do THIS. The *order*—why, that is nothing but sounds, ink-marks. –"

Every sign *by itself* seems dead. *What* gives it life?—In use it is *alive*. Is life breathed into it there?—Or is the *use* its life?[16]

Pure sound, isolated words, "ink-marks," are sapped of meaning so that signification might only be found in the *use* of signs. Hence the lovely image: the sign breathes in its usage. It must be proposed, however, for it to have some meaning. But to whom is the game of signs proposed, if not the reader? The sign, after all, requires that the reader breathe for it. The word needs the reader to live. What remains is this sort of war, or battle, to which writers, critics, historians, or sociologists are all fated (the true *fatum*, here). A battle with words, against the enchantment of our intelligence, to follow Wittgenstein further. In the end, one should seek to reveal the word in the heart of its text and context, through the complex interaction with those who are playing.

Beyond a few blatant errors in Giselda Mota's bibliography, Buarque de Holanda critiques her excessive concern with terms to the detriment of syntax. After all, syntax is what articulates the meaning of the text. In the composition and sowing of the words, the word lives, and the sign may breathe:

Her lack of concern with syntax, which she seeks to compensate for with a fallacious interest in the magic of words highlighted out of context, may explain not a few of the imprecisions and misunderstandings from Ms. Giselda. Here I am referring not to grammatical syntax, as the topic often exceeds my expertise, although a certain lack of grammatical awareness [*desgramática*] may also be partly at fault.[17]

Here, the historian is perturbed by the act of highlighting words in the text and considering them as meaningful in isolation. In this play of words, there is a provocation. Grammar—as a technique, in its original sense—may fall into "desgramática" without the balance of the discourse necessarily being lost. What is important is not the letter in itself—or its weight, taken out of context—but all the letters as a whole, properly arranged. Hence the irony in the zealous use of quotation marks, as if the inverted commas were enough to save a word from possible misunderstandings:

Well, in doubt, there is no harm in quotation-marking whatever may appear ambiguous or multivocal. In this sense, one should write "Independence" so the reader may know that I know that, in Brazil, "Independence" was not truly independence. Nothing against it, but I believe that, deep down, this is provincialism. I spent a few months, quite a long time ago, in Cachoeiro do Itapemirim, in [the state of] Espírito Santo, and the director of a newspaper there, called *O Progresso*, who fancied himself a bit of a humorist, made such abundant use of quotation marks and capital letters, to show that such words should be understood *cum grano salis*, that in the end the newspaper had more quotation marks than words. As for me, I find the practice of adorning ambiguous terms with little horns gallant, but I must confess with some frustration that I am too old to endorse such excesses.[18]

Freeing oneself of quotation marks simply means facing down the multivocality of words, consciously establishing a language game in which they complete each other such that we may discover, in the very act of playing, meanings that renew themselves beyond, or even in spite of, the authorized writing technique. To free oneself of quotation marks is, above all, to strip oneself of the smug air of those who take themselves to be far from imprecision, shielded by the bright sun of science. This said, we should not confuse history with a literary genre. Historians are writers as well, but their writing calls for an appropriate objective approach, not subject to the evaluation of scientific laws, but to the reader's judgment, which may reanimate the text along with the writer.

We have seen that the text lives and breathes in the use of signs. The word breathes in the readers' imaginations, or even in their ear (we cannot deny the musicality of certain texts, even those apparently far removed from poetic forms). It is the readers who mobilize the terms of the text, finding the thread of its narrative, or creating new threads with which to draw it out, recreating the thrust of the text. They become active, eager interlocutors, true partners in the game. But this does not make any reading a reasonable one. When one reads a text, it is not as if readers are faced with a void and are called upon to fill it with what they may—or may not—understand. Nor do texts simply contain hermetic meanings that resist any explanation. Here we are on the path of understanding, wrestling with objects that shy from any presumptive scientific sterilization, which even the hard sciences no longer embrace, as Buarque de Holanda notes in the letter in question. He refers to "unsuspected" authors like Popper or Einstein, for whom "empathy"—despite the imprecision of the translation from the German word *Einfühlung*—is inevitably called upon in objective approximation. Nor does "speculation," the recourse of the social scientist or the historian, equal to "subjective, wordy explanations bereft of self-criticism, set apart from logic and confrontation with reality."[19] The issue is that the complexity of the material one is dealing with, and the density of historical reality, call for special gifts as a writer. Style becomes an indispensable weapon, to be handled with precision, in the interminable task of reconstructing historical connections.[20]

Here we are cast into the realm of the historiographical essay. And in the presence of good essayistic prose, there is no room for categorical affirmations or for closed-off texts. In sum, we are before the circle of the eternal return executed by all texts, which is the path of signification itself—from the sign to us and from us to the sign, from the words to the reader and from the reader to the words—with the reader as constant mediation. The reader is the motive force, moving the text, winding up the music box. The movement of meanings, seeking to recover or hint at meanings lost in time, lies beneath the fabric of words. If the text is a good one, then it will always attempt to sweep readers off their feet. The active readers will not refuse this, taking it on as a proposition and a challenge; and only then, with the game proposed and accepted, will they dive into the half-gloom of signification itself. There will always be a chiaroscuro here, able to reveal or conceal. One must accept the game, rejecting the illusion of a single, utterly illuminating sense.

The comparison between the language of the historian and painting may be a productive one. In his *The Story of Art*, Ernst Gombrich reflects on movement in the paintings of Leonardo da Vinci. Why are his figures not static, as so many earlier works had been? According to the author, this is because

> only Leonardo found the true solution to the problem. The painter must leave the beholder something to guess. If the outlines are not so firmly drawn, if the form is left a little vague, as though disappearing into a shadow, this impression of dryness and stiffness will be avoided. This is Leonardo's famous invention which the Italians call "*sfumato*"—the blurred outline and mellowed colours that allow one form to merge with another and always leave something to our imagination.[21]

Thinking of painting and writing at the same time, *sfumato*, with its only partially defined spaces, calls on the imaginative eye of the spectator. This is where movement is born. Here the figure awakes from its sleeping-beauty slumber and breathes.

The metaphor of breath suggests a text that is alive, able to move and morph. Just as the essayistic text strives to be, refusing Scholastic rigidity for the free movement of the body or whatever the issue at hand may be. If there is a playful streak here, there is no air of irresponsibility in it. On the contrary—once outside the safe harbor of unambiguity, we are inevitably thrown into the adventure of multivocal language, which gives us even greater responsibility over the movement that the text puts forth and brings about.

Buarque de Holanda's prose is the result of a hand given to willful sowing. One might call it rigorous, although its rigor comes through in the elegance with which it delves into the realm of historical documents, never in the rigidity of the terms it proposes. The articulation of words, sans geometric regularity, may leave space for the imagination, like a sort of *sfumato* within writing, with the spaces between words only partially defined, to be filled by the light of reading.

Since Montaigne, the essay has been winking at the reader, offering a seductive form for the imagination. Theodor Adorno compared it to a carpet into which one might weave a variety of thoughts: "The fruitfulness of the thoughts depends on the density of this texture."[22] Such fruitfulness must be demanded of the writer whenever approaching a dense object. And all historical objects are, deeply so. Calling our attention to language, then, is not a way of losing oneself in the rhetorical void, but rather proposing that we once again recognize the complexity of rhetoric, simplified and impoverished by rigid formulas for thinking and writing. Calling attention to writing is a way of putting it to the service of enlightenment, turning language into its own target. This suggestion from the Frankfurt philosopher seems to be echoed by the author of *Roots of Brazil* when he comes to see himself as a writer, with all the zeal inherent to the profession.

The essay contains a dual dialogue. On one hand, there is the writer's search for the *logos*; and on the other, the reader finds it again. Mediation—the text—is all. The text is a repository of words, but it will always be up to the reader to interrogate them when they are offered up by the text. While the disposition of the words still belongs to the writer, the open form of the essay serves as an invitation to the reader, offering up the chance to let oneself go and slip into its seduction. Halfway along, we find ourselves cradled by the movement of a form that opens itself up to a critique of language, setting itself the task of rethinking and reorganizing ideas, and—why not?—words as well. The syntax that brings the terms together and blends them is shared by the writer and the reader. But it is the reader who will ultimately give life to the signs and make them breathe.

Perhaps the reader's rights are exaggerated here. Perhaps they are given more importance, or more weight, than they are due. However, this may be the appropriate spirit to keep in mind when heading down the paths that the oeuvre of Sérgio Buarque de Holanda opens up for its readers. After all, words can awake only when we take ownership of them. To an extent, they begin to breathe only when all reverence is lost, all the authority of the term drains away, and we are permitted to play with words that are not our own.

CHAPTER 9

In a Thread of Time

Chico, Sérgio, and Benjamin

The stories around musician and writer Chico Buarque (b. 1944) and his father, Sérgio Buarque de Holanda, include curious episodes. Of these, the least familiar may be Chico's observation about his childhood—a time when his father was, for the most part, the sound of a typewriter rattling away in an office.[1]

It is difficult to hear the sound of writing, and it may be trying. In this chapter, I will suggest not a clear relationship but more of an inference born of literature. I will not be reading Chico Buarque's *Benjamin* (1995) exactly through the lens provided by "Chico's dad" (as Sérgio Buarque de Holanda sometimes introduced himself in public) but simply put forth a relationship between the writings of the two.

At the start (and finish) of his second novel, Chico Buarque places the title character, Benjamin, before a firing squad, on the brink of his own death. It is here that the narrative takes off, echoing an old trope in Latin American literature, as critics have noted.[2] After all, in *One Hundred Years of Solitude* (1967), by Gabriel García Márquez (1927–2014), Colonel Aureliano Buendía is also facing a firing squad—just then, the moment that his father took him to see the ice for the first time returns in a flashback.[3] But there are striking differences here. The instant of death, in García Márquez's novel, paves the way for a fable whose tragedy winds up bolstering the grandeur of the condemned family line rather than destroying it; in *Benjamin*, the glimpse of life just before death closes out a story devoid of any epic tones, in a shorter, more agitated narrative, which reveals to us a world in which poetry itself seems impossible, or unattainable.

Let us hear the first, drawn-out, indispensable first paragraph of *Benjamin*:

> The execution squad was lined up; the order to fire was forceful and the shots produced a single report. But to Benjamin Zambraia they sounded like a drum roll, and he might even be able to tell the order in which the dozen weapons in front of him had discharged. Even if blind, he would identify each rifle and say from which barrel had come each of the projectiles that now tore into his chest, his neck, his face. Everything would be extinguished with the swiftness of a bullet between the skin and its first vital target (aorta, heart, trachea, medulla), and in that instant Benjamin witnessed what he had expected: his existence was projected from beginning to end, like a motion picture, on the blindfold of his eyes. Faster than a bullet, the film could be projected again on the inside of his eyelids, in reverse, when the succession of events might prove more acceptable. And there would still be a small thread of time for Benjamin to see himself once more here and there in situations that he would prefer to forget, the images ricocheting in the recesses of his skull. The allotted time would end to be succeeded by an ultimatum, a whistle, a cry of alarm, but Benjamin would interpret them as the threat of a child counting to three—one . . . two . . . two and a half . . .—and would pause a little longer on moments that belonged to him, and that he had not known how to appreciate before. He would also learn to penetrate into spaces he had never known, into times that were not his own, with the senses of other people. And suddenly he would catch himself walking simultaneously in all directions, and he would take in everything at a single glance, and all that he perceived would never cease, and infinity itself would fit inside a bubble in the interior of a dream of a man like Benjamin Zambraia, who does not remember ever having died in a dream.[4]

The cinematographic narration sets the tone for the novel, with the protagonist seeing himself as possessed of a camera that has followed him ceaselessly since adolescence. Beyond this paranoia of surveillance (we should think of this interminable dream as a life sans the tranquilizing horizon of death), and beyond what critic José Paulo Paes has referred to as a "hyper-realist gaze," linking the author to an illustrious trio (Dostoevsky, Kafka, and Camus),[5] there lies the point—a supreme, providential moment—in which the man finds himself before the absolute fact of his life and personal history: "suddenly he would catch himself walking simultaneously in all directions, and he would take in everything at a single glance."

The passage from the individual to the collective, and its proper understanding, is a topic that Sérgio Buarque de Holanda would long follow. There is no need to go over his fine discussion of the German Historical School, as immortalized in one of his most beautiful pieces, a little-read work that I have referenced a few times over the course of this book, namely, the essay that he wrote, by then a septuagenarian, for the *Revista de História*, titled "O atual e o inatual na obra de Leopold von Ranke" [The Current and Uncurrent in the Work of Leopold von Ranke].[6] Rather, we simply shall draw a few elements from it that may speak to the intersection of literature and history.

After discussing the meaning of a misunderstood formula of Ranke's (where he suggests the need to show the event "as it actually happened"), Sérgio Buarque de Holanda turns to a broad consideration of the works of the Prussian historian. In referring to Ranke's scientific notion of history, however, he notes, taking several perspectives into account, that the author's *ocularidade* [visual focus] ultimately ties him to the *moment*, robbing the world as the historian describes it of many of its potentialities: shackled to the instant, the historian's time takes in history itself (what has passed) and the gleam of the present (what is passing) but excludes the future (what will come to pass).

If we go through the door that Sérgio Buarque de Holanda has opened for us, we will soon realize that the problem before him, when he discussed the historian's craft (he being a writer as well, as he liked to recall), was precisely the "end" of history—or, in other terms, its *meaning*. I shall not linger over Ranke here, who sought to discuss and overcome the canon of historical reflection in his time. Rather, looking back to *Benjamin*, we should understand that the absence of the "end" is a problem with far-reaching consequences for history and philosophy, because it forces us to face down the lack of continuity and stability in their own narratives, traditionally anchored in a logic that necessarily rejects the fragile, open-ended nature of the writing of history. It is a history that then leans, after a discussion like Ranke's, closer to uncertainty over its meaning than the certainty of a just, lofty end.

In the case of the literature of Sérgio's son, we should note that the circularity of the narrative (abundant in the prose of Chico Buarque) tends to enclose the character's history in the *instant*, cast in the minute timescale of gaze, thus refusing the comfort of a meaning to be revealed after life, or after the end of history. In Benjamin's perfect circle, there is nothing beyond death, which itself evades contact even in dreams. There is nothing beyond a life robbed of transcendence. We are thrust into a world that inevitably verges on the nonsensical, made prisoners of a story almost completely devoid of meaning, as it is limited to the instant, sans death to arrive as an ultimate resolution.

It is agonizing to see the very much alive Benjamin, just as a bullet tears through his body, speaking of a "thread of time," of an ultimatum and the possibility of lingering over moments that are his but which he never appreciated in life. This is the moment of true anguish, as there blossoms doubt as to what belongs to him, in the very moment that he seems to be feeling through others, just as a perfect historian would dream of doing: "penetrate into spaces he had never known, into times that were not his own, with the senses of other people." Thinking of the composer, this may be what Heloisa Starling dubbed a "time of delicateness," marked by an ability to "absorb time and turn it into memory."[7]

Warning us that the insistent presence of God in Ranke's works does not equal a concession to religious principles, Sérgio Buarque de Holanda recalls that, for the eminent Prussian historian, the value of an era (or, might we say, of a life?) is certainly not found in the results it may produce, but rather "in its very existence, in whatever that may be." This is what would have led Ranke to imagine that, "in the eyes of God, all generations are equally justified, as they must be for the historian."[8] We need not imagine the historian (or the narrator, or the cinematographer) occupying a transcendent space, as if the "visual focus" in question equaled some sort of omniscience. The idea of seeing all, through all eyes, is nothing more than a logical possibility that consumes itself just as we believe we have attained it, much like Benjamin in the instant before his death. The omniscience of the protagonist crumbles (he *would learn* to penetrate . . .) because the narrative may not go farther than the desire to recover the meaning of life, nor may it avoid failure in the attempt to understand or decipher it. Let us suppose that death is meaning revealed, as a long literary and philosophical tradition would have it: but death itself slips away at the very moment that we feel closest to it, at the start and finish of the novel. The death of the narrator remains outside the book, hanging over it, just as it haunts us readers.[9]

Benjamin recounts the days before his death, dividing up "the ingot of his remaining lifetime into monthly slices," all his savings in a single bar of gold that he intends on using to support himself in his old age.[10] However, the fiduciary value of his life does not lie in shining metal, but in the massive, animalesque Rock that he sees every day from his window. (The mountainous landscape of Rio de Janeiro is of key importance for the poetics of Chico Buarque.) Then comes the most interesting fantasy of the book: the rock also sees him, every day, but in reverse, as rocks "appear to grow younger with time," becoming smooth and hard, unlike Benjamin's body:

> In the eyes of the Rock, the appearance of the Benjamin who came to live in the building in front of it, who every morning opened the three windows, did push-ups on the parapet, thrust out his thorax and said "Good morning, Rock," would be that of someone thirty years older than this man with the battered face who contemplates it in silence. Benjamin does not reject the hypothesis that the rocks are right and that real time runs in reverse to that which we normally compute. It's possible that the moments we have just lived suddenly wipe themselves from our awareness and become transformed into fear, desire, anxiety, premonition. And in what we believe is remembrance there is perhaps a fate that, if we have the knack, we can determine, elude, refuse, or enjoy with redoubled intensity.[11]

With events in reverse gear, ends are jumbled up, and destiny becomes past, with all its ramifications. The future is erased, as it were (just like death, which sits at the start of this backwards-traced circle), and we find ourselves immersed, along with Benjamin Zambraia, in the fate of memory. There is no destiny possible but that which is created by projecting the past outward—but not in the direction of the future, rather in the circularity of memories and reminiscences that the subject only partially controls, though he or she might wish to master them completely.

The projection of the ghost of Castana Beatriz in the body of Ariela Masé occurs precisely within this circularity, in the possibility of reconstructing, in the narrative, the time that precedes death. But the sole, agonizing chance of re-tying the knots of life lies in recounting the past—an open past, as it is still in the process of being realized—and forgetting the future, leaving it alone, to run at the expense of the bar of gold. After a sleepless night, Benjamin "has the clear notion that his future is bound," and then imagines it as a string wrapped around the tuning peg of a guitar and that snaps once stretched taut, leaving the other end loose, whipping around aimlessly. This is the past that he is (re)imagining, and in which he may relocate his fantasies, although without total control over them—given the strength with which the snapped string moves through the air.[12]

The land of memory that opens up from here is none other than (duly swathed in the fantastical reminiscences of Benjamin Zambraia) Rio de Janeiro during and after the military dictatorship (1964–1985). In the landscape of the city, there swells an electoral monster with its origin in the curdled genetic formation of a people: in the present, aging and decadent, Benjamin is asked to play professor and social scientist Diógenes Halofonte on television, declaring that the con man Alyandro Sgaratti "is the citizens' xiphopagus." Marcelo Ridenti has already suggested, in detail and vivid imagination, the stage on which memory, society, and politics come together to form the narrative fabric of *Benjamin*.[13] Here, however, I suggest that some movement springs from the very breast of the narrative, tying the narrator's life to the minefield of the past, although certainty is unable to take a foothold, nor should it. *Benjamin* may be suggesting that the political future of Brazil has been abolished, as Ridenti suggests; and this is where the individual and the collective, the political and the literary, intersect. The powerlessness of narrative, which unfolds under the sign of death, unable to achieve any end (and thus meaningless), is also the impossibility of writing the future, because we are content to play with the remnants of the past. Rather, we are the prisoners of a circle that never breaks, the perfection of which is far from edifying, or even touching. Perhaps in this we may understand Chico Buarque's taste for ruins—which, fully present in his songs, is brought to fruition in his fourth novel, *Spilt Milk*.[14] The problem is still the end of men, and the end of writing.

* * *

One final text may be called in, by way of contrast. But this is the son speaking about the specter of his father.[15]

On November 22, 1996, upon the release of the critical works of Sérgio Buarque de Holanda through a long and admirable editorial undertaking (*O Espírito e a letra*, in two volumes edited by Antonio Arnoni Prado, presented that night at the São Paulo Museum of Art—MASP), Chico Buarque rose to the occasion before an admiring audience and read two old texts of his father's, one of which was the 1925 piece "Perspectives." Those of us in attendance heard the young modernist's declaration of principles, as read by his son:

I, Sérgio Buarque de Holanda, believe it indisputable that in all things there is a limit, an end, beyond which they lose their instability, which is one of the conditions of life, so as to settle comfortably into what we euphemistically call their expression, and what is in truth nothing more than their reflection. Only already lived thoughts, those that may be considered not over the course of their duration, but objectively, previously dissected, may find an end. I mean to say: this end only comes about at a breaking point with life.[16]

This approach to language leads us to distrust the very act of writing; each word, then, is nothing more than the pale reflection of something not completely understood, shut within the ineffability of life, stubbornly resisting death and the silence of definitive words, written in stone. We might say that life contains a secret that words themselves are unable to fix and offer back to man. Although Benjamin may be given the opportunity to review his life (literally), his attempt to understand what has happened fails miserably. Ultimately, a film played in reverse might make the "succession of events ... more acceptable."

The crisis of writing and the writer must have intrigued the author of *Benjamin*, if his third novel, *Budapest*, is any indication; there, the narrative, whose senseless production we follow, mingles with the uncontrollable course of events.[17] In the case of *Benjamin*, however, nonsense reveals itself at each step; there is no chance of an ending, which would be that "breaking point with life," able to frame the moment in which words and men make their peace, when narrative itself might fall still and breathe no more. On the contrary, in the story of Benjamin Zambraia, the narrative obstinately survives, while the hero in crisis agonizes at every line. That story, we should recall, recovers and recaptures the precarious meaning of the narration, just as the bullet enters the body. A single blast—the imagined death—is substituted by the whistling of the bullets, making the end of everything close and distant at the same time, bringing death close, albeit suspending it above the narrative thread, which entwines itself in the infernal circle of a life that stubbornly refuses to consummate it.

At the end of this brief jaunt through the texts of father and son, we are left with noises. It seems that hearing the rattling of the typewriter made the father both distant and forbidden, at some point in the past. Amusingly enough, however, Chico Buarque notes that later on, with his adolescent interest in the books of his father's formidable library, he was finally able to draw closer to Sérgio Buarque de Holanda. The two recognized each other in literature, enchanted by writing. Or, perhaps, they were enchanted by the limits and the precariousness of words and their impotence before life.

EPILOGUE

Roots of the Twenty-First Century
Wisnik and the Horizons of the Essay

Everything that I do not invent is false.
—Manoel de Barros, *Livro sobre nada*, 1996

Why does no one write essays of national interpretation anymore?
Some may believe, for the reasons discussed in this book, that such essays have simply run out of steam; there would be no reason to return to a genre marked by the desire to address totalities at a moment when the very notion of totality has entered into profound crisis. There are those who see the tradition of classic essays in Brazil as a moment already made outdated by systematic studies of culture and history. After all, when Gilberto Freyre and Sérgio Buarque de Holanda wrote, respectively, *The Masters and the Slaves* and *Roots of Brazil* in the 1930s, we simply didn't know as much as we do today, thanks to intervening decades of work by social scientists and historians. While this accumulated knowledge allows us to write about Brazil with greater nuance, it also stays our hand with the reminder that any attempt to set down national characteristics will be a merely impressionistic exercise, unable to stand up to a rigorous analysis of society and history.

But we should recall that essays of national interpretation never cast themselves as the product of accumulated facts. These essays don't speak of Brazil as it is. Their horizon is another. As we have seen, the essay is also a battle with language, which may become, as in the case of *Roots of Brazil*, a sinuous conversation about the insufficiency of the national sign. Even so, as paradoxical as this may seem, the essay contains questions of an ethical, almost transcendent nature, sounding out the nature of the collective. The essay asks not only how we arrived where we are, but also where we are headed and even where we should be going. Its field of vision encompasses the past, present, and open-ended future in a single continuum, taking a long view of history, as if we were navigating on a current without knowing where it carries us. The true essayist may be he or she who dares to name our possible destinations, making them into a fable where readers may or may not recognize themselves. Faced with the path not yet taken, one must write.

After decades of development in social sciences and historical studies, then, is there still room for essays that announce Brazil's purpose? Can we still ask after that open future that letters, shackled to the instant as they are, can barely graze?

I believe that the answer came a few years ago, in the form of a book that may be read as a *Roots of Brazil* for the twenty-first century: *Veneno remédio: O futebol e o Brasil* [Poison/Cure: Soccer and Brazil], by José Miguel Wisnik.[1] It's odd that the book hasn't yet provoked larger debates, especially in Brazilian academic circles. Perhaps this bespeaks some reticence regarding the book's subject material, since not all intellectuals are prepared to take soccer seriously. But perhaps the problem is that the book points to an issue that remains unresolved, although it has been worked over in a number of ways and to a number of degrees in Brazilian essayism: *miscegenation*. Not simple miscegenation, of genetic or phenotypic traits, but miscegenation as the fundamental rupture of patterns associated with order and discipline—a point at which we might bring Buarque de Holanda and Freyre together, once again. This is an attempt to consider mixture on another level as well: as the composition of civilizational structures and principles in constant dialogue.

For Wisnik, soccer is not an escape valve for social tensions, or a banal form of entertainment, or the simple expression of economic and commercial interests. Rather, it is principally a symbolic system that brings wide sectors of society closer to real experiences of gain and loss, felt and lived collectively: either all lose, or all win. The temptation to see a populist drive behind all this, a possible manipulation of the masses, is powerful but misleading.[2] True, fans' devotion may be a form of wiping out any respect for difference (hooliganism is a reality), but aside from fanaticism there is an immense gradation of associative possibilities, various ways of identifying with what's going on down on the field. The reader of *Veneno remédio* will not fail to notice Wisnik's psychoanalytical framework: discussion of soccer turns into the analysis of complex mechanisms of transference. The movements on the field have implications for the subject watching the match, because it bears the cipher of a history and a destiny that may not be his or hers alone. This is the horizon where the essay operates, always aware of the possibility that the collective may appear faintly in the experience of the subject.

A fundamental difference between the game and manipulative mass phenomena like fascism, Wisnik would say, is that the fascist masses exist in a hypnotic state that moves them forward, avoiding anything that might give them a reality check (or an encounter with "the Real," in psychoanalytic terms), while the game favors a mesmerizing battle always on the edge of the Real and which will inevitably fall into it. In fact, as mesmerizing as the game may be, when one plays for keeps, the risk of defeat is both assumed and lived, as if loss formed part of the dialogue between the subject and destiny. In playing, one learns how to lose. The fascist model sustains itself through the negation of any and all loss, avoiding the shadow of frustration and always searching, irritably and brutally, to sweep from the map those who might contribute to an unacceptable defeat.

Why "poison/cure," the term Wisnik uses to characterize Brazilian soccer? The formula recalls the *pharmakon*, which contains within itself the seeds of both healing and destruction.[3] The book's argument is fairly simple, partly intuitive and unfailingly accurate: in its vision, Brazil lives in an imaginary oscillation between success and disaster. Either we're the best or we're worthless. Nothing is possible between the two poles. The most perfect satire of this state of the collective soul is the Brás Cubas Poultice that Machado de Assis puts into his protagonist's imagination; Brás Cubas dies even as he conjures up a providential solution to alleviate "our melancholy humanity" once and for all. Against profound sadness, eternal happiness. Machado's lesson is that we'll die of this yet.

Wisnik's is a book in which soccer-related erudition is paired with cultural and philosophical analysis. But if the argument that it proposes is closer to the radical uncertainty of Sérgio Buarque de Holanda regarding Brazil's future, the elliptical and dense nature of Wisnik's prose brings him, at least stylistically, alongside Freyre. Or perhaps we can say that *Veneno remédio* plays midfielder between the two essayists, since the goalposts Wisnik uses come from their thinking.

I shall limit myself to one question, a fundamental one even for those who don't follow soccer. It has to do with something that, in the book, is termed "the nonlinear nature of Brazilian soccer." Why are nonlinearity, ellipses, and sinuous curves called upon to say something that goes far beyond the soccer field? How can this resistance to the rectilinear help decipher an entire social matrix and pose questions about collective destiny? The answer comes from a realization born of literature. *Veneno remédio* takes its initial inspiration from the distinction made by the Italian filmmaker and poet Pier Paolo Pasolini, who, in the early 1970s, imagined the opposition between soccer played in *prose*, which he associated with European teams, and in *poetry*, a style identified with South American soccer, and Brazilian soccer in particular. The provocation has profound consequences for understanding the game from within. But at the same time, it points toward different ways of approaching the social contract—different ways of exploring the spaces of society. On one side, the European style (capitalist, urbane, First World, and so on), "linear and goal-oriented," with "triangular passes, defensive emphasis, counter-attacks, crosses, and follow-through"; on the other, the Latin American mode (peripheral, rural, Third World, and so on), with its "creation of empty spaces, feints, autonomous dribbles, [and] a congenital tendency towards the attack."[4] Two systems of playing and two proposed civilizations facing off, although the principles in question are present in each and every society.

Even with the proviso that the two methods aren't exclusive, this brings us to a delicate moment when more irritable readers, suspicious of approaches that praise tropical civilization in all its malleability and ductility, will pin Wisnik with an apology for tropical swing, as if each effective dribble, in all its dazzling material beauty, were the proof of the superiority of a society that sidesteps conflict, being unable to face it. Here one might see a superficial reading of Buarque de Holanda's "cordial man," which the unwary tend to identify with the elimination of violence and the triumph of a "technique of goodness" fully realized in this blessed homeland—as we saw in Cassiano Ricardo's interpretation, sprung of the national imaginary of Getúlio Vargas's Estado Novo. Readers, however, are invited to swallow their irritation and put their lips back in their original position for a moment before trying out an ironic smirk in the face of one more thinker stepping into line behind Gilberto Freyre. Discussing whether Wisnik is more or less Freyrian is frankly useless. Evidently there is something quite *modernist* in the study of the consequences of these dribbles, something in these "irruptions" (to recall Édouard Glissant's *irrué* once more) that end up short-circuiting the linear order of clear objectives defined by the logic of means and ends, which is perhaps closer to Mário and Oswald de Andrade than Freyre. Or perhaps that something is Tropicalist, dreaming of a civilization that constructs itself against the threatening order of technique and predictability, valuing a Dionysian freedom born of the pleasure and the fully realized joy of the body.[5]

The soccer coach, in this sense, is an unwanted but necessary castrator. If the situation calls for it, he will ask the genius to put aside his creative outbursts in the name of efficiency, because what matters is the result. This is not to say that castration and technique are unnecessary. Any psychological organization (including collective ones) develops in the space between the assumed and internalized rule on the one hand and the space normally identified with "freedom" on the other. This "free" space would not exist without the established order. Not only does transgression not exist without laws, freedom also depends on the breaking of an internally fixed rule that functions on the subjective plane. Turning to the old psychoanalytic jargon, one doesn't play well when the superego dominates, but one can't let one's instincts run wild, either—the id, that is, the "this" that, if uncontrolled, would plunge all into a war against all, with no truces and no end.

I shall leave aside some of the book's internal mirages, such as Wisnik's enchantment with the unique character of soccer—which, as opposed to American football, supposedly lives on the edge of the imponderable, set against the cumulative and progressive strategies of the most popular American sports. There is something very interesting, in fact, about a sport in which the slightest and least expected details can decide the game. Soccer tends to give the sense that the best team isn't always the one that wins, as if in the end there were a certain poetic justice waiting to redeem even the weakest. Meanwhile, sports like basketball and American football function via the linear accumulation of points, making it practically inevitable that the best will win in the end—the team with the best strategy, preparation, and talent, that is—thereby eliminating, so to speak, the power of chance.

Stéphane Mallarmé is also central in *Veneno remédio*. The power of *chance* is at stake when the "superiority" of Brazilian soccer at its best (which Pasolini identified in the 1970 national team) comes into play. But this is not chance as cosmic punishment, or as mythical determinant of history. The chance in question points toward the fertile power of uncertainty, of that which opens into a myriad of possibilities. After all, nothing can close off or control the environment when one is talking about a truly poetic soccer move—and there are many, minutely described in Wisnik's book.

Poetry (and soccer as well, with its epiphanic moments) lives on the edge of uncertainty, testing and pushing the boundaries of the possible, in that "band of structural spontaneity" that Wisnik attributes to soccer. Technique, on the other hand, works with the boundaries of the possible, bending itself to them and respecting them in a kind of reverence for the given. One can then imagine the range of the "nonlinearity" discussed as a national characteristic by *Veneno remédio*. Instead of constituting a fixed and inescapable trait, it is simply one more element in play, which Brazilians should come to terms with and which might even benefit them. From a "rational" perspective (developed, controlling, technical, and so on), nonlinearity is a cardinal flaw. But it is from this drug that Brazil will extract its cure; rather, it is through this poison that Brazil can dialogue with the masters of the world. In this sense, soccer can be thought of as a "successful Brás Cubas Poultice," in yet another allusion to Machado de Assis.[6] The idea is tempting, amusing, and provocative and made Wisnik call another Buarque de Holanda to the field halfway through the match—this time, and again in this book of mine, the son of the author of *Roots of Brazil*, Chico Buarque.

Observing a scrimmage between European boys and the sons of immigrants in Paris in 1998, Chico Buarque noted that the rich boys played like "masters of the field," preferring "control of the ball as a way to occupy the field in an organized way," while the poor boys were merely "masters of the ball." The passage is worth reproducing for its touching conclusion: the immigrants' sons, says Wisnik, echoing Chico, "take advantage of the opportunity in soccer to instruct themselves as best as they can in the art of intimacy with the ball (developing, within the game, the splendid and wasted expertise that we know so well from the fleeting spectacle of the 'stoplight jugglers'). Some people are *equilibrados* [well-balanced], others are *equilibristas* [acrobats]."[7]

Between the well-balanced and the acrobats, there emerges a question of the mastery of codes and how much one can trust in the rules. The well-balanced rich boy plays as if the field were his natural plane, since every millimeter of it can and should be occupied rationally. The exception, of course, is the exact, wandering point where we find the ball, because it is there that the "poor boy" shows up to balance himself (and the circus-like aspect of Ronaldinho Gaúcho's play is probably what leaps to the mind of a soccer-following viewer of a certain generation). After all, nobody told the poor boy that the field is his as well. This is why he should not limit himself to simply occupying the field in a rational, horizontal fashion; he must construct his marvels up and to the sides, always around himself, without losing the precious ball in its capacity as unstable point of equilibrium.

Still passing the ball between fathers and sons, José Miguel moves on to the observations of Guilherme Wisnik, reminding us that the occupation of space is revealing when it comes to the history of the United States and the nation's march to the West. In this one can see "the imperialist vocation for conquest," the tendency to advance point by point across the territory—this recalls not only the American football field, but also a grand poetic lineage leading "from Walt Whitman to Herman Melville, including John Ford, Frank Lloyd Wright and land art."[8] Meanwhile, we Brazilians (an imaginary "we," naturally, as essays tend to employ) find our balance wherever and however we can. In *Veneno remédio*, however, nonlinearity is called in not simply to speak to the truth of a "*jeitinho*" or a "*bossa*" as an original swing—"our things," as the great samba composer Noel Rosa (1910–1937) put it. It would be no use to gild these "things" and hang them on the wall of our illusions like trophies, telling ourselves that we are the best even if the rest of the world doesn't know it. In short, this is neither self-condescension nor self-glorification. *Veneno remédio* is an urgent question about what to do with what we have: how to evolve, given this state of "things"?

At one point in the book when various authors are pulled in to say something about soccer, Wisnik recalls Mário de Andrade, who, writing about Brazil's defeat to Argentina in 1939, imagined the Brazilians as "eleven hummingbirds" defenseless before the oiled platinum machine, as if a "Minerva-Argentina" delivered a masterful slap to the face of an "adolescent, completely drunk Dionysius," who, in his divine stubbornness, still invented "a few subtle slides, a few samba-like deceptive moves," and "a few lightning-swift volleys, a radiant, Pan-like thing, full of the most sublime promises."[9] Here may lie the secret of *Veneno remédio*: the sublimity of an unrealized promise, a spasm of beauty and genius that consumes itself as it is materialized, which empties itself without becoming productive— a fleeting and useless spectacle, like the boys juggling at the stoplight. But how to turn this unproductive productivity, this glorious moment without consequences, into a project, a chain of clear and stable consequences for society? How, out of the incessant pleasure that drives a character like Macunaíma, to construct something?[10] Must Macunaíma be sent to school so he may be taught a technique that he ignores and scorns on principle?

The star player and illustrious dribbler Manuel Francisco dos Santos, "Garrincha" (1933–1983), was a sort of Macunaíma. Beyond the "biographical" similarities with Mário de Andrade's character— exceptional birth, abnormal growth, simultaneous precocity and retardation—this semimythical creature with crooked legs was the master of the dribble, taking it to unimaginable extremes of grace and curvature. For Wisnik, Garrincha's Macunaímian dribble is the conjunction of three elements: ellipse (a flight from linearity which produces a poetic effect on the rhetorical plane); slip (a flash of the unconscious, in Freud's terms), and syncopation (a contrametric accent found in the intersection of European and African rhythms).[11] All three are dribbles in their own way: the *ellipse* is a way of getting around the next logical step, creating a suspension and an unexpected swerve in the discourse; the *slip* is the shift that gets around the censorship of the conscience and lets loose that which was guarded in the unconscious; *syncopation* makes it possible for the body to slide between the beat and the backbeat, doubling over to fit into a space that resists the military step of the march and then expanding outward in those swaying capoeira-tinged moves that, to the eyes of the more traditional writers at the turn of the twentieth century, seemed simply like a regressive element, dangerously Africanized—and which in the modernist view was a treasure, something closer to our purest essence (or, perhaps, in Mário de Andrade's words, our most "sublime promises").

But nations aren't made with Garrinchas alone, and we may ask up to what point a "stubborn" and "premodern" amateurism can still exist in an advancing society that is starting to seriously test the waters of its future. *Veneno remédio* came out, not by chance, in 2008, at a moment when Brazil was beginning to sound out the strange and halting feeling that, just maybe, there might be a place for it at the table of developed nations. Evidently, the tension between technique and freedom, predictability and spontaneity, virtual and real, becomes an agonizing question for the country and explains, at least in part, why the "essay of national interpretation" has been reborn exactly now, in the midst of the thrust of the past decade. When the transcendent question—about a possible path forward—starts making sense and increasing its volume, the essay becomes urgent, releasing critical imagination from the ties of strict objectivity, just as necessary as it is limiting. This is not to say that the essay lays out an iron-wrought vision of what is to come. Its malleability (or its "texture," in Theodor Adorno's term, as we saw) makes it possible to feel out possibilities, entering into a realm of pure imagination, although it engages head-on with the harsh concreteness of the present.

Best not to get into the case of Edson Arantes do Nascimento (b. 1940), Pelé. Soccer lovers may strike out on their own in search of the dialogue that Wisnik strikes up with retired player and columnist Tostão (b. 1947) and poet Décio Pignatari (1927–2012) in order to understand the utterly exceptional player who seems to have "brought the virtual into the present," as we read in the paean to Pelé.[12] Let us remain with the unresolved (and unresolvable) pendulum between technique and freedom, the well-balanced and the acrobats, which throws us into a sort of tunnel in the history of ideas, with the luminous debates of Brazilian modernism at the end, which in turn become relevant in the discussion that, in the midst of the dictatorship, critic Antonio Candido sparked around the constant swing between "order" and "disorder." A restless, provocative swing, which Candido would famously name—not without irony—the "dialectic of malandroism." Let us see.

When he published his essay in 1970, Antonio Candido analyzed Leonardo, the protagonist of *Memoirs of a Militia Sergeant* (1852), by Manuel Antônio de Almeida (1831–1861). Here we can see precisely the problem that Wisnik tackles in his essay and which opens the way for a better understanding of Sérgio Buarque de Holanda. In the novel, according to Candido,

> we might say that there is ... a positive hemisphere of order and a negative hemisphere of disorder, functioning as two magnets that attract Leonardo, having already attracted his parents. The dynamic of the book presupposes a seesaw of the two poles, with Leonardo growing up and participating now in the one, now in the other, until he is finally absorbed by the conventionally positive pole.[13]

In a critical reading of a clearly modernist bent, Antonio Candido put forth—according to Wisnik—"a surprisingly positive reading" when he concluded that the nineteenth-century work produced, in its atmosphere of negotiations, "an enchanting 'world without blame' of a democratic and tolerant spirit, against all stigmatization and witch-hunts."[14] In this, Wisnik sees a discreet preference for the paradoxically positive value of disorder. It's as if Garrincha and Macunaíma had won the battle, if perhaps not the war.

If we wish to understand how Wisnik's thought advances through *Veneno remédio*, we must understand that he is rethinking the balance between *order* and *disorder* by way of the classic essays of the 1930s. This journey ultimately leads him to find, in Sérgio Buarque de Holanda, the ambiguous formula for expressing the *pharmakon* produced by the formation of Brazilian society. But if the impasse in this shapes *Roots of Brazil*,[15] we should note that Buarque de Holanda also parallels Freyre in the conclusion of *Veneno remédio*. The paradigmatic figure of the mulatto is raised to the status of an emblem, bringing out Freyre's reading of cordiality as seen in the second (1951) edition of *Sobrados e mucambos* [The Mansions and the Shanties]—where he explicitly associated the "cordial man" to the figure of the mulatto, hewing closer to Cassiano Ricardo's terms and distancing himself from the problem as configured by Sérgio Buarque de Holanda, as we have seen in a previous chapter.

To paraphrase the poet, in *Veneno remédio* there is something that whispers to us, reminding us that "down here, uncertainty is the rule."[16] But, as with Caetano Veloso, the dance of Brazil is the other side to a brutal lack of rights: the democratic potential of the cordial man, his ability to mold himself, to yield and negotiate, not rolling over before the norm, is also a sort of efficacy in confusing the public and private spheres, steamrolling strangers to save friends, elevating the renowned *jeitinho brasileiro* (the famous, or rather infamous, "Brazilian way" of doing things and slipping around the rules), which can get around anything and is always just outside the law and social norms. On the issue of social class, the cordial man is both completely beneficent (as a potential defense against the arbitrary power imposed from above) and utterly malign (as the rich man who places a squeamish distance between himself and society's lower elements, giving new life to centuries-old prejudice against the poor, and as the poor man who sets himself apart from the poor, allying with the rich).[17]

In calling on a potentially beneficent historical legacy here (*poison* become *cure*, we might say), the optimism of the Tropicalist impulse, which overtakes Wisnik himself, has provoked a reaction among those who take up the arms of sociological evidence and proclaim the deplorable state of the country, this the ultimate result of the Brazilian historical experience. This struggle begins on an aesthetic level, encoded in images that may be either liberating or suffocating, and then opens up into a whole range of questions as to the future of the country and its place in that which was once called the march of civilization.[18]

The "poison" that the Tropicalists reacted to springs from the visible historical wreckage of Brazil's formation. Here, *Veneno remédio* turns to historian Caio Prado Júnior, for whom the colonization of Portuguese America stands as a sort of "far-flung and displaced chapter" of capitalism on a global scale,

> an enterprise built on "incoherent and unstable population" efforts, "poverty and economic calamity," the "dissolution of customs," and "inertia and corruption in both lay and ecclesiastical officials" [quotations from Prado Júnior's *The Colonial Background of Modern Brazil*]. This incoherent, fragmentary agglomeration, poorly amalgamated atop precarious bases, lacking in vision, justice, limits, and character, constituting a society oriented exclusively by long-distance economic exploitation, knows no other popular existence than the group degraded by slavery, on one hand, and the marginal portion of free men with no prospects, on the other. In the painstaking, implacable realism of his productivist view, Caio Prado Júnior can find no place for the emergence of any original cultural production.... We may recognize in [his] vision not only an individual perspective, but also the foundation of a paradigm for approaching Brazil, with its corresponding critical lineage, in which Paulista and USPiana [of

the Universidade de São Paulo] sociology takes center stage. In this area, emphasis falls upon the identification of Brazil's being backwards and out of place in the world order, with no space for original popular cultural phenomena, seen as of little relevance in economic and political terms. This diagnosis would produce a theory of dependence, and an analysis of [the country's] peripheral condition. If applied to soccer, it turns its demystifying tone to an analysis of the socioeconomic conditions around the sport, with no breath spent on the contemplation of redemptive *gingas* [hip-swaying] and bodily expressions—and without giving due relevance to the singularity of its cultural overlaps.[19]

Beyond the institutional geography where such ideas are produced, it becomes clear that the diagnosis of an unfeasible civilization is inseparable from a critique of the noxious effects of peripheral capitalism in Brazil. Tropicalism, meanwhile, as a vector of questions around Brazilian civilization, will always have sociological evidence hot on its heels, presenting a full-color portrait of the miserable figure "we" Brazilians cut in the world.[20]

Whether we belong to the circle that gave rise to these debates or not, *Veneno remédio* is greatly enriched once one considers the institutional geography around it. A complex map unfolds from the foundational sociological debates emanating from the Universidade de São Paulo, especially in the 1960s. This is a Paulista issue, but it speaks to the great questions about the future of Brazil, calling once again on the three essayists whom Antonio Candido evoked in his preface to *Roots of Brazil*, suggesting that their works shaped the imagination of his generation: Caio Prado Júnior, Gilberto Freyre, and Sérgio Buarque de Holanda.[21] In this triangulation, Wisnik vigorously resists Prado's somber reading; delicately resists Freyre's happy synthesis; and suggestively alights on Buarque's ambiguity, elevating it to the status of a hermenutical framework—not by virtue of what it resolves, but precisely because of the answers it refuses to provide.

Ambiguity (the poison that is the cure, and vice versa) plays an important role in the works of both Freyre and Buarque de Holanda.

In the case of *Veneno remédio*, it must be said that Freyre's ambiguities, laid out carefully through the readings of Ricardo Benzaquen de Araújo, are seen in a retrospective view that appropriately touches on not only *The Masters and the Slaves* (from 1933, we should recall), but also *Sobrados e mucambos* (1936). While Wisnik takes as his starting point a glaring silence in Caio Prado Júnior's analysis (the voices of the slaves), he does it so as to highlight that here, in what he provocatively dubs a "place outside ideas,"[22] Freyre finds his own kind: "Gilberto Freyre, in his own way, and with very different assumptions, is simply giving shape to the Dionysian side of that presence which is silenced in Caio Prado Júnior—the leftovers, or the human surplus, invested in this colonial undertaking."[23]

This attention to the "silenced presence" of the slaves would be the novelty of a history of private life *avant la lettre* with Freyre, seeking out in the domestic sphere a framework for understanding a society marked by the mingled eroticism and merrymaking of Indians, Portuguese, and blacks, with due attention to the sadistic aspect of the master-slave relationship, all tempered by patriarchal despotism and shot through by the antagonisms that, as readers of Freyre are well aware, constitute the strength of his prose.

In a remarkable reading, Wisnik recalls that the equilibrium of antagonisms that sustains the colonial society laid out in *The Masters and the Slaves* is lost in the new urban geography that marks the "decadence" of an entire world, or a project, starting in the nineteenth century—and this will be the topic of *Sobrados e mucambos*:

> And thus the Europeanization of the mansions, now distant from the shanties, sends Gilberto Freyre's historico-ideological project in another direction: in the newly independent country [after 1822], the promiscuous poles of *The Masters and the Slaves* now move away from each other, losing their ambivalent vigor and threatening to split that symbiotic, unconscious base that the essayist sees as the only cement, albeit a slippery one, able to fix any national unity. Against this diverging tendency (towards Europeanization and civilization), Gilberto Freyre then juxtaposes

the almost-miraculous emergence, like a *deus ex machina* coming not from on high, but up from Hades: the mulatto.[24]

A reader looking carefully at the whole will see that here, "high" and "low" are projected in the figure of the mulatto, who emerges shambling (or perhaps swaying, hiding some unsuspected perfection in the unhandsome body which nobody cares for) out of Hell, not from the heavens. Those who have read Euclides da Cunha will certainly recall the *sertanejo*, dubbed a "Hercules-Quasimodo." Readers of José Miguel Wisnik, meanwhile, may turn to his insistent inquiries into what Brazilian music has produced, in the meeting of the "elevated" realm of the erudite and the "low" element come from the streets, from the depths where the Brazilian popular experience roils in its syncopated, polyrhythmic step, revealing an "other place whose instinctive truth cannot be denied."[25]

Here we may venture a hypothesis before returning to Sérgio Buarque de Holanda. Wisnik had already responded to the artificial nature of the mulatto as a Freyrian deus ex machina, in the extraordinary essay "Machado maxixe," with that brilliant mulatto Machado de Assis, with a prose obedient to the primmest of styles but bearing the figure of a musician thrown between the highs and the lows of his inspirations and references, inscribed in codes of irony and subtlety. Pestana, Machado's protagonist in the story "Um homem célebre" [A Famous Man], cannot compose sonatas, because his swift fingers inevitably produce the liveliest polkas (where the Afro-Brazilian mark of the maxixe is evident by this time, although not named). One day Pestana sends the polkas to hell—but, in what Wisnik calls a "wonder of [Machadian] irony," the polkas "preferred not to go down so far."[26]

All that is banished to this "low" universe, in the "depths" of an experience of a lineage mingled with slaves—which the Europeanizing superego of the nineteenth century will sweep under the carpet—will return through the back door of the unconscious. Or, rather, once past the derepression of Brazilian modernism, it all returns in the composite matter of a perennially hypothetical Brazilian culture, which leads us, meanwhile, to the great project of the recovery of the popular, as explored by those like Mário de Andrade. But let us linger on Gilberto Freyre, still through Wisnik's lens:

> The ethnic output of the "agrarian, slaveholding, and hybrid society," in its tardy transition to the modern, forms the basis for the implicit operation, by which Gilberto Freyre's work fulfills its original, unconfessed design: something like a transition from the *vira-lata* [the stray dog] to the *vira-ser* [the soon-to-be]. Here he puts his money on the transmutation of a mixed-race people, their value denied by nineteenth-century scientific determinism, seeing them paradoxically become what they are, bringing out the power of the *pharmakon* and extracting from the poison of slaveholding colonization the cure of an original civilization in the tropics. This reversal was shaped in the modernism of the 1920s: in the words of Oswald de Andrade, it meant devouring the frightening aspects of the other, "transform[ing] taboo into totem," turning repression on its head and making the traumatic impediments of Brazilian formation into the stuff of liberation.[27]

Not by chance, it is at this moment in *Veneno remédio* that Wisnik interrupts the Freyrian melody to recall that it would later curdle into an "ideological crystallization," with the "aestheticized sublimation of Brazil's looming social violence, fulfilled through soccer and popular music, as a sort of sociopolitical panacea with the power to reconcile both nation and the danger [posed by] an untamed people."[28] But why the interruption? Why does he avoid giving into the Freyre ballad, waking up just as the tune threatened to consume all with its lulling dream of universal harmonization?

Whatever the limits of their ideological crystallization, especially *a posteriori*, Gilberto Freyre's books from the 1930s produced the impact of a paradigm shift, resting on their authorization to *jump to the other extreme* and contemplate the stigmas of Brazilian colonization *through its opposite*. The *race-mixing violence* behind all this, once revealed—the name of which, if pronounced, would be an appalling *amorous rape*—takes on a cathartic, redeeming strength: a trauma, or a store of historical *karma*, which paradoxically would have given rise to a new humanity open to differences.[29]

The equation thus formulated expresses itself in the medical, or curative, metaphor that sustains the book. The first diagnosis, from Caio Prado Júnior, had stalled out in the *poison* sprung of the historical formation of Brazil. In the second diagnosis, Freyre, guided by an optimism that would soon fall into severe conservatism, arrives at the other extreme in his suggestion, from some angles, that *cure* alone produces the peculiar historical destiny of the Lusitanian tropics. Then we find ourselves before the privileged place reserved for Sérgio Buarque de Holanda, whose crucial and radical indeterminacy leads Wisnik to identify, in *Roots of Brazil*'s diagnosis, the *poison/cure* that provides the book with its title.

His reinterpretation of the enigma on display in *Roots of Brazil* is supported, as I have noted, by Antonio Candido's reinterpretation of the novel by Manuel Antônio de Almeida; there, the critic had compared

the exclusive character of Puritan societies, such as North America's monoreligious and monoracial arrangement (where the powerful introjection of the law hardens the individual and the group, conferring a certain identity and resistance, but dehumanizing relations), to the potentially dialogic and open nature of spontaneous sociability in Brazil (where the softening of conflicts between norm and conduct disburdens conflicts of conscience, allowing for a greater acceptance of the Other). Thus, at that point in the dictatorship when [Candido's] text was written [1970], the "dialectic of malandroism" (and the "world without shame" to which it is associated) emerges to Antonio Candido as an advantage held over the Protestant ethic and the spirit of capitalism, and as a "triumph for the hypothesis of our becoming part of a more open world" (in the review by Roberto Schwarz). Inspired by the reading of *Memoirs of a Militia Sergeant*, Antonio Candido thus opts for an affirmative take on a Sérgio-Buarquian ambivalence and introduces into the USPian [from the Universidade de São Paulo] paradigm an uncommon paean to Brazil's congenital peculiarities.[30]

"Introduces into the USPian paradigm...." Once the drug is injected, the interpretation machine creaks to life, and the bipolar oscillation between maximal pessimism and extreme optimism (represented by Caio Prado Júnior and Gilberto Freyre) gives way, allowing for free transit from poison to cure and vice versa. Here we find Sérgio Buarque de Holanda, and here there is also room for a quick and rare approximation on Wisnik's part to Roberto Schwarz's rereading of the "dialectic of malandroism." In his interpretation of Candido's text, Schwarz noted that the world which operates in a space prior to all rules would lead to a state of pure arbitrariness (even more so in a state of exception like the Brazilian dictatorship), justifying the unjustifiable, in the end. Schwarz's take demanded greater attention to the price of an enchanting freedom, amidst the calamitous political situation of the crackdown known as the "coup within a coup" in the dictatorship, post-1968.[31]

In indicating the ways in which social structure weaves its way into the form of the novel, Candido's theses would later be crucial for Schwarz—as much as the latter took issue with the former's enchantment with the pole of disorder, at a moment when Brazil desperately needed some sort of judicial order to temper arbitrary political power. But before we lose ourselves in this thicket of interesting issues, we must note that the "dialectic of malandroism" refers to a balance, a "seesaw" between two poles, without necessarily indicating that either will prevail. Neither poetry nor prose, neither technique nor epiphany, neither Brazilian soccer nor American football—what we have is, first and foremost, radical irresolution.

The reading of *Veneno remédio* demands not only that readers take the title's provocation seriously, but also that they pay attention to the fact that its argument is carefully set up in successive oppositions, rich in their irresolution and tension: "prose and poetry," "leather ball and capital," "ritual and game," "mud and grass," and so on. One need only note how the essay is constructed to see that Wisnik is writing about an indivisible unit of contradictory forces, a perpetual pendulum that proclaims itself an inescapable truth. Not an essential truth, frozen in space and time and buried in the geological depths of being, but a truth of tension and irresolution, with the perennial impression that it may slide and fall toward the pole of disorder, because it is there that clashes are softened and the world is potentially more open, poised to flee from the arbitrariness of law.[32]

Here we return to the bone of contention, because the malleable and porous experience born of this break with law may point us towards a bloodless confrontation, cordiality in its most generous aspect, opening the curtains of the past to reveal the thorny question of the legacy of slavery and how it was established and developed in Brazil. One can't accuse Wisnik of fleeing from the problem. On the contrary, he tries to take the bull by the horns when, taking up the dialogue of the exiled critic Anatol Rosenfeld (1912–1973) with sports writer Mário Filho (1908–1966) about the presence of blacks in soccer, he suggests that the game gives rise to a sort of "racial democracy on the field."

In the wake of the first debates about inclusion and affirmative action in Brazil, the passage merits a full citation:

> We might say that racial democracy in Brazilian soccer prescribes (in the medical sense, of recommending a cure), but does not describe Brazil. Or perhaps that it describes realized and significant possibilities that do not form a complete system. In other words, the country does not align with itself; racial democracy has to be thought of as something which both is and is not. This paradox is the crux of the problem.[33]

The question is how to leave the soccer field and materialize that which is realized only as a fleeting and spectacular moment—how to spread this promise and turn it into reality, or a "system" that might allow society to dribble the harsh opposition between classes and races. The problem becomes even more glaring when class and race overlap and mingle so much and so often as they do in Brazil (although not only there, of course). Here, the essayist calls Machado de Assis back onto the field:

If Machado de Assis creates in his works, albeit surreptitiously, that which the stifled society that he describes would present as impossible (the preemptive contemporaneity of an original creation in the intellectual field), Brazilian football [soccer] made possible on the field that which Brazilian society systematically failed to fulfill (racial democracy in action, the elevation of the poor to a position of maximum importance, unequivocal competence in the mastery of an international code). For those gifts to spread to less ludic areas, there would have to come something like a second abolition of inequality (beyond the dichotomy of races) and, at the same time, the cure for the unwholesome framework that casts the country as either the recipe for happiness or a dead-end failure—totality or null, panacea or bait, paradise or hell. As I see it, this is the incorporeal precondition for any other change.[34]

Miscegenation is, nevertheless, not a simple promise of mixture. No "cosmic race" is emerging on the horizon of this civilization, nor is there any intention to deny racism in Brazil or negate the importance of black movements, for example. What we have in *Veneno remédio* is a vote for the plurality of a composite formula, as if a new, more "porous" model of civilization could spring from it, one with a healthy disregard for the straight lines that clarify, with no margin of error, who is on which side. The path is treacherous, and Wisnik knows its traps well. The biggest is Gilberto Freyre's "Lusotropicalism," which, as has already been noted here, in its most unfortunate and reactionary moment, flirted with Salazarist Portugal and sung the praises of the exceptionality and the gentleness of Portuguese dominion over the tropics (while Portugal still held its African colonies, moreover). One might argue that the political solutions of a Lusotropicalist Freyre weren't fully revealed back in 1933, in *The Masters and the Slaves*, nor even in *Sobrados e mucambos* in 1936.

The ungovernable principle—which Wisnik calls, with entertaining and ironic precision, "anthropological π"—suggests that something indefinable awaits us whenever we approach the laboratory that is soccer. The Tropicalist wave, of which Caetano Veloso and José Miguel Wisnik are both a part, albeit in very different ways, bases itself off the belief in a limit-space where order slips and gives way, making way for the entrance of an unexpected element that resists classification. This might give rise to racial (or postracial) theorems, which not a few critics would identify as a perverse form of self-negation in a country that has yet to pay its historical debt to its Afro-Brazilian population. But that would be a way of placing authors like Wisnik or Caetano under a bell jar, making them the unwilling representatives of a resuscitated, poorly interpreted Freyrianism. This violent, reductive interpretation is a way of not hearing what they're saying.

Work on and reflections about the limits of order are a vital way of thinking about the limits of classification as well as the limits of social spaces. Which doesn't mean, of course, that playful dis/order on the field can break down the real, cruel barriers off the field. The problem is that this problem doesn't solely exist on the plane of ideas, and as such forces us to face historical and sociological questions. After all, the "alchemy" of the poison/cure—Brazilian soccer—has yet to produce the formula to bring democracy into the plane of the Real, to provoke that "Reality check" or "fall into the Real" that Wisnik proposes, and which may be the only effective way of breaking the enchantment of any magical formula. But once the spell is broken, what will become of Brazil?

* * *

It is certainly ironic that, having sprung from a desire to pick apart the traps of national discourse, this book should end with that very question.

The issue may call for a wider focus. Shielding ourselves from essentialization and exceptionalism as we may, the question about "Brazil" points to a recognizable entity, one often associated with global development, "unequal and combined"—to recall Trotsky's old formula and the long shadow it has cast around the peripheries of the world. In short, whenever we take up the arms of a discourse around

Brazil, the idea of an ineluctable path looms ahead and the developmentalist paradigm that reigned for so long furtively introduces itself, in the process marking the uncomfortable spot left for a book like *Roots of Brazil*, called on to give answers while it merely offers up new and broader questions.

Or perhaps we might simply accept that questions about Brazil's destiny no longer make any sense, and in this case the essay might finally be relieved of the burden of blazing a trail for us, finding a way to shape the country's problematic insertion into a global order. When asked about destiny, after all, the essayist creates a sort of brilliant and incomplete fable, refusing the image of a single, imperious path to be taken. The essay is not the history of the future.

We should also recall, to borrow the words of another essayist, that "we are not the realization of the dream of the 'national-developmentalist' project, nor its nightmare, but a combination of both." Neither cure, nor poison, between "subordination" and an "unprecedented autonomy in decision-making," the "Brazilian reality" continues to shout in our ears, and yet we are charged to react to it without succumbing to the fantasy of a collective path.[35] The truth is that, from the margins where "we" Brazilians stand, it is difficult to know where to place our bets with the little that we have. For that matter, and thinking of Sérgio Buarque de Holanda, Antonio Candido, and José Miguel Wisnik, it is simultaneously tempting and challenging to suppose that "indefinition" might be the greatest value of the collective experience to which we are witness: our most precious stake, keeping the spell just on the edge of unraveling, so to speak. But here we are again, flirting with the sensation of ultimately possessing a magical pill that will soothe all our ills.

In its own way, *Veneno remédio* returns in great style to the adventure of the essay, updating it on its own terms, setting Prado Júnior against Freyre and finding, in the ambivalence of Buarque de Holanda in *Roots of Brazil*, the potency of the undecidability of the *pharmakon* as the bearer of solutions and questions, thus raising up the impasse that emerges whenever the personalist bonds that hold the family together are broken. To see in Wisnik's work nothing more than an invitation to enchantment would be to read only half of it.

This, of course, is not to deny that the question about the Brazilian experience may stubbornly spark the imagination of two worlds: one enchanted, the other disenchanted. The fact that it may always be easier to locate disenchantment with the world in a space from which we might see ourselves as protected—as if something were separating us from a distant and strange land—is an intricate problem that we may have barely begun to understand.

* * *

Steering clear of belief in a universal panacea, I hope to have suggested over the course of this book that that which we generally associate with "identity"-related discourse may inadvertently reveal the limits of the national sign. In this sense, *Roots of Brazil* is an example of a text that breathes precisely whenever it oscillates, going to and fro, delving into paradox, which is, after all, the essay incarnate. The reader is thus invited to surrender to the power of the trails and residues of thought, relinquishing the unbearable burden of a final synthesis.

To allow myself one last metaphor, the discourse of the essay is insular, because it tends toward escape, evasion: a "promise made present," as Spanish philosopher María Zambrano wrote, thinking of islands as a space for flight.[36]

In the end, the crisis of identity discourse may be a crisis in reading, not in the texts themselves. Perhaps the stiffening may lie in our own eyes, not always up to the task of identifying, in the essay, that which paradoxically escapes any identity.

APPENDIX

Excerpts from *Roots of Brazil*

From Chapter 1, "European Frontiers"

The effort to implant European culture in an extensive stretch of territory under conditions largely foreign, if not adverse, to Europe's thousand-year tradition is the dominant fact in the origins of Brazilian society and the one that has yielded the most valuable consequences. We have brought our forms of association, our institutions, and our ideas from distant countries, and though we take pride in maintaining all of them in an often unfavorable and hostile environment, we remain exiles in our own land. We can accomplish great things, add new and unexpected features to our human nature, and forge the type of civilization that we represent—nevertheless, all the fruits of both our work and our sloth seem to belong to an evolutionary system from another climate and another landscape.

Before asking to what extent such efforts at development will attain success, we should ask how far we have been able to represent those inherited forms of association, institutions, and ideas.

* * *

Our lack of social cohesion, then, is not a modern phenomenon. And that is why those who imagine that the only possible defense against our disorder lies in a return to tradition, a certain tradition, are mistaken. The rules and regulations developed by those erudite men are really ingenious spiritual products, which are detached from and adverse to the world. In their opinion, our anarchy and incapacity for solid organization are nothing more than the absence of the only possible order they deem necessary and effective. If we think about it carefully, the hierarchy they glorify needs such anarchy to justify itself and win approval.

* * *

Among the Spanish and Portuguese, a strong work ethic was always an exotic fruit. Not surprisingly, their ideas of solidarity are precarious.

To put it clearly, they have such solidarity only when the connection is one of feeling, that is, in the domestic circle or among friends, rather than interest-based relations. These circles are by nature restricted and particularistic, and more hostile than favorable toward associations formed on a broader group or national basis.

The individual's autonomy and the extreme glorification of personality, a fundamental passion that does not tolerate compromise, can give way only when it is necessary to renounce that personality in the service of a greater good. On the rare and unlikely occasion when that happens, the Iberian peoples hold obedience as the supreme virtue above all. Such obedience—blind obedience, which differs fundamentally from medieval or feudal principles of loyalty—has so far been their only truly strong political principle. The desire to command and the propensity to carry out orders are equally peculiar to them. Dictatorships and the Holy Office seem to be aspects as typical of their character as the inclination to anarchy and disorder. Their outlook includes no kind of well-conceived discipline other than that based on excessive centralization of power and on obedience.

From Chapter 4, "Sowers and Builders"

The primacy of rural life in colonial Brazil is in harmony with the spirit of Portuguese domination, which refrained from imposing imperative and absolute rules. Rather, the Portuguese always made concessions where immediate convenience so advised, and they paid more attention to achieving riches within easy reach than to constructing, planning, or planting foundations.

* * *

On our own continent, Spanish colonization was broadly characterized by what the Portuguese lacked: an insistent use of methods that ensured the mother country's military, economic, and political predominance over the conquered lands, mainly through the creation of large centers of stable and orderly settlements. Meticulous zeal and foresight guided the founding of Spanish cities in America.

From Chapter 5, "The Cordial Man"

Contrary to what some theoreticians assume, the state is not a broadening of the family circle, and it is even less an integration of certain groupings or of certain particularistic desires best exemplified by the family. There is no gradation between the family circle and the state, but rather discontinuity and even opposition. The fundamental lack of distinction between the two is a romantic prejudice, which had its most enthusiastic supporters during the nineteenth century. Those who espouse that doctrine maintain that the state and its institutions descended in a straight line and through simple evolution from the family. The truth is quite different: they essentially belong to different orders. The state is born, and the simple individual becomes a citizen, taxpayer, voter, eligible for office, a potential recruit, and responsible to the laws of the city only by transgressing the domestic and family order. This fact reveals a clear triumph of the general over the particular, of the intellectual over the material, and of the abstract over the corporeal, rather than a succession of purges, a spiritualization of more natural and rudimentary forms, or a procession of substances, to speak in Alexandrian philosophy. The family order in its pure form is abolished through transcendence.

* * *

Wherever the notion of family prospers and has a very solid base—usually where the patriarchal type of family predominates—the formation and development of society along current lines tend to be precarious and face strong limitations. The difficulty of individuals to adapt to social mechanisms is especially acute in our times, given the decisive triumph of certain antifamily virtues, such as those based on the spirit of personal initiative and on competition between citizens.

* * *

A joyful expression states that the Brazilian contribution to civilization will be that of cordiality—we will give the world the "cordial man." The affability in relationships, hospitality, generosity, and virtues extolled by visiting foreigners are indeed well-defined traits of the Brazilian character, at least to the extent that the ancestral influence of patterns of human relations, formed in a rural and patriarchal environment, remain active and flourishing. It would be a mistake to think that those virtues can mean "good manners," or civility. Above all, they are legitimate expressions of an extremely rich and overflowing emotional base. There is something coercive in civility—it can be expressed in commands and judgments. Among the Japanese, as we know, politeness, which involves the most ordinary aspects of social relationships, can at times become conflated with religious reverence. Some observers note, significantly, that the external forms of venerating the divinity in the Shinto ceremonial are not essentially different from social ways of showing respect.

No person is further from this ritualistic idea of life than the Brazilian. Our ordinary form of social relations is fundamentally the very opposite of politeness.

* * *

For the "cordial man," social life is, to some extent, a true liberation from the panic that he feels from living with himself and from depending on himself under all the circumstances of existence. His way of revealing himself to others continually reduces the individual to the social and peripheral part of life, which, for the Brazilian—like a good American—tends to matter most. More than anything, he lives through others. Nietzsche addressed this type of human being when he wrote, "Your inadequate self-love makes you a captive of isolation."

From Chapter 7, "Our Revolution"

If the date of abolition of slavery [1888] in Brazil marked the end of agrarian predominance, then the political framework established the following year was an attempt to adequately respond to the demands of a new, recomposed society. A secret link connects these two events and several others with a slow, but sure and planned, revolution—the only one that we have truly experienced over the course of our nation's existence. Granted, this revolution took place without great fanfare, which historians often exaggerate through their detailed and easy zeal for recording the external changes in peoples' lives. Compared to this revolution, most of the agitation during our republican period, similar to that in Spanish American nations, seems like a simple change in direction of the political and legal life of the state, comparable to those old "palace revolutions" so familiar to connoisseurs of European history.

* * *

That our cultural formation is still broadly Iberian and Portuguese should be attributed especially to the inadequacies of "Americanism," which can be largely summed up as a kind of exacerbation of foreign features—that is, of decisions imposed from the outside that are foreign to the country. Inside, we are still not American. "The blood is chemically reduced by the nerves, in American activity," said one of the great poets of our time [D.H. Lawrence].

* * *

Abolition, among other factors, dealt a heavy blow to the old, rural proprietors, rendering them powerless and leaving them no way to become involved in the new institutions. The republic, which created a plutocracy—if that term can be used—but not an aristocracy, ignored them completely. This class of individuals, which during the empire [1822–1889] had directed and inspired the institutions that ensured a certain national harmony, one that was never again restored, was thus reduced to melancholy silence. Such effects resulted not necessarily from the monarchical regime but rather from the structures that supported the monarchy, which disappeared forever. The continuous, progressive, and overwhelming urbanization, a social phenomenon complemented externally by republican institutions, destroyed the rural support that was the foundation of the decayed regime, without succeeding in replacing it with anything new.

* * *

Experience has already amply shown that simply replacing those who hold public power is an uncertain remedy, especially if it is not preceded—and somewhat determined—by complex and truly structural social transformations.

Another remedy, which is more plausible only in appearance, is to pretend to regulate events according to systems, laws, or rules of proven virtue, or to believe that a dead letter, if carried out energetically, can influence by itself a people's destiny. Rigidity, impermeability, and completely homogeneous legislation seem to us to be the only mandatory requirements leading to a good social order. We have no other recourse.

We have not grasped the truth that laws written by specialists in jurisprudence cannot legitimately guarantee a people's happiness and national stability. Rather, we habitually think that good laws and obedience to abstract principles represent the ideal flowering of a pure political education, of literacy, and of acquired civilized habits and other equally excellent conditions. We are different from the English, for instance, for although they lack a written constitution and rule themselves through a confused and outmoded legal system, they nevertheless show a capacity for spontaneous discipline that is unrivaled by any other people.

* * *

On the opposite pole from democratic depersonalization, caudillismo, or dictatorship, can often be found in the same circle of ideas to which the principles of liberalism belong. It can be the negative form of the liberal thesis, and its rise is understandable if we remember that history has never given us the example of a social movement that did not contain the germs of its own negation—a negation that necessarily falls within the same space. Thus, Rousseau, the father of the social contract, belongs to the family of Hobbes, the father of the Leviathan state; both come from the same nest. The negation of liberalism, which was unconscious in a Rosas, a Melgarejo, or a Porfirio Díaz, is affirmed today as a body of doctrine in European fascism, which is nothing more than a critique of liberalism in its parliamentary form erected on a positive political system. The victory of democratic doctrine will only really be possible when its antithesis, liberalism-caudillismo, is overcome.

* * *

If the revolutionary process that we are witnessing—the most important stages of which have been suggested in these pages—has a clear meaning, then it will be that of the slow but irrevocable dissolution of the surviving forms of archaism that have yet to be successfully eradicated since our establishment as an independent state. More precisely, it is only through such a process that we will finally revoke the old colonial and patriarchal order, with all the moral, social, and political consequences that it implied and continues to imply.

That revolution may not take the visible form of catastrophic convulsions, which attempt to transform long-established values with one mortal blow, along lines articulated in advance. Perhaps some of those final phases have already been bypassed without our being able to immediately assess their transcendental importance. We could be living between two worlds: one definitely dead and the other struggling to be born.

* * *

What is most significant is that the coincidence between the ideas proclaimed by liberalism and the social comportment defined as particular to our people is, in the end, more apparent than real. All liberal thought can be summed up in Bentham's famous phrase: "The greatest good for the greatest number." Clearly, this idea contrasts directly with any kind of human relation based on emotion. All affection between men is perforce based on preference. To love someone is to love him more than others. This one-sided view is frankly adverse to the legal and neutral point of view on which liberalism is based. In this sense, democratic benevolence is comparable to politeness, the result of a well-defined social behavior that tries to balance selfish tendencies. The humanitarian ideal preached by this benevolence is, at best, paradoxically impersonal; it is based on the idea that love in its highest degree is necessarily love for the greatest number of men, thus subordinating ideals of quality to quantity.

* * *

If the principles of liberalism have been useless, onerous, and redundant at the political and social levels, yet experimenting with other ingenious formulas will not bring us, someday, face to face with reality. We can try to organize our disorder by following wise plans of proven virtue, but a more intimate and essential world will continue to exist, always intact, irreducible, and disdainful of human invention. To wish to ignore that world is to renounce our own spontaneous rhythm, the law of ebb and flow, in favor of a mechanical beat and a false harmony. We have already seen that the state, a creature of the mind, is opposed to and transcends the natural order. But opposition must also be resolved through counterpoint if the social framework is to be internally consistent. There is only one possible order, superior to our calculations for making a perfect whole out of such antagonistic parts. The spirit is not a normative force, except where it serves and adapts to society. Higher forms of society must be hereditary complements to, and inseparable from, society: they continually emerge from its specific needs, never from capricious choices. However, a perfidious and pretentious demon is busy obscuring these simple truths from our eyes. It inspires men to see themselves as different from the way they are and to create new likes and dislikes; only rarely do they choose good ones.

Notes

Introduction

1. In the body of the text, when works lack published translations, the Portuguese original title will be followed by a translation between brackets. Future occurrences within the same chapter will revert to the original title. Where published translations exist, they will be cited directly in English (as in the case of *Roots of Brazil*).
2. Meira Monteiro, *A queda do aventureiro*. In this book, I use "Buarque de Holanda," thus avoiding the other ways in which he is commonly referred to in Brazil (whether "Sérgio Buarque," or in the cordial custom of simply using a famous author's first name, "Sérgio"). For other names of Portuguese origin, I will follow convention in citing only the paternal surname ("Prado," for "Antonio Arnoni Prado," for example). For Hispanic names, I will also follow convention, citing both the paternal and maternal surnames ("García Márquez" for "Gabriel García Márquez"). As for the critic Antonio Candido de Mello e Souza, usually cited as Antonio Candido, his name will simply be reproduced as Candido, or Antonio Candido.
3. As for the academic context that produced those first reflections, I might recall that *A queda do aventureiro* is a version of the master's thesis in sociology defended in 1996 at the Universidade Estadual de Campinas. Under the supervision of Elide Rugai Bastos, the thesis was written in circumstances which, at that point, allowed for a "rehabilitation" of the essay as an acceptable genre within sociological reflection. This had been happening in Brazil since at least the late 1980s, when the importance of narrative in the discourse of social sciences was a subject of intense discussion, and crossovers with literature seemed more and more promising. In this sense, my first book owes much to Octavio Ianni himself, Elide Rugai Bastos, Fernando Antonio Lourenço, and Niuvenius Junqueira Paoli, as well as committee members Rubem Murilo Leão Rego and Laymert Garcia dos Santos, the latter the author of *Tempo de ensaio*, a book that deeply influenced me at that moment. My posterior shift toward literary studies, under

the guidance of Luiz Dantas, who would write the preface to *A queda do aventureiro* (a preface I will return to later on), may also be explained by the circumstances that, to recall an expression that Ianni used quite often at the time, allowed for a reflection on the "crisis of paradigms" in the social sciences. See Ianni, "A crise dos paradigmas na sociologia: problemas de explicação."

4. Said, *Orientalism*. See also the work by Uruguayan critic Ángel Rama, produced during his own exile in Venezuela in the 1970s. See Rama, "La riesgosa navegación."

5. S. Holanda, *O espírito e a letra: Estudos de crítica literária* (2 vols., hereafter cited as *O espírito e a letra*).

6. Translator's Note: While there is an existing English-language version of *Sobrados e mucambos*, translated by Harriet de Onís, the edition was (with Freyre's evident consent) so heavily abridged that its text often bears little resemblance to the original. With this in mind, we have opted to retranslate the passages quoted from Freyre's work; and the Portuguese title will be used in the body of the text so as to reflect that choice.

7. This tension may be understood, in Richard Morse's terms, in the opposition between a "genetic" focus and a "situational" focus. See Wegner, "Os EUA e a fronteira na obra de Sérgio Buarque de Holanda." For the investigation of the types presented in *Roots of Brazil*, via an oscillation between "mental" and "social" structures, "psychogenesis" and "sociogenesis," with an eye to Sombart and Simmel, see Goldfeder and Waizbort, "Sobre os 'tipos' em *Raízes do Brasil*."

8. In the case of Gilberto Freyre in the "Latin Americanist" sphere, I might recall Jossianna Arroyo's study and the book edited by Joshua Lund and Malcolm McNee, both indications of interest in Freyre outside Brazil over the past decade. See Arroyo, *Travestismos culturales* [Cultural Travestisms], and Lund and McNee, *Gilberto Freyre e os estudos latino-americanos* [Gilberto Freyre and Latin American Studies]. For an understanding of Sérgio Buarque de Holanda in the context of Latin America, within "inter-American dialogues," see also Newcomb, *"Nossa" and "Nuestra América."*

9. Richard Morse's book was written in English and has not yet been published in its original language, despite its important impact in Brazil, where it was published in 1988, and in Hispanic America, where it was published (in Mexico) in 1982. When I cite Morse here, it is from his English-language manuscript, kindly provided by Dain Borges.

10. One of the inescapable references in this investigation is Ronald de Carvalho, with his *Espelho de Ariel* [Ariel's Mirror] and *Toda a América* [All America], with whom Buarque de Holanda had a falling-out in 1926 over the

article "O lado oposto e outros lados" [The Opposite Side and Other Sides], as we will see here. On Ronald de Carvalho, see Botelho, *O Brasil e os dias*.

11. The first review that Buarque de Holanda published, at age eighteen, was of José Enrique Rodó's *Ariel*. See S. Holanda, *O espírito e a letra*, 1:42–46.

12. As for Vico (to recall his *corsi e ricorsi*), Maria Odila Dias has mapped and suggested his influence on Buarque de Holanda. See Dias, "Sérgio Buarque de Holanda, historiador." In Spengler's case, beyond his presence in the first edition of *Roots of Brazil*, I might call attention to the mapping of Buarque de Holanda's library, which helped João Kennedy Eugênio to postulate the importance of Ludwig Klages in the historian's imagination but also demonstrates the presence of the author of *The Decline of the West* in the body of his readings, many apparently dating from his experience as a correspondent in Germany from 1929 to 1930. Eugênio also proposes that the "law of ebb and flow," as *Roots of Brazil* puts it, comes directly from Klages's *The Science of Character*. See Eugênio, *Ritmo espontâneo*, 151, 212.

13. See Leite, *O caráter nacional brasileiro*, esp. 317–25. Leite's first analysis of *Roots of Brazil* dates from the first half of the 1950s and emphasizes the ideological aspects behind the affirmation of a "Brazilian national character."

14. Sometimes translated into English as "rogue," the *malandro* has become a stereotypical figure of the Brazilian—more specifically *carioca*, or Rio de Janeiro–born—individual who bounces and dribbles so as to swerve around the law, surviving in a space that the state usually fails to reach completely. The character was personified in the 1940s by Walt Disney's Zé, or Joe Carioca, a *malandro* parrot from Rio.

Chapter 1. Marking the Starting Point

1. Written in December 1967 in São Paulo, the preface was included in the fifth edition of *Roots of Brazil*, published in Rio de Janeiro in 1969. Since then, with the later addition of a 1986 postscript, it has become an inseparable part of the book. Here I will reference the recent North American edition of *Roots of Brazil*: S. Holanda, *Roots of Brazil*. When necessary, I will turn to the edition released on the seventieth anniversary of *Roots of Brazil*, published in Brazil in 2006 with critical commentary: S. Holanda, *Raízes do Brasil*. In the case of key discrepancies, over the course of the book I will refer to the first edition of *Roots of Brazil*, from 1936: S. Holanda, *Raizes do Brasil*.

2. Arantes, *Sentimento da dialética na experiência intelectual brasileira*.

3. Waizbort, *A passagem do três ao um*.
4. Gaspari, "Uma cabeça que bate contra a maré." João Kennedy Eugênio has recently written on the issue of the "invention" of *Roots of Brazil*. See Eugênio, *Ritmo espontâneo*.
5. A.C. Souza, "Prefácio." This was the preface to Miceli's *Intelectuais e classe dirigente no Brasil (1920–45)*, first published in 1979 and later included in *Intelectuais à brasileira*.
6. A.C. Souza, "The Significance of *Roots of Brazil*."
7. The phrase appears in Oswald de Andrade's landmark "Manifesto of Pau-Brasil Poetry." See O. Andrade, "Manifesto da poesia pau-brasil," in *A utopia antropofágica*, 41–45. In English, cf. O. Andrade, "Manifesto of Pau-Brasil Poetry." The now-centenarian formulation of the "advantages of backwardness," meanwhile, is from Thorstein Veblen. On the mysticism of "fits of modernization," as opposed to the "search for modernity," in Brazil, with tragic results in terms of citizenship, see Faoro, "A questão nacional."
8. There is quite a broad bibliography that situates the intellectuals sprung from the modernist movement (in São Paulo in particular) in a context of political and economic losses and ideological reshuffling post-1930. In terms of literary criticism, we might look to Lafetá, *1930: A crítica e o modernismo*; in sociology, Miceli, *Intelectuais à brasileira*. As for the rearranging of forces after 1930 and the importance of Pernambuco native Gilberto Freyre's essays in the consolidation of a new political pact outside of Paulista fantasies around Brazilian progress, see Bastos, *As criaturas de Prometeu*.
9. Many of the texts that Buarque de Holanda produced in Germany may be found (prefaced by a study from Antonio Candido) in S. Holanda, *Raízes de Sérgio Buarque de Holanda*. Others are contained in Holanda, *Sérgio Buarque de Holanda: Escritos coligidos*, 1:24–64. The time the young Sérgio Buarque de Holanda spent in Germany would also feature in his son's latest novel. While Buarque de Holanda abandoned a pregnant German woman in late 1930, in his son's novel, the character "Sergio de Hollander" leaves a German son whom the narrator discovers to be his half brother. See F. Holanda, *O irmão alemão*. See also Meira Monteiro, "O pai, lá em cima."
10. As I will discuss further on, the critical reception of *Roots of Brazil* has not only grown, but has also progressively opened up to the metamorphoses of the text, with special attention on the significant revisions in the second (1948) and third (1956) Brazilian editions, but also on the layers of meaning added to the work by readings of it. An exemplary hypothesis in this vein is Luiz Feldman's, who argues that the notion of a "born classic," in Antonio Candido's words, ought to be substituted by the idea of a book that "ripens" into a classic. Cf. Feldman, "Um clássico por amadurecimento."

11. S. Holanda, *Capítulos de literatura colonial*.
12. This topic was recently the subject of a study by João Cezar de Castro Rocha. Rocha, *Crítica literária*.
13. A.C. Souza, "Introdução," in *Capítulos de literatura colonial*. On Sérgio Buarque de Holanda as historian and critic in the 1950s, see Nicodemo, *Urdidura do vivido*. For a perspective on his formation as a literary critic, see Wegner, "Criação e crítica literária na trajetória modernista de Sérgio Buarque de Holanda (1921–1926)."
14. A.C. Souza, "Introdução," 8.
15. On Capistrano de Abreu's position in Brazilian historiography, see S. Holanda, "O pensamento histórico no Brasil nos últimos 50 anos," or Bottmann, *A propósito de Capistrano*.
16. Reyes, *Antología de Alfonso Reyes*, 93. See also Reyes, *Capítulos de Literatura Española (Primera serie)*, as well as the letter from Ribeiro Couto to Alfonso Reyes from Marseilles in 1931, with what appears to be the first reference to the "cordial man" in the Portuguese language, despite Couto's title in Spanish. Cf. R.R. Couto, "El hombre cordial, producto americano." On Reyes's relationship with Brazil, see P. Moreira, *Literary and Cultural Relations between Brazil and Mexico*.
17. S. Holanda, *Roots of Brazil*, 139.
18. Here I refer to the turns of phrase enshrined by Ángel Rama's essay (*La ciudad letrada*) and *Clélie, Histoire romaine*, by Madeleine de Scudéry ("la carte de Tendre"). Also at play is the tradition that emerges as a problem, in which its very principles are an imaginary space that is as rich as it is undetermined. The question that one poses to a book—where to begin?—is also the question put to tradition: where does it start? I began writing this chapter under the influence of my reading of Arcadio Díaz-Quiñones's book. See Díaz-Quiñones, *Sobre los principios*.
19. S. Holanda, *Raízes de Sérgio Buarque de Holanda*. See also Barbosa, "Verdes anos de Sérgio Buarque de Holanda."
20. Avelino Filho, "As raízes de *Raízes do Brasil*."
21. Benjamin, *Illuminations: Essays and Reflections*, 253–64.
22. See, in this vein, Foucault, *Dits et écrits*, vol. 1, esp. 1008. On the relationship and the tension between "genealogy" and "archaeology" in Foucault, see Dreyfus and Rabinow, *Michel Foucault*, esp. 104–25.
23. Baudrillard, *Oublier Foucault*.
24. For a critique of the "functionalist" character of the autonomist principle in *Roots of Brazil*, albeit with an eye to the rhizomatic potential of the baroque allegorization in Buarque de Holanda, see Antelo, "Rizomas del Brasil." For an examination of Buarquian ambiguity from an openly

deconstructionist angle, see Santiago, *As raízes e o labirinto da América Latina*. A preliminary critique of Santiago's and Antelo's arguments may be found in Meira Monteiro, "Desfazendo gênero." For a quick approximation deliberately inspired by Deleuze and Guattari, exploring the "weak" nature of Luso-Brazilian colonization as well as the limits and range of phytomorphic metaphors in *Roots of Brazil*, see M. Veloso and Madeira, "Sérgio Buarque de Holanda: Raízes e rizomas do Brasil," in their *Leituras brasileiras*. In a different vein, but still exploring multicausality in *Roots of Brazil*, see also Leenhardt, "Frente ao presente do passado."

25. "Sérgio, o radical," "Radicalismos," and "A visão política de Sérgio Buarque de Holanda," all by A.C. Souza.

26. If we also consider Sérgio Buarque de Holanda's legendary erudition, one might ask if it isn't also through Antonio Candido's eyes that we look back and see young Sérgio devouring Joyce and Eliot alongside "Plotinus and the Fathers of the Church." And isn't the anecdote about the letters in seventeenth-century English, or in Latin, or in archaic Portuguese, that his friend sent him from abroad, very Candido-esque as well? See A.C. Souza, "Sérgio em Berlim e depois," 122; A.C. Souza, "Amizade com Sérgio."

27. A.C. Souza, "Sérgio em Berlim e depois," 124.

28. Ibid., 124–25.

29. We should avoid the tremendous error of associating Candido's vision to a strict rationalism. In this vein, I must recall his courageous 1946 essay in defense of Nietzsche. A.C. Souza, "O portador." On the importance of "scenes of reading" for understanding the genesis of a thought, see Piglia, *El último lector*. Finally, in the study already referenced here, João Kennedy Eugênio proposes an inversion of Wanderley Guilherme dos Santos's *boutade*, suggesting that "Candido (as a reader of *Roots of Brazil*) is actually an invention of Sérgio Buarque's." Eugênio, *Ritmo espontâneo*, 399.

30. Buarque de Holanda would meet up with Brazilian Communist Astrojildo Pereira in Berlin to plan a trip to the Soviet Union; but the project fell through—in part, according to Candido, out of Sérgio's fear of the Muscovite winter. A.C. Souza, "Sérgio em Berlim e depois," 119–20. See also the good-humored article from poet Manuel Bandeira in *O Jornal*, from 1931, which stands as the introduction to the third part of *Raízes de Sérgio Buarque de Holanda*. Bandeira, "Introdução." In addressing the ideological oscillations of *Roots of Brazil*, recalling Buarque's critique of Bovarism and the tensions between it and the renewed value placed on Portuguese realism and even cordiality, Alfredo Cesar Melo affirmed that the complexity of the essay lies "in the author's uncertainty as to the

ideological stance from which to launch his criticism. One may, in the end, criticize the ethos of cordiality either from the right or the left: either from a fascist viewpoint or from a socialist or liberal one. There is a subtle tension in Buarque's essay in his search for an ideological foundation from which to make his criticism of Brazilian reality; a tension which relates to the very ideological conflicts of the anxious years of the 1930s in Brazil, arising from the crisis of Liberalism and the rise of Fascism and Socialism as models of social organization." Melo, "Lusitanian Roots and Iberian Heritage in *Raízes do Brasil*," 79.

31. S. Holanda, *Roots of Brazil*, 155. The reference to the demon at the end of the book refers to the first of Descartes's *Meditations*, in which the "suspension of judgment" allows the subject to resist that "malignant demon, who is at once exceedingly potent and deceitful, [and who] has employed all his artifice to deceive me." Descartes, *Meditations on First Philosophy*. On Descartes as a reference in Buarque de Holanda, see Ramirez, *Sérgio Buarque de Holanda e a dialética da cordialidade*, 175–182.

32. S. Holanda, *O espírito e a letra*, 2:191.

33. Ibid., 2:190.

34. Ibid.

35. The key references here are the Machadian reflections from Lúcia Miguel Pereira, Eugênio Gomes, and Afrânio Coutinho. However, even comments from Richard Morse, then (in 1951) a young assistant professor of Latin American history at Columbia University with an interest in Machado de Assis, are fodder for Buarque de Holanda's criticism. S. Holanda, *O espírito e a letra*, 1:305–12, 317–21; 2:158–64, 189–94, 327–30, 340–45. As for the image of the "man who writes with a liana-wreathed pen [*estilo de cipó*]," it had been coined by Joaquim Nabuco in referring to Euclides da Cunha. See O. S. Andrade, *Joaquim Nabuco e o Brasil na América*, 119–22.

36. In a 1981 interview with Ernani da Silva Bruno, Maria Tereza Petrone, Bolívar Lamounier, and Laura de Mello e Souza, Sérgio Buarque de Holanda spoke about *Roots of Brazil* in these terms:

> I published my first book, *Roots of Brazil*, in 1936. I was still at the Universidade do Distrito Federal [in Rio de Janeiro] at the time. It's a book I don't quite agree with, but which has had tremendous exposure. It's on its fourteenth edition and has been translated into multiple languages—even Japanese. In Japanese, the title became "What the Brazilian Is." Of course I would never have given it that title or authorized it, but they didn't ask me. In Italian, there was a similar problem. They wanted to

leave it as "Radici del Brasile." I found that odd: for me, *radici* means sweet potatoes, manioc, that sort of thing. I knew the Italian editor, who was a professor at the University of Rome. He said that there was no problem, that there was an ambiguity in the Portuguese title as well, but I proposed *Alle radici del Brasile*, "On the Roots of Brazil," and that's what we went with. The book took a long time to get a second edition, which only came in 1947 [1948]. After that one, the most important edition was the fourth, by the Universidade de Brasília, at the request of Darcy Ribeiro. Antonio Candido wrote the preface, and I have the impression that it was good luck, because after then the book started to be reprinted quite often, sometimes two runs a year. I don't know if I have anything more to say. (L. Souza, "Corpo e alma do Brasil," 5–6)

"Corpo e alma do Brasil" [Body and Soul of Brazil] was an early title for *Roots of Brazil*, one that was soon discarded.

37. Rocha, "'Nenhum Brasil existe.'" See also Rocha, *O exílio do homem cordial*, and, in English, Rocha, ed., *Brazil 2001*.

38. In praising Antonio Arnoni Prado for his edition of practically all of Sérgio Buarque de Holanda's literary criticism, Walnice Nogueira Galvão suggests that "the steadfastness and constancy of the researcher may be seen in the fact that, while he had sought to publish the collection within four years, [Arnoni] bowed to Antonio Candido's requests that he include *everything*, a task that would take three more years of work." Galvão, "Presença da literatura na obra de Sérgio Buarque de Holanda," 122.

39. Schwarz, *Misplaced Ideas*. For a new approach to Schwarz's propositions and the discussion around their influence on contemporary theoretical debates, see Palti, "The Problem of 'Misplaced Ideas' Revisited."

40. S. Holanda, *O espírito e a letra*.

41. Galvão, "Presença da literatura na obra de Sérgio Buarque de Holanda," 123.

42. See Graham, "Dr. Sérgio." On *Do Império à República* and the author's "horizon of political expectations," see Assis, "A teoria da história como hermenêutica da historiografia." More recently, one might compare and contrast *Do Império à República* and the posthumous *Capítulos de história do Império*. See S. Holanda, *Capítulos de história do Império*. In addition, see Graham, "O teatro das eleições no Brasil imperial."

43. A. A. Prado, "Introdução," 30.

44. Here I return to Alcir Pécora's line of argument, in his provocative homage to Buarque de Holanda. See Pécora, "A importância de ser prudente."

45. A.A. Prado, "Introdução," 31. On Sérgio Buarque de Holanda and New Criticism, turn to Moraes, "Críticas cruzadas," and Thiengo, "A crítica entre a literatura e a história."
46. For more on the understanding of Sérgio Buarque de Holanda's literary criticism, with a focus on the debates and political context of modernism in Brazil and its successors, see again the introduction to *O espírito e a letra*, as well as later essays by Antonio Arnoni Prado. A.A. Prado, *Trincheira, palco e letras*, 257–84; A.A. Prado, "Sérgio e Mário: Um diálogo entre críticos." I addressed the link between the critic and the historian in the study that accompanies the correspondence between Sérgio Buarque de Holanda and Mário de Andrade. See Meira Monteiro, "Coisas sutis *ergo* profundas." Also, see Thiengo, "A crítica entre a literatura e a história," and Moraes, "Críticas cruzadas."
47. See Nogueira et al., eds., *Sérgio Buarque de Holanda: vida e obra*. Also, *Revista do Brasil* 6 (special issue dedicated to Sérgio Buarque de Holanda).
48. See Dias, "Estilo e método na obra de Sérgio Buarque de Holanda"; Dias, "Sérgio Buarque de Holanda, historiador"; and Dias, "Negação das negações."
49. In referring to the changes in the text of the second and third editions, as I mentioned earlier (further alterations up through the fifth edition, in 1969, would not be substantive), Luiz Feldman recalls that

> few evaluations of the extent of these alterations could be less precise than that which greeted readers in the preface to the third [Brazilian] edition of the book, mentioning "some modifications that do not affect the content of the work in general." The new expository order had first been introduced in 1948 [with the second edition], but at that stage the author had not yet decided to announce them at the *incipit* of the text [this in reference to the alteration of the opening paragraph of *Roots of Brazil*, which would be introduced in the third edition]. When he did so in 1956, his topic sentence would confirm the dynamic that now ran through the work as a whole. Here, exile may be seen as the problematic existential condition sprung from the antithesis between cordiality and civilization, which refused to resolve into any sort of synthesis over time. Exile became the visible form of that aporia, in this text. (Feldman, "Um clássico por amadurecimento," 136)

João Kennedy Eugênio has given us a detailed examination of what he would call, in a playful reference to Buarque de Holanda's later terms, a "plausible attenuation" of the organicist framework in *Roots of Brazil* from the first to the second editions, especially around the seeming emergence of a clearer "progressive political vein" in the text, largely in reaction to the uncomfortable confluence of the original 1936 theses and subsequent popular authoritarian developments. See Eugênio, *Ritmo espontâneo*, 369–451.

Chapter 2. A Familial Tragedy (in Hegel's Shadow)

1. Freyre, *The Masters and the Slaves: A Study in the Development of Brazilian Civilization*; Freyre, *Sobrados e mucambos*. In this chapter, I will be referencing the latest edition of *Roots of Brazil*, except in cases of important discrepancies, when I will turn to the first edition. As for *Sobrados e mucambos*, translated by Harriet de Onís as *The Mansions and the Shanties*, we have opted not to use the published translation, given the considerable abridgement of the text.

2. Roberto Vecchi dubbed *Raízes do Brasil* an "essay-aphorism." Vecchi, "Atlas intersticial do tempo do fim," 164. To better understand the narrative that shapes the modern drama of the individual in an urban environment, with Dyonélio Machado's *Os ratos* [The Rats] as a counterpoint in comprehending *Roots of Brazil*, see Vecchi, "Ratos cordiais e raízes daninhas."

3. The passage in question was a pair of Johnson's lines added to the poem "The Traveller," by Oliver Goldsmith, published in 1764:

In every government, though terrors reign,
Though tyrant kings, or tyrant laws restrain,
How small, of all that human hearts endure,
That part which laws or kings can cause or cure.
Still to ourselves in every place consign'd
Our own felicity we make or find:
With secret course, which no loud storms annoy,
Glides the smooth current of domestic joy.

The Complete Poetical Works of Oliver Goldsmith. The section of English literature in the Sérgio Buarque de Holanda Collection at the Universidade Estadual de Campinas (Unicamp) is quite varied, with an emphasis on the Elizabethan period. The historian seems to have read Johnson with some frequency, to judge from a passage in an article of his from 1973, where he refers to a concept which, "if I am not mistaken, the illustrious Dr. Johnson [remarked upon] something like two centuries ago." S. Holanda, *Para uma nova história*, 116. In *Roots of Brazil*, moreover, Dr. Johnson is brought up in terms of his frank praises of the rod as a pedagogical instrument. S. Holanda, *Roots of Brazil*, 116. In the first edition of *Roots of Brazil*, the man renowned for publishing Shakespeare in the eighteenth century is referred to as "the prodigious Dr. Johnson." S. Holanda, *Raízes do Brasil* (1936), 98.

4. The copy of Pareto's *Mind and Society* (in French) presumably consulted by Buarque de Holanda still sits on the shelves of his private collection at Unicamp. Pareto, *The Mind and Society*, 2232. Buarque de Holanda's inspiration also, of course, points us in the direction of Simmel's reflections on the "adventurer." Simmel, *On Individuality and Social Forms*, 187–98. See also, again, the article by André Goldfeder and Leopoldo Waizbort, which draws different conclusions from those I present here. Goldfeder and Waizbort, "Sobre os 'tipos' em *Raízes do Brasil*." Also on Simmel and *Roots of Brazil*, see Cohn, "O pensador do desterro."

5. Thomas and Znaniecki, *The Polish Peasant in Europe and America*. Although Sérgio Buarque owned a 1927 copy of the book, his contact with the work likely came only later, if we are to judge by the fact that references to Thomas appear only in the second edition of *Roots of Brazil*, in 1948, or by a reference to his 1941 trip to the United States, when in addition to works "on the so-called New Criticism," he brought "back to Brazil works on the social sciences, especially of the 'Chicago School' of sociology." Graham, "An Interview with Sérgio Buarque de Holanda," 15. On the influence of North American thought in Buarque de Holanda's work, especially on his research around forays into the backlands via São Paulo, see Wegner, *A conquista do oeste*. In English, Wegner, "America, Joy of Man's Desiring."

6. Park and Burgess, *Introduction to the Science of Sociology*. In a previous book, I investigated the presence of Thomas and Znaniecki, and of Pareto as well, in *Roots of Brazil*. Meira Monteiro, *A queda do aventureiro*, esp. 91–145.

7. Here I turn to Nicolau Sevcenko's literary-historiographic approach to the topic. Sevcenko, *Orfeu extático na metrópole*. Nor can I neglect to mention the tormented characters of the expressionist cinema that Buarque de Holanda saw firsthand during his time in Germany.

8. O. Andrade, *A utopia antropofágica*, 157–59.

9. In the second half of the 1970s, prefacing a book by Carlos Guilherme Mota, Alfredo Bosi juxtaposed Freyre and Buarque de Holanda, recognizing the "rich and fascinating reading" that both offered but reproaching them for their use of an "antiquated social psychology, given to humoral typologies and rhetorical contrasts, all complacently wrapped up in literary prose—more flowing in the former, more halting, in the old classical style, in the latter—where both sinuously avoid the dialectic of classes, bending its

sharper edges under the weight of erudite notations and picturesque documents." Bosi, "Um testemunho do presente," ii.

10. A.C. Souza, "The Significance of *Roots of Brazil*," xxv.

11. In his famous lecture on "science as a vocation," Weber, with a strikingly tragic tone, establishes the impotence of science when faced with questions about *meaning*. Weber, *The Vocation Lectures*. For an understanding of the collapse of the prophetic discourse, see Goldman, *Politics, Death and the Devil*.

12. Hegel, *Phenomenology of Spirit*.

13. S. Holanda, *Roots of Brazil*, 112. In the French translation of the book, Marlyse Meyer corrects the error but without alerting the reader. See also S. Holanda, *Racines du Brésil*, 224. In the North American edition, the mistake was highlighted in a note from Daniel Colón. See *Roots of Brazil*, 176n1.

14. Dantas, "Prefácio."

15. Bataille, *L'érotisme*.

16. Dantas, "Prefácio," 19.

17. Gomes, "Dialética da tradição."

18. Mattos, "A vida política."

19. A.C. Souza, "Radicalismos."

20. On the importance of conservative Catholic thought as a target of Sérgio Buarque de Holanda's criticism, see Meira Monteiro, "Coisas sutis *ergo* profundas." See also Thiengo, "A crítica entre a literatura e a história," 83–118. On the "misunderstanding" of democracy in *Roots of Brazil*, see Sallum Jr, "Sobre a noção de democracia em *Raízes do Brasil*," and Waizbort, "O mal-entendido da democracia."

21. Sophocles, *Antigone*.

22. A.C. Souza, *Os parceiros do Rio Bonito*, 253.

23. The debt here is unmistakable; even so, we should revisit Antonio Candido's dedication to his *compadre* in the copy of *Os parceiros do Rio Bonito* (2nd ed.) currently held in the Sérgio Buarque de Holanda Collection, at Unicamp:

> Dear Sérgio: upon rereading this book for the proof corrections, I was struck to see just how much it is influenced by your work, "Bandeirantes e Mamelucos" [Frontiersman and Mamelucos] and *Monções* in particular. I already knew that, of course, and I say so in the preface; but the impregnation is greater than I'd thought. It's not your fault. But if the book has anything useful in it, then there lies the credit. This is the reason spurring a simple republishing, improved (in my view) by Ana Luisa's cover. Affectionate hug, etc.

The cover is by Ana Luisa Escorel, Antonio Candido's daughter. A.C. Souza, "Amizade com Sergio."
24. S. Holanda, *Roots of Brazil*, 112.
25. The verse is from eighteenth-century *arcadista* poet Cláudio Manuel da Costa and is the key line for a study that Buarque de Holanda elaborated around him. S. Holanda, *Capítulos de literatura colonial*, 227. On the condition of exile, for an examination of the *topos* in both Ovid and the wavering Republic of letters in the Luso-Brazilian colonial context, see Alcides, "O lugar não-comum e a república das letras."

Chapter 3. Rural Roots of the Brazilian Family

1. The inescapable reference here is the already-referenced preface by Antonio Candido to *Roots of Brazil*, which brings the experience of reading into the realm of interpretation: "People who today [1967] are around fifty years old were deeply influenced in their understanding of Brazil by three books: *The Masters and the Slaves*, by Gilberto Freyre, published when we were in middle school; *Roots of Brazil*, by Sérgio Buarque de Holanda, published when we were in high school; and *The Colonial Background of Modern Brazil*, by Caio Prado Júnior, published when we were in college. These books, which we consider key, express the mentality linked to the intellectual radicalism and social analysis that burst out after the 1930 Revolution, one which even the *Estado Novo*, or New State (1937–1945), could not smother." A.C. Souza, "The Significance of *Roots of Brazil*," xxi.
2. Barbosa, "Verdes anos de Sérgio Buarque de Holanda," 37.
3. D'Andrea, *A tradição re(des)coberta*, 64. On the Regionalist Manifesto and the controversy around when it was composed, see Dimas, "Um manifesto guloso."
4. Freyre, "Sergio, mestre dos mestres," 117. This "encounter" became especially well-known for Hermano Vianna's use of it in his study of samba. H. Vianna, *The Mystery of Samba*. In terms of erudition, Freyre also recalls the competition allegedly invented by Manuel Bandeira one day in Santa Teresa, to see which of them—Buarque de Holanda or Freyre—knew the most about English literature. The former, it seems, was one of the few scholars rival to the Pernambucan in this aspect, the latter a proud Oxfordian with experience in the North American academic world. Freyre, "Sergio, mestre dos mestres," 117. The topic of their bohemian encounters in Rio de Janeiro would be revisited in particularly jocose tones during an interview with Elide Rugai Bastos. Bastos, *As criaturas de Prometeu*, 211–12. We might

also compare Freyre's vision to the even serener recollections of an elderly Sérgio Buarque de Holanda, who would recall how young modernists in Rio were taken out to see samba players by Blaise Cendrars, who had met the Oito Batutas in Paris. S. Holanda, *Tentativas de mitologia*, 26. On the "discovery" of Brazil by the modernists, and the mediation and intermediation of the European gaze, see Eulalio, *A aventura brasileira de Blaise Cendrars*. For the intersection of primitivism and cosmopolitanism in a comparative study, see Garramuño, *Primitive Modernities*. For a broad reading of the period, with emphasis on the mediators of the musical universe of Rio de Janeiro, see Hertzman, *Making Samba*.

5. S. Holanda, *Tentativas de mitologia*, 31.
6. P. Prado, *Retrato do Brasil*.
7. Cohn, *Crítica e resignação*, 5.
8. On Buarque de Holanda's short stint at the Universidade do Distrito Federal as assistant to Professors Henri Tronchon and Henri Hauser, who taught comparative literature and history, respectively, see M.V.C. Carvalho, "Outros Lados."
9. In keeping with his habit of referring to himself in the third person, the "Introduction" to the second Brazilian edition of *The Mansions and the Shanties* (written in 1949, published in 1951), reads: "Hence the method— or the plurality of methods or techniques—of inquiry and study, adopted by the author in this essay and the one that preceded it [The Masters and the Slaves]. From a simultaneously psychosociological and historico-social angle of study, in the attempt to reveal, comprehend, and interpret the topic, multiple techniques, rather than a single one, were employed: ecological, sociological, psychological, anthropological, and folkloric [approaches]." Freyre, *Sobrados e mucambos*, 48.
10. For a broad vision and historical perspective on the debates around region and nation in Brazil, see Bastos, "Região e nação."
11. On Buarque de Holanda's trajectory, from the erratic character of his modernist militancy to his academic institutionalization, see Wegner, "Latas de leite em pó e garrafas de uísque."
12. One example of the ambiguity of this discomfort with essayists' eclecticism may be found in the comments of a "reader of the Brazilian generation of 1968," he himself bouncing, in his interpretation of *Roots of Brazil*, between enchantment and disenchantment:

> Decades of academia and the search for a more objective approach to outlining [Brazilian] history have made us unused to such a tenacious effort, to use the object to illuminate the gaze that illuminates it in turn.

This effort, while it is not exclusively so, has been a characteristic of the essay since its origin; it is especially characteristic of the interpretative essayism around Brazil in the '20s and '30s, from the melancholy gaze of Paulo Prado to Gilberto Freyre's gluttonous look, running down the full gamut of humours and appetites. The matter of gaze has been substituted by a consideration of method; the reader of old documents has given way to the researcher of structural relationships, and this has been fruitful, one might note, in many cases. (Aguiar, "A moldura e o espelho," 69)

On Sérgio Buarque de Holanda and the Instituto de Estudos Brasileiros, see Caldeira, "Sérgio Buarque de Holanda e a criação do Instituto de Estudos Brasileiros da USP."

13. Freyre, *Sobrados e mucambos*, 48–49.

14. Freyre, "Camerado Whitman." Here we might also note Morse's tart critiques of the Freyrian use of Proust's and Whitman's names. Morse, "Balancing Myth and Evidence." On the "sentimental" dimension of the empathic revival of an "absolutely personal and uncontrollable truth," see Araújo, *Guerra e paz*, esp. the conclusion, "Dr. Jekyll and Mr. Hyde," 185–208.

15. Pallares-Burke, *Gilberto Freyre*; see also Bastos, *Gilberto Freyre e o pensamento hispânico*.

16. Alencastro, "Introdução."

17. Bastos, *Gilberto Freyre e o pensamento hispânico*, 52n20. For a fresh angle on what might be called modern conservatism in Gilberto Freyre, see Melo, "Os mundos misturados de Gilberto Freyre."

18. S. Holanda, *Tentativas de mitologia*, 100.

19. Two fundamental references here are the works by Maria Odila Leite da Silva Dias, and more recently from Marcus Vinicius Corrêa Carvalho. Dias, "Estilo e método na obra de Sérgio Buarque de Holanda"; M.V.C. Carvalho, "1936: Tradição, cultura e vida."

20. S. Holanda, *Tentativas de mitologia*, 101.

21. This is what Fernando Novais would call, in a preface to the most recent edition of *Caminhos e fronteiras*, "a study of material civilization in a Braudelian style, *avant la lettre*." Novais, "Prefácio," 7–8. See also Blaj, "Sérgio Buarque de Holanda." Other references include Finazzi-Agrò, "Caminhando entre fronteiras," and Vangelista, "'Sua vocação estaria no caminho.'" On Buarque de Holanda and ethnology, especially after 1946, when he returns from Rio de Janeiro to live in São Paulo again, this time to head up the Museu Paulista, see Françozo, "Um outro olhar"; also Françozo, "Os

outros alemães de Sérgio." For a broad view of Buarque de Holanda's work as a director in various cultural institutions, see Nicodemo, "Sérgio Buarque de Holanda e a dinâmica das instituições culturais no Brasil 1930–1960."

22. S. Holanda, *Tentativas de mitologia*, 106. (I have altered the original paragraph division.)

23. Ibid., 105. This is the dilemma that, in the Brazilian historical and sociological imagination, sets up the poles of "Americanism" and "Iberianism." As for Buarque de Holanda on this score, see Wegner, *A conquista do oeste*. In terms of the bridge between *Roots of Brazil* and his studies of material civilization (*Monções* and *Caminhos e fronteiras*), see also Wegner, "Um ensaio entre o passado e o futuro."

24. Elide Rugai Bastos suggests that the act of moving a "purely cultural" analysis to the "social and political plane" illuminates one of the most important differences between the two authors. "Social content" and "sociological forms," and the primacy of one or the other, are at the center of this debate. See Bastos, "*Raízes do Brasil—Sobrados e mucambos.*"

25. Freyre, *Sobrados e mucambos*, 59. Recall, for example, Freyre's idealized reflections on the architecture of patriarchal residences, where, "as in women," there were qualities "that compensate, at times, for the absence of pure physical beauty: a welcoming sweetness, honesty, or dignity tempered by simplicity, for example." Ibid., 59.

26. Fonseca, "Arquitetura e paisagismo." On Brasília as a space where "politics met poetry," in a sort of apotheotic, violent conquest of the frontier, see the harsh critique—albeit one in a productive dialogue with Ángel Rama's *ciudad letrada*—by Eduardo Subirats. Subirats, "Writing and Cities."

27. Freyre, *Sobrados e mucambos*, 106.

28. Ibid.

29. Ibid., 148.

30. Ibid., 253.

31. Ibid., 156.

32. Ibid., 750.

33. Ibid., 558.

34. For a reflection on the "historical tenacity" of the tension between public and private in terms of Brazilian social thinking, but also in terms of its consequences for the exercise of citizenship, see Botelho, "Público e privado no pensamento social brasileiro."

35. S. Holanda, *Roots of Brazil*, 51. This passage did not appear in the first edition.

36. Meira Monteiro, *A queda do aventureiro*.

37. DaMatta, "'Do You Know Who You're Talking To?' The Distinction between Individual and Person in Brazil," in *Carnivals, Rogues, and Heroes*.
38. Freyre, *Sobrados e mucambos*, 115.
39. S. Holanda, "Carta a Cassiano Ricardo," in *Raízes do Brasil*. See, in the same edition, Ricardo, "Variações sobre o 'homem cordial.'" One might also consult Cassiano Ricardo's 1959 book, which includes a favorable review of *Caminhos e fronteiras*, by Buarque de Holanda, who (in the reviewer's opinion) drew closer to Freyre in his examination of the inroads forged by Paulista frontiersmen: "Now his approach ... is that put forth by Gilberto Freyre, of the dynamism of culture as well, in relation to the ecological area, laying out the multiple relationships between men and animals, men and plants, the animals and the soil, some men and other men." Ricardo, *O homem cordial e outros pequenos estudos brasileiros*, 379–80. To understand Ricardo's political and ideological side, mainly through his poetry, see L. F. Moreira, *Meninos, poetas e heróis*. For a brief examination of the controversy that pitted Sérgio Buarque de Holanda against Cassiano Ricardo, see Bertolli Filho, "Sérgio Buarque e Cassiano Ricardo."
40. S. Holanda, *Roots of Brazil*, 114.
41. Freyre, *Sobrados e mucambos*, 199–200.
42. Ibid., 790–91.
43. On the semantic plurality of "cordiality" and its political implications, see Rocha, "As origens e os equívocos da cordialidade brasileira." For an explanation of the literary rivalry between Freyre and Buarque de Holanda, see Rocha, "*Raízes do Brasil*: Biografia de um Livro-Problema." The idea of the mulatto as *deus ex machina* in Freyre's narrative was recently taken up again by José Miguel Wisnik in his interpretation of soccer as a symptom of the impasses of Brazil's social formation. The topic will reappear at the end of this book in the discussion of the presence of *Roots of Brazil* in Wisnik's *Veneno remédio*.
44. H. Vianna, "Mestiçagem fora de lugar."
45. Telles, *Race in Another America*, 6. As for the permanence of the imaginary of Brazilian essayism from the 1930s through recent times, it is significant that a broad investigation into racism in Brazil, conducted in the mid-1990s, should have resulted in a book that returns to the lexicon born of Buarque de Holanda and Freyre's readings, featuring a free use of categories like "cordiality" and "racial democracy." See Turra and Venturi, *Racismo cordial*. For a discussion of the affirmative action policies of the past decade, especially in the context of public universities, see Cicalo, *Urban Encounters*.
46. Freyre, *Sobrados e mucambos*, 743.

47. S. Holanda, *Roots of Brazil*, 118. On Buarque de Holanda's readings of Nietzsche, see Chaves, "O Historicismo de Nietzsche segundo Sérgio Buarque de Holanda."
48. Eulalio, "Antes de tudo, escritor," 268.

Chapter 4. Wandering Origins

1. On the relationship between travel and the formation of a narrator of fiction, with "origins" as a reference, see Süssekind, *O Brasil não é longe daqui*.
2. Joyce, *Ulysses*, 25.
3. Rocha, *Nenhum Brasil existe: Pequena enciclopédia*.
4. In his dialogue with his son, Adeodatus, Saint Augustine recalls the etymology of the word "signify"—*signa facere*, literally "to make signs." Augustine, *Against the Academicians and the Teacher*, 102.
5. Saussure, *Words Upon Words*, 5.
6. It never hurts to recall that the theoretical corpus under the generic umbrella of "postcolonial studies," which has taken on a special importance and influence in the Anglophone academic and cultural sphere, would be inconceivable outside of French poststructuralism. For a particularly instigating essay in terms of analyses of the national sign, see Bhabha's "DissemiNation: Time, Narrative and the Margins of the Modern Nation," in his *Nation and Narration*. For an "interstitial" reading of *Roots of Brazil*, see Vecchi, "Atlas intersticial do tempo do fim: 'Nossa revolução.'"
7. Abelard, "On Universals," 534.
8. Ibid. Here I am referring to Eco's best seller, *The Name of the Rose*.
9. In a Romance language like Portuguese, the Latin infinitive *esse* is split into two, making way for that which, in Caetano Veloso's words, would be called the "pleasure of *ser* and *estar*" (from "Língua"). In Abelard's original phrasing, the last sentence is: "*nulla rosa est.*" *Incipiunt Glossae Secundum Magistrum Petrum Abaelardum Super Porphyrium*.
10. The epithet "Hegelian," so easily thrown around, and the general antipathy to any sort of philosophy of history, may be hiding the problem—maybe even a symptom—of a moment in intellectual history where we find ourselves unable to make peace with finalist thinking in any form. It is as if belief in the end of history, which after all takes in all classical utopian thinking, were simply an undesirable demon that we would be better off exorcising. Note, however, the signification and etymology of the word "end" [*finis*], which is related precisely to the "frontier," and even the frontier of

thought. It never hurts to recall that, in More's text, it is a Portuguese traveler, Raphael Hythloday, who reveals the secrets of the island of Utopia to a riveted More and Peter Giles. More's conclusion is the quintessence of utopian thinking: "In the meanwhile, though it must be confessed that he [Raphael Hythloday] is both a very learned man and a person who has obtained a great knowledge of the world, I cannot perfectly agree to everything he has related. However, there are many things in the commonwealth of Utopia that I rather wish, than hope, to see followed in our governments" (*"permulta esse in Utopiensium republica, quae in nostris ciuitatibus optarim uerius, quam sperarim,"* in the original). More, *Utopia.* See also *De optimo statu reipublicae deque nova insula Utopia.* Note that the "wish" to "see" (*optarim uerius*) does not necessarily lead to a belief in the annihilation of history.

11. S. Holanda, *Roots of Brazil,* 1–2.

12. The first paragraph of *Roots of Brazil* is striking, if we place the book in contrast with the works of Paulo Prado and Mário de Andrade, where "sloth," name-checked here by Buarque de Holanda, plays a crucial role. See P. Prado, *Retrato do Brasil.* Also, M. Andrade, *Macunaíma.*

13. Homi Bhabha asks,

> How do we conceive of the "splitting" of the national subject? How do we articulate cultural differences within this vacillation of ideology in which the national discourse also participates, sliding ambivalently from one enunciatory position to another? What comes to be represented in this unruly "time" of national culture, which Bakhtin surmounts in his reading of Goethe, Gellner associates with the rags and patches of every-day life, Said describes as 'the non-sequential energy of lived historical memory and subjectivity' and Lefort re-presents again as the inexorable movement of signification that both constitutes the exorbitant image of power and deprives it from the certainty and stability of centre or closure? What might be the cultural and political effects of the liminality of the nation, the margins of modernity, which cannot be signified without the narrative temporalities of splitting, ambivalence and vacillation? (Bhabha, "DissemiNation," in *Nation and Narration,* 298)

Recently I sought to bring the discussion around this "movement of signification"—and the theoretical and political ties that draw the intellectual's eye to "margins"—closer to the critical debate in Brazil, suggesting a contrast between Bhabha's theses and Alfredo Bosi's examination of the "dialectic of colonization." See Meira Monteiro, "The Dialetic of Resistance." Also, Meira Monteiro, "Literatura e resistência."

14. See Sommer, *Foundational Fictions: The National Romances of Latin America*.

15. The phrase is Gabriel Cohn's, from the text where he proposes that the Weberian influence in *Roots of Brazil* is limited to the exploration of paradoxes of action—to wit, the disconnect between intention and consequences. Buarque de Holanda's "German" framework, for Cohn, is much closer to the "sinuous and indirect" style of Simmel: "each, the Brazilian and the German, is, in his own way, a thinker of exile, of inadequacy, of the distance between the spontaneous flow of vital impulses and the form that it takes as it is shaped by the ordering forces of culture." Cohn, "O pensador do desterro." The theme had already come up in *Roots of Brazil*'s critique of Bovarism, "an abnormal growth" (144), and the creation of an "out-of-this-world existence." S. Holanda, *Roots of Brazil*, 131. For a nuanced reading of the problem, with a productive comparison between Gonçalves Dias and Keats, see Pereira, "Cordialidade, ressentimento e lírica," 101.

16. I elaborated on this topic in another text. Meira Monteiro, "The Other Roots: Sérgio Buarque de Holanda and the Portuguese."

17. Pratt, "Arts of the Contact Zone."

18. For more on the Brazilian language, see Pinto, *A gramatiquinha de Mário de Andrade*.

19. Here I refer the reader once again to a text of mine, this time addressing the debate around culture and the place from which one speaks of Brazil in the United States. See Meira Monteiro, "The Impertinence of Belonging."

20. Here I refer to Rimbaud's famous formula, from a letter to Paul Demeny, dated May 1871: "Car Je est un autre." Rimbaud, *Correspondance*, 68.

21. Lacan, *L'Angoisse*.

22. S. Holanda, *Visão do paraíso*.

23. It would be well worth it to investigate to what extent the recent return to Freyrian theses around Brazil has coincided with the rediscovery, in Anglophone circles (and perhaps beyond them), of the desire to recognize a miscegenation that may ultimately be a variation on the golden promise of a future of multiple identities and differences that come together and coexist on cultural and political terms. I might recall here—among some of the most articulate proposals in terms of the critical recuperation of Freyre's work—the works of Hermano Vianna, where *mestiçagem* and multiculturalism may find an improbable, generous equilibrium. See H. Vianna, "Mestiçagem fora de lugar."

24. Ribeiro, *A carta de Caminha e seus ecos*. Still in the vein of the "legacies" of *Roots of Brazil*, I will return to the topic of the letter describing the finding of Brazil in the chapter on João Moreira Salles's documentary on Lula, in the third part of this book.

25. Lourenço, "Portugal: Entre a realidade e o sonho," in *A Nau de Ícaro*. See also B. de S. Santos, "Entre Próspero e Caliban."

26. Apud Baptista, "A lusofonia não é um jardim ou da necessidade de 'perder o medo às realidades e aos mosquitos.'"

27. See, on this note, Castro Rocha's interpretation of the canonical Romantic poem by Gonçalves Dias. Rocha, *O exílio do homem cordial*, 125–41. Finally, one should recall that, upon introducing Oswald de Andrade's "Brazilwood" poetry style in the 1920s, Paulo Prado wrote,

> Brazilwood poetry is the egg of Columbus—the egg, as an inventor friend of mine was fond of saying, that nobody believed in, and which wound up making the Genovese [explorer's] fortune. Oswald de Andrade, on a trip to Paris, from atop a studio off Place Clichy—the navel of the world—discovered, awestruck, his own land. His return to the homeland confirmed, in the enchantment of the discoveries under King Manuel I, the surprising revelation that Brazil existed. This, which some had already hinted at, opened his eyes to the radiant vision of a new, unexplored, mysterious world. "Brazilwood" poetry was created.

Prado, "Poesia pau-brasil," 57.

28. On this note, one may consult Rocha, "O exílio como eixo: bem-sucedidos e desterrados. Ou: por uma edição crítica de *Raízes do Brasil*," in *O exílio do homem cordial*, 105–41. For a more detailed examination of the alterations between the first, second, and third editions, see Feldman, "Um clássico por amadurecimento." The current version of the opening paragraph of *Roots of Brazil*, after all, was set in the third edition, from 1956. The first edition began as follows:

> Any comprehensive study of Brazilian society must emphasize the truly fundamental fact that we constitute the only successful large-scale attempt to transplant European culture into a zone of tropical and subtropical climate. Across a territory that, if populated at the same density as Belgium, could hold a number of inhabitants equal to the current population of the globe, we have undertaken an unparalleled experiment. (S. Holanda, *Raízes do Brasil* [1936], 3)

29. Camões, *The Lusiads*; Antonio Vieira, *História do futuro*; Pessoa, *Message*; Antunes, *The Return of the Caravels*.

30. "For the first time, a shudder of fear went through the peninsula and nearby Europe." Saramago, *The Stone Raft*, 21.

31. Rocha, *O exílio do homem cordial*.

32. Rosa, *The Third Bank of the River and Other Stories*, 189–96.

33. The critical bibliography on Rosa is a vast one. Here I shall note the works of Walnice Nogueira Galvão, José Miguel Wisnik, Ettore Finazzi-Agrò, and Luiz Fernando Valente. Galvão, *Mitológica rosiana*; Wisnik, "The Gay Science"; Finazzi-Agrò, *Um lugar do tamanho do mundo*; Valente, *Mundivivências*.

34. Alighieri, *The Inferno of Dante*.

35. "If medieval life aspired to beautiful harmony and rested on a hierarchical system, nothing would be more natural, since even in Heaven there are degrees of blessedness, as Dante's Beatrice tells us. The natural order is nothing more than an imperfect and distant projection of eternal order and is explained in terms of it." S. Holanda, *Roots of Brazil*, 4.

36. The formula in question took on new importance in the wake of Lucien Goldmann's work. Goldmann, *Le Dieu caché*.

37. Freud, *General Psychological Theory*, 203–4.

38. Here we have a Pascalian motif. In the famous dialogue (*le pari*), one plays a game where it is not possible to get around the bet and refuse to embark. After all, not betting is a form of betting. Pascal, "Pensées," 515.

39. Rosa, *The Third Bank of the River and Other Stories*, 196.

40. Refusing the father may lead us in other directions. The radical distancing might also suggest the opposite of paternal substitution, opening up to the subject the possibility of reencountering the function of father in an Other outside the home. In terms of the migratory experience, some have imagined a structural proximity with hysteria in this case. Contardo Calligaris, an Italian psychoanalyst living in Brazil, addressed the topic, intrigued by the absence (or failure) of the paternal function in Brazilian culture, although looking to conceive of the migratory experience in its totality:

> Indeed, the emigrant leaves his country of origin, and with it he leaves behind and represses the filiation in name of which he is or might have been a subject, for reasons that are homologous to those that lead the hysterical figure to deny her own filiation. The misery promised by the socioeconomic situation in the country of origin, in compromising citizenship, stands as powerfully as a maternal discourse depriving the Father of his ability to symbolically sustain a lineage. When the

subject becomes an immigrant, approaching a new land, he seeks out some filiation with a new Father, who—not being the symbolic Father left behind—emerges as Real. The reasons for this are clear: the father of the lineage is a name that attaches a symbolic debt to us; leaving it and seeking out another means requesting filiation from someone who—precisely because they are not yet our father—we will find in the real, and with which we may have to grapple in the real before we can finally be awarded symbolic recognition. The hysterical figure, then, just like the immigrant, can only attempt to please the new Father, and runs the risk that this new Father will demand a tribute in the Real to accept the new child. The position is an uncomfortable one, and the hysterical figure may ultimately choose a sort of permanent exile, where one avoids paying a tribute to the new father that will always seem exorbitant. She stands in a position of otherness outside any filiation, while still requesting entrance. The drama here is that the cost of this exile is the repression of desire that only the acceptance of filiation will permit. (Calligaris, *Hello Brasil! Notas de um psicanalista europeu viajando ao Brasil*, 153)

It would be interesting to put this perspective in dialogue with the notion of a "canon of empty fathers" in the context of Lusophone literature. See Rothwell, *A Canon of Empty Fathers*.
41. Rosa, *The Third Bank of the River and Other Stories*, 196.
42. Ibid.
43. Finazzi-Agrò, "Caminhando entre fronteiras," 422.

Chapter 5. Seeking America

1. In his study on Leopold von Ranke, Buarque de Holanda recalls that Otto Hintze had already proposed a description of history on two levels, or in two fundamental rhythms, which recall Braudel's classic formations. In Hintze the analogy returned to old geological theories from the Neptunists and Vulcanists. See S. Holanda, "O atual e o inatual na obra de Leopold von Ranke."
2. On this, see Eugênio, "Um horizonte de autenticidade"; Franco, "*Visão do Paraíso*."
3. S. Holanda, *Tentativas de mitologia*, 30. On Buarque de Holanda's German readings, see Chaves, "O Historicismo de Nietzsche segundo Sérgio Buarque de Holanda." As for the impact of "irrationalist" ideas in the

vocabulary and progression of *Roots of Brazil*, with a particular focus on Klages, Eugênio's recent work, to which I will return shortly, is indispensable. See Eugênio, *Ritmo espontâneo*.

4. For a broad reading of the Weberian legacy in Buarque de Holanda, see Machado, "*Raízes do Brasil*." For more on the Weberian influence in Buarque de Holanda, see Faoro, "A aventura liberal numa ordem patrimonialista"; Meira Monteiro, *A queda do aventureiro*. On the presence of Simmel in *Roots of Brazil*, Cohn, "O pensador do desterro." See also Goldfeder and Waizbort, "Sobre os 'tipos' em *Raízes do Brasil*"; Eugênio, *Ritmo espontâneo*, esp. 264–339.

5. João Kennedy Eugênio's recent book, which I have just referenced, however, offers a broad mapping of these Romantic remains—in his interpretation of Buarque de Holanda's formative years, they emerge as a network of counterpoints, with emphasis on the interplay between "organicism" and the "philosophy of life," examining the 1936 edition of *Roots of Brazil*. See Eugênio, *Ritmo espontâneo*.

6. On metaphors in *Roots of Brazil*, see Vecchi, "Contrapontos à brasileira"; De Decca, "Decifra-me ou te devoro."

7. S. Holanda, *Tentativas de mitologia*, 30. On the "Theory of America," see the first chapter of the third part of this book, "Cordiality and Power: The President and Politics between Film and Essay."

8. The decision to read Buarque de Holanda's essay with an eye to Iberian "constants" does not, of course, invalidate a discussion of the development of Peninsular models in the Americas, which highlights the impasses of citizenship in a civilization "of rural roots," as one reads in the most recent editions of *Roots of Brazil*. In adopting a stance that focuses (although not exclusively) on what is preserved and resists in a society that has undergone urbanization and civilization, I do not wish to propose an abandonment of discussions around *civility* and *cordiality*, which have been rightly privileged by criticism. I simply believe that we might also inquire into the "constants," given that, in investigating the specificities of an Ibero-American civilization, *Roots of Brazil* does pay a tribute, however cautious, to Iberian tradition. I believe that a typology of reading may emerge here: on one side, those readings that address the more static dimension of the essay, looking to identify the forces holding back "modernization," which may ultimately reveal legacies that are as undesirable as they are seductive; and on the other, readings that emphasize the dynamic of posterior development, seeking out the impasses that surface in the clash between opposing civilizational models, opening up to speculations around the future of national politics. In privileging the first sort of reading here, I wish to suggest that the reader

of *Roots of Brazil* may legitimately feel the seduction of the Iberian legacy without this necessarily leading to a sugarcoating of the colonial or precolonial past. Interestingly, in these interpretations, that which more "progressive" readings see as an obstacle to modernization may be conceived of from another angle as the driving force behind new utopias. On the clash between cordiality and civility, see Avelino Filho, "Cordialidade e civilidade em *Raízes do Brasil*"; Esteves, "Cordialidade e familismo amoral." For a discussion of *Roots of Brazil* in terms of modernization vs. backwardness, see Piva, *Ladrilhadores e semeadores*; Lamounier, "Sérgio Buarque e os 'grilhões do passado.'"

9. See Cunha, *Rebellion in the Backlands*.

10. The image of men as foreigners in the landscape recalls the theme of exile. When João Cezar de Castro Rocha localizes and discusses a cultural experiment founded on the tension between exile and acclimation—the end point of which calls into question the rationales that proclaim the essential nature of Brazil—his guiding thread comes from Buarque de Holanda. See Rocha, *O exílio do homem cordial*. In a comparative perspective, one must highlight Robert Wegner's illuminating investigation into the frontier in Buarque's oeuvre, understood as a space in which the Iberian tradition both finds its limits and reveals its reach. See Wegner, *A conquista do oeste*. Also along the lines of this dislocation, which lays out and recreates Iberian singularity, one would be well-advised to follow Silviano Santiago's reflections in a book structured around the essays of Octavio Paz and Sérgio Buarque de Holanda. Santiago, *As raízes e o labirinto da América Latina*. For a different parallel between Paz and Buarque de Holanda, see Monasterio, "*Raízes do Brasil* y *El laberinto de la soledad*."

11. Significantly, Freyre shifted the Iberian Peninsula toward Africa, postulating a "softening" of European medieval institutions, thanks to the "oil of African mediation." Freyre, *The Masters and the Slaves*, 78–79. Let us recall once again that in 1936, Freyre would write the preface to the first volume of the Documentos Brasileiros series of publishing house José Olympio, namely the first edition of *Roots of Brazil*.

12. In *The Stone Raft*, José Saramago ironically takes the geographical conception of Iberian singularity to its limit, as the Pyrenees "split open" and the whole Peninsula drifts away from "nearby Europe," as I mentioned in Chapter 4. See Saramago, *The Stone Raft*.

13. Here is the passage in question:

> At its beginning, Christian asceticism had fled from the world into the realm of solitude in the cloister. In renouncing the world, however,

monastic asceticism had in fact come to dominate the world through the church. Yet, in retreating to the cloister, asceticism left the course of daily life in the world by and large in its natural and untamed state. But now Christian asceticism slammed the gates of the cloister, entered into the hustle and bustle of life, and undertook a new task: to saturate mundane, *everyday* life with its methodicalness. In the process, it sought to reorganize practical life into a rational life *in* the world rather than, as earlier, in the monastery. Yet this rational life in the world was *not of* this world or *for* this world. (Weber, *The Protestant Ethic*, 101)

14. It is interesting to think in terms of Buarque de Holanda's relationship with the United States, from the biting anti-Americanism of his early articles to his travels as an academic in the decades following the publication of *Roots of Brazil*, with emphasis on the influence of Frederick Jackson Turner's hypotheses in Buarque de Holanda's examinations of Brazil's western frontier. See S. Holanda, *O espírito e a letra*, vol. 1; S. Holanda, *Cobra de vidro*, 23–27; Wegner, *A conquista do oeste*; J. Souza, *O malandro e o protestante*.

15. Prado Jr, *The Colonial Background of Modern Brazil*; R.M.L. Rego, *Sentimento do Brasil*; Ricupero, *Caio Prado Jr. e a nacionalização do marxismo no Brasil*; Ricupero, "Celso Furtado e o pensamento social brasileiro."

16. S. Holanda, *Roots of Brazil*, 10.

17. João Kennedy Eugênio, in his study, goes back to Plato's reaction to the principles of movement in Heraclitus, allowing for the conception of an Ionic rhythm as opposed to an (regular, orderly) Attic rhythm, leading in turn to a distinction between inner rhythm and exterior tempo in Buarque de Holanda's imagination, a concept mediated by Klages. Eugênio, *Ritmo espontâneo*, 309. The discussion is continued in terms of the definition of "form" in Aristotle, in dialogue with the "spontaneous form" in *Roots of Brazil* and *Gestalt* (form) and *Bildung* (formation) in German thinking, particularly around the debates within Stefan George's circle, to which Buarque de Holanda was exposed during his German years. Ibid., 339–64.

18. On such an intersection, see Lafetá, *1930*.

19. On Buarque de Holanda as both modernist and historian, in addition to the works already cited here, I might highlight C. Castro, "Com tradições e contradições"; M.V.C. Carvalho, "Outros Lados."

20. Meira Monteiro, "Coisas sutis *ergo* profundas"; Wegner, "Criação e crítica literária na trajetória modernista de Sérgio Buarque de Holanda (1921–1926)"; Vecchi, "Atlas intersticial do tempo do fim."

21. S. Holanda, "O lado oposto e outros lados," in *O espírito e a letra*, 1:226.

22. S. Holanda, *Roots of Brazil*, 10.
23. Ibid., 5.
24. "Cum enim gratia non tollat naturam, sed perficiat, oportet quod naturalis ratio subserviat fidei; Sicut et naturalis inclinatio voluntatis obsequitur caritati." *Summa Theologiae*, I, q.1, a.8, ad.2.
25. Beyond the evident specter of populism, aren't we drawing close here to that which, in the fiction of Machado de Assis (1839–1908), emerges from the comfortable leisure of the cynical gentleman as a ridiculous universal cure-all? In criticizing the super-affectation of Brazilian Romanticism and its creation of an "out-of-this-world existence," Buarque de Holanda tosses a lightly poisoned dart in the direction of Brazil's greatest writer: "Machado de Assis was the flower of this greenhouse plant." S. Holanda, *Roots of Brazil*, 131. See also Machado de Assis, *Epitaph of a Small Winner*.
26. João Cezar de Castro Rocha has examined the significance of the alterations made in the first paragraph of *Roots of Brazil*; in the first edition, it reads, as we have seen, that Brazil had stood as a most "successful large-scale attempt to transplant European culture," while in more recent editions the success of that cultural transplant has been tempered by natural conditions "largely foreign, if not adverse, to Europe's thousand-year tradition." Rocha, "O exílio como eixo: bem-sucedidos e desterrados: Ou: por uma edição crítica de *Raízes do Brasil*," in his *O exílio do homem cordial*. The topic was addressed most recently by Luiz Feldman, as noted. See Feldman, "Um clássico por amadurecimento."
27. Hence the witticism that closes out Buarque de Holanda's letter to Cassiano Ricardo, published in 1948 in response to the latter's allegedly incorrect reading of the cordial man: "And at times, I sincerely worry that I have spent far too much time flogging this poor dead horse." S. Holanda, *Raízes do Brasil*, 396.
28. I examined the topic of "evanescent" categories in: Meira Monteiro, "A cordialidade evanescente em *Raízes do Brasil*."
29. A.C. Souza, "A visão política de Sérgio Buarque de Holanda."
30. I agree with Brasilio Sallum Jr's critique of Leopoldo Waizbort, when the latter aligns the Buarque de Holanda of the first edition of *Roots of Brazil* with an ultimately conservative, antiliberal vein of thought that bloomed during the interwar period. See Sallum Jr, "Sobre a noção de democracia em *Raízes do Brasil*," 54. See also Waizbort, "O mal-entendido da democracia." We should recall that, contrary to Sallum Jr's postulations, and beyond Waizbort's suggestions, the context of enunciation of the first edition of Buarque de Holanda's essay and the subsequent singularity of his text have been examined at length for quite some time, by critics

including João Cezar de Castro Rocha, Sandra Jatahy Pesavento, Jacques Leenhardt, Marcus Vinicius Corrêa Carvalho, João Kennedy Eugênio, Conrado Pires de Castro, and myself. (More recently, among the work that I have been able to follow over the past few years, I should highlight the pieces by Alfredo Cesar Melo and Luiz Feldman referenced over the course of this book.) But it is true that the systematic contextualization of ideas, shedding light on the changes of tone between *Roots of Brazil*'s first (1936), second (1948), and third (1956) editions, largely remains to be done. Coincidentally, João Kennedy Eugênio's arguments as to the importance of Klages for Buarque de Holanda, also referenced here, emerged just as Waizbort, in the article cited above, was unveiling his critique of the "vitalism" present in *Roots of Brazil*, especially in its 1936 incarnation. As for Waizbort, he nonetheless fails to consider the meaning of "vital" gestures in the context of the previous decade's vanguards, when the defense of "life" against "spirit" fell into step with the "Romantic" gesture of liberating modern art (from surrealism to expressionism), in a political context whose "regressive" side would become particularly clear in the 1930s. In short, and despite their differences, I believe that Eugênio and Waizbort's critiques err in placing Buarque de Holanda's arguments within a body of irrationalist readings (although the philosophical arc of Eugênio's investigation is indeed quite broad, extending back to the Pre-Socratics), without paying due attention to what the vitalist principle had meant in the decade prior to the publication of *Roots of Brazil*, especially in discussions of the "primitivism" and creative principles (the unconscious, impulses) making their way through avant-garde aesthetics, mainly radiating outward from Paris and which a young Buarque de Holanda would receive with critical glee, most of all from 1924 to 1926. In the end, the singularity and strength of Buarque de Holanda's work may lie in the sheer ambivalence of his formulations, the richness of which is compromised whenever one aligns the author to the Left (Antonio Candido, for example) or to the Right (Waizbort, although somewhat cautiously). As a possible response to the problem, I might recommend my own considerations on the role of "looseness" in Buarque de Holanda's own literary criticism during the 1920s and 1930s, as already cited. See Meira Monteiro, "Coisas sutis *ergo* profundas," esp. 174–291.

31. S. Holanda, *Raízes de Sérgio Buarque de Holanda*, 298–301.

32. Coelho, "Entrevista: Sérgio Buarque de Holanda." See also L. Souza, "Corpo e alma do Brasil," 10.

33. Romero, "Richard McGee Morse, 78, Latin America Expert," n.p.

34. Morse, "Prospero's Mirror," 9.

35. Ibid., 54. For an understanding of the problem from a different angle, examining the role of the myth in Mariátegui's thought, see Bosi, "A vanguarda enraizada: O marxismo vivo de Mariátegui," in his *Entre a literatura e a história*.
36. Morse, "A miopia de Schwartzman," 168.
37. Morse, "Balancing Myth and Evidence," 52.
38. Morse, "Prospero's Mirror," 11.
39. For an analysis contrasting Oliveira Vianna and Sérgio Buarque de Holanda, see Brasil Jr and Botelho, "Próximo distante."
40. S. Holanda, *Roots of Brazil*, 155.
41. See Williams, *Marxism and Literature*. Luiz Werneck Vianna's analyses are, for their part, required reading for those venturing into the topic of Iberianism and Americanism in the history of Brazilian social thought. L.W. Vianna, *A revolução passiva*. More recently, see also L.W. Vianna and Perlatto, "Iberismo e americanismo."

Chapter 6. "El hombre cordial" and Specular Poetics

1. Darío, *Selected Writings*, 400.
2. Ibid., 402–3. The Calibanic theme would return some years later, in the context of North American intervention in the Caribbean, in a text of Darío's titled "The Triumph of Caliban," published originally in *El Tiempo*, in Buenos Aires, May 20, 1898. Darío, *Selected Writings*, 507–12.
3. Darío's portrait of Poe bears remarkable similarities to Baudelaire's. See Baudelaire, "Edgar Poe, sa vie et ses oeuvres," in *Curiosités esthétiques et l'art romantique et autres oeuvres critiques*.
4. Zabus, *Tempests after Shakespeare*. See also Renan, *Caliban, suite de La Tempête*.
5. For a discussion of the origins of the concept of Latin America, see Newcomb, *"Nossa" and "Nuestra América*," 11–20; Diniz, "O conceito de América Latina"; Santos Jr, *A trama das ideias*. While asserting that "the term Latin America appears for the first time in 1836, in an article by Michel Chevalier, [and is then] vigorously taken up by Colombian writer and diplomat José María Torres Caicedo," author of the 1865 treatise *Unión Latinoamericana*, Jorge Schwartz suggests that the idea that the term was coined by the ideologues of Napoleon III, as a justification for the invasion of Mexico, is simply an error. See Schwartz, "Abaixo Tordesilhas!" For a broad debate on the imperial logic that guides the concept of the "*hispanoamericano*," see Díaz-Quiñones, *Sobre los principios*, 65–166.

6. Castro, "Introducción," 53.

7. See the chapter titled "Genealogy" in Machado de Assis's *Epitaph of a Small Winner*.

8. Díaz-Quiñones, *Sobre los principios*, 131.

9. Ibid., 131–32. On Rodó and the term "*iberoamericano*" as comprising Brazil as well, Newcomb, *"Nossa" and "Nuestra América,"* 57–86.

10. S. Holanda, *Roots of Brazil*, 139.

11. Martí, *En los Estados Unidos*.

12. Foucault, "Nieztsche, Freud, Marx," 278.

13. The declaration—"inside, we are still not American"—is associated with D.H. Lawrence ("one of the great poets of our time," Buarque de Holanda says), the Brazilian writer having found in his *Studies in Classic American Literature* the idea that "the blood is chemically reduced by the nerves, in American activity." S. Holanda, *Roots of Brazil*, 139n2, 181.

14. For a consideration of a "subtle sublimation of *bandeirante* activity" in Sérgio Buarque de Holanda, see Bosi, *Colony, Cult, and Culture*, 48. The *bandeirantes* were the explorers of the Brazilian backlands who engaged in private and official expeditions to the interior of the colony, seeking Amerindian captives, gold, and precious stones. These expeditions frequently departed from the Piratininga highlands, where the town of São Paulo (founded by the Jesuits in the mid-sixteenth century) was located. The *bandeirantes* were especially active during the seventeenth century, at which time they were in constant conflict with the Jesuits who sought to protect the Amerindians from the *paulistas*, as the *bandeirantes* were often termed. Traditional historiography and iconography have tended to idealize the figure of the *bandeirante*, projecting the image of an intrepid explorer-as-civilizing agent and frequently obscuring the extremely violent character of the *bandeirantes'* simultaneously economic and civilizational crusade. For information on the *bandeirantes* in English, in a book that includes an essay by Sérgio Buarque de Holanda, see Morse, ed., *The Bandeirantes*.

15. Rodó, *Ariel*, 99–100.

16. Castro, "Introducción," 94.

17. S. Holanda, *O espírito e a letra*, 1:35–41.

18. Ibid., 1:42–46. For a broad consideration of the importance of Rodó for young Buarque de Holanda, which proposes a connection with his failed "Theory of America" and the subsequent writing of *Roots of Brazil*, see, again, Newcomb, *"Nossa" and "Nuestra América,"* 183–210.

19. On the monarchism of young Buarque de Holanda, see Eugênio, "Um horizonte de autenticidade."

20. S. Holanda, *O espírito e a letra*, 1:43.

21. For more on Weber's presence in Buarque de Holanda's imagination, see, in addition to the works previously referenced, the volume edited by Jessé Souza, *O malandro e o protestante*, particularly the essays by the editor himself ("A ética protestante e a ideologia do atraso brasileiro," 17–54), Luiz Werneck Vianna ("Weber e a interpretação do Brasil," 173–93), and Roberto Moreira ("Weber e o mal-estar colonial," 195–210). For an understanding of Reyes's role as an interlocutor in the dialogue on cordiality, highlighting the "deep undercurrents" that may draw unexpected connections between Brazil and Mexico, see P. Moreira, *Literary and Cultural Relations between Brazil and Mexico*, 37–51.

22. R.R. Couto, "El hombre cordial, producto americano," 397.

23. Darío, *Selected Writings*, 509. See also Darío, *Los raros*, 86–87. Note that I have altered the original paragraph division.

24. Darío's reference to the "Yankees" blends into the passage in which Don Quijote and Sancho react to the "yangüeses" (natives of the highlands of Soria, in the north of Spain; note that the English translator missed the reference and translated the term as "Yankees"), who give Rocinante a whipping after he tries to take liberties with their mares. The result is a David-and-Goliath battle, with Sancho and Quijote against a hundred men, and the knight and his faithful squire end up taking a beating. Cervantes, *Don Quijote de la Mancha*, 159–67.

25. Vasconcelos, *The Cosmic Race*, 20–22.

26. Jáuregui, "Calibán: Ícono del 98." To follow Jáuregui's arguments further, we should recall that the furious Darío of '98 does not totally jibe with the poet of "Saluting the Eagle," in 1907, where we read,

Tráenos los secretos de las labores del Norte,
y que los hijos nuestros dejen de ser los rétores latinos
y aprendan de los yanquis la constancia, el vigor, el carácter. (125)

Give us the secret of the way you labor in the North,
the way our children might cease to be cut from Latin cloth
and learn perseverance, vigor, character from the Yankees.

27. Schwartz, *Vanguardas latino-americanas*.

28. Rodó, *Ariel*, 91.

29. On Rodó, esp. through *Motivos de Proteo* (1909), see Draper, "Entre política y crítica cultural."

30. A curious case with some similarities to Buarque de Holanda's is that of Dominican sociologist Pedro Henríquez Ureña, who in 1904 wrote

a review of *Ariel*, expressing more or less the same degree of enthusiasm (if somewhat less unconditional than Buarque de Holanda's). See Henríquez Ureña, "Ariel," in *Obra crítica*.

31. In *"Nossa"* and *"Nuestra América,"* Robert Newcomb wonders if young Buarque de Holanda mightn't be "a lost child of Ariel" (186).

32. S. Holanda, *Roots of Brazil*, 145–47.

33. Ibid., 146–47. In the first edition of *Roots of Brazil* (1936), Machiavelli appears in place of Hobbes, the former as "the pioneer of the doctrine of power." S. Holanda, *Raizes do Brasil*, 149.

34. S. Holanda, *Raízes do Brasil*, 155. The topic had already come up in an article published in the *Folha da Manhã* in 1935, in which Buarque de Holanda reviewed Schmitt's *The Concept of the Political*. S. Holanda, "O Estado totalitário," in *Raízes de Sérgio Buarque de Holanda*.

35. S. Holanda, "A Chiméra do Monroismo."

36. Fernández Retamar, *Todo Caliban*.

37. Zabus, *Tempests after Shakespeare*, 32.

38. Merquior, "O outro Ocidente," 71.

39. For an examination of the specter of racism hanging over the image of Brazil as a racial laboratory in the nineteenth and early twentieth centuries, see Schwarcz, *The Spectacle of the Races*.

40. Bosi, *Colony, Cult, and Culture*, 91.

41. For a broad understanding of the use of the concept of "racial democracy" in the postwar period, see Guimarães, *Classes, raças e democracia*, 137–77. In English, see Guimarães, "Racial Democracy."

42. Santí, "Esta edición."

43. Glissant, *Introduction à una Poétique du Divers*, 11–12.

44. For an examination of the Latin American vanguards as a whole, in a spectrum that spills over the borders between Brazil and Hispanic America, see Gelado, *Vanguarda e cultura popular nos anos 20 na América Latina*. From Lezama Lima, *La expresión americana*.

45. See, on the topic, Schwartzman, "O espelho de Morse"; Schwartzman, "O gato de Cortázar"; Morse, "A miopia de Schwartzman"; Merquior, "O outro Ocidente"; Arocena, "Ariel, Caliban e Próspero"; Velho, "O espelho de Morse e outros espelhos"; Oliveira, "Anotações sobre um debate"; Bomeny, "Saudades do Brasil de Richard Morse." Also on Morse, see the special number of the *Luso-Brazilian Review* 32, no. 2 (1995), ed. Thomas Cohen and Dain Borges, as well as the fundamental work *O código Morse*, ed. Domingues and Blasenheim. Also see M.A. Carvalho, "Morse e o mar," in *Quatro vezes cidade*.

46. Schwartzman, "O espelho de Morse," 192.

47. Luiz Inácio Lula da Silva was defeated in that race by the candidate of the traditional right wing, Fernando Collor de Mello, who would later, in 1992, be impeached and leave the office to his vice president, Itamar Franco. Franco remained in power through 1994, when Fernando Henrique Cardoso was elected. Finally, Lula, running for the fourth time, would become one of the most popular leftist leaders in modern history, governing Brazil from 2003 to 2010. The 2002 election that first brought him to power was the subject of a documentary by João Moreira Salles, as I will discuss in the next chapter.

48. Morse, "A miopia de Schwartzman," 168.

49. Tenorio, "Profissão: Latin Americanist," 119–20.

50. Velho, "O espelho de Morse e outros espelhos," 96.

51. Morse, *New World Soundings*, esp. 131–66. A nuanced analysis of this redemptive vision of Latin America ought to take into account Morse's youth at Princeton University, where, as he puts it, Augusto Centeno "opened [his] eyes to García Lorca, San Juan de la Cruz, [and] Ricardo Güiraldes," and where Américo Castro, "the great man of '98 in Spain," was teaching. See Bomeny, "Saudades do Brasil de Richard Morse," 130–31. On Morse, see also Meira Monteiro, "Richard Morse."

52. Morse, *New World Soundings*, 227–51.

53. Brioso, "De la desaparición de los oráculos y de la muerte y resurrección de los dioses," 87.

54. Ibid., 99.

55. Here I refer to the final verses of Caetano Veloso's song from the album *Cê*, "O herói" [The Hero], which takes the "cordial man" as its protagonist, proclaiming: *Eu sou o herói / Só Deus e eu sabemos como dói* [I am the hero / Only God and I know how it hurts].

56. The use of Nietzschean categories in interpreting *Roots of Brazil* was proposed by Luiz Dantas. See Dantas, "Prefácio."

Chapter 7. Cordiality and Power

1. Here I might once again mention João Cezar de Castro Rocha's reflections on exile and literature, which, again, have Buarque de Holanda as their most prominent character. See Rocha, *O exílio do homem cordial*.

2. S. Holanda, "Corpo e alma do Brasil: Ensaio de psicologia social" (1935), in *Raízes do Brasil*, 399–420; S. Holanda, "O lado oposto e outros lados" (1926), in *O espírito e a letra*, 1:224–28; S. Holanda, "Apresentação," in *Tentativas de Mitologia*, 7–35.

3. At the time, Buarque de Holanda was living off the money he was making with his texts. L.M. Souza, "Corpo e alma do Brasil: Entrevista com Sérgio Buarque de Holanda," 8.

4. João Kennedy Eugênio, I should repeat, has produced the deepest investigation into the extent to which the roots of Buarque de Holanda's thought give rise to an organic imaginary, with its broad strokes already evident in writings prior to *Roots of Brazil*. See Eugênio, "Um horizonte de autenticidade"; Eugênio, *Ritmo espontâneo*.

5. See Mello, "*Raízes do Brasil* e depois"; Wegner, "Um ensaio entre o passado e o futuro."

6. The polemic, waged in the pages of *Colégio* magazine in mid-1948, may be found in full in the fourth edition of *Roots of Brazil* (1963) as well as in the seventieth anniversary edition of the book. S. Holanda, *Raízes do Brasil*, 365–96.

7. Leite, *O caráter nacional brasileiro*; C.G. Mota, *Ideologia da cultura brasileira (1933–1974)* (preface by Alfredo Bosi). In the following chapter, "Sérgio Buarque de Holanda and Words, or Evoking Wittgenstein," I address the controversy over word usage as sparked by a savage argument between Sérgio Buarque de Holanda and Carlos Guilherme Mota.

8. Among the vast critical bibliography around Caminha's letter, a special place must be reserved for the study and anthology drawn up by Maria Aparecida Ribeiro. Ribeiro, *A carta de Caminha e seus ecos*. See also Jorge Coli's proposal of a rereading of the letter by way of the nineteenth century and visual arts, with particular attention paid to Victor Meirelles's painting *The First Mass in Brazil*. Coli, "Primeira missa e invenção da descoberta."

9. O. Andrade, "Manifesto of Pau-Brasil Poetry." Decades later, Andrade would return to the topic of the promises of a Brazilian civilization (at once matriarchal and mechanized) in a discussion of, as it so happens, cordiality. See O. Andrade, "Um aspecto antropofágico da cultura brasileira: O homem cordial," and "A crise da filosofia messiânica," in *A utopia antropofágica*, 101–59; O. Andrade, *Pau-brasil*. See also Bary, "Oswald de Andrade's 'Cannibalist Manifesto.'"

10. S. Holanda, *Raizes do Brasil* (1936), 101–2 (translation adapted from *Roots of Brazil*, 117–18).

11. Salles, *Entreatos*; Coutinho, *Peões*.

12. Given widespread cries for a political opening, which had begun in 1979 with amnesty for those persecuted by the dictatorship, a constitutional amendment restoring free and direct presidential elections was proposed in 1984. A broad conservative coalition in Congress rejected the amendment, despite massive popular pressure, which meant that the transition to

a civil government in 1985 came through indirect elections, with Tancredo Neves chosen for the office of president by an electoral college. As Neves passed away before taking office, José Sarney, his vice president, fresh out of the alliance that had long supported the military government, would lead the country until the 1989 election of Fernando Collor de Mello (who ran against Lula) in the first free election for president since the dictatorship had taken hold of Brazil in 1964.

13. The case of the *mensalão* was a vote-buying scandal in Brazil's congress from 2005 to 2006, with investigations that led to the resignation or firing of figures in the highest echelons of the federal government, thereafter sentenced to prison in trials that veered toward the side of spectacle and led to the public atonement of those found guilty. Corruption schemes would not end, though. The so-called *operação lava-jato* (car wash operation), a federal investigation into bribery schemes connecting politicians, political parties, and big corporations is still developing as I am writing this. Such investigation started in 2014 and led to the impeachment of President Dilma Rousseff in 2016, as I discussed in the preface.

14. Interestingly enough, during the campaign that culminated in Lula's reelection to the presidency in 2006, adversaries used excerpts from Salles's documentary in television ads as a sort of "evidence" that the scandals involving all-powerful chief of staff José Dirceu were already being devised before the first election cycle—as if cinema could reveal a Machiavellian plot cooked up behind the scenes on the campaign trail, and as if the camera had probed into private space to capture glimpses of the infamies that would later be revealed in the public arena.

15. On this note, I should direct readers to the book that Paul Firbas and I edited on Argentine filmmmaker Andrés Di Tella. See Firbas and Meira Monteiro, eds., *Andrés Di Tella*.

16. See chapter 2 above, "A Familial Tragedy (in Hegel's Shadow)."

17. In an article published in the *Folha da Manhã* in June 1935, Buarque de Holanda elaborated on the distinction between "friend" and "enemy," proposed by the "wise professor at Bonn" in his *The Concept of the Political*. S. Holanda, "O Estado totalitário," in *Raízes de Sérgio Buarque de Holanda*, 298–301. As I suggested earlier, there remains to be conducted a careful examination of Buarque de Holanda's uneasiness with the tension between liberal and totalitarian principles as he began to work up *Roots of Brazil*.

18. Panizza, *Populism and the Mirror of Democracy*, 9. On a somehow less optimistic take on populism, think of Perón's case in Argentina and his "hostility toward liberal democracy." Mainwaring and Pérez-Liñán, *Democracies and Dictatorships in Latin America*, 137.

19. Funnily enough, scenes of future presidents beholding themselves in the mirror may have become a sort of cinematographic *topos*, as a documentary register of the moment in which two images meet: on one side, the private person, and on the other, the public individual, increasingly internalizing his or her role before the collectivity. Along these lines, see the scene of Evo Morales before the mirror at the barber's, in Alejandro Landes's documentary. Landes, *Cocalero*.

20. See Schwarcz, "Sérgio Buarque de Holanda e essa tal de 'cordialidade.'"

21. This passage remained unaltered from the first edition. S. Holanda, *Roots of Brazil*, 118. Ernani Chaves examined this passage in depth as a way of shedding light on the German debates that form the basis for Buarque's notion of cordiality. See Chaves, "*Raízes do Brasil* e Nietzsche"; Chaves, "O historicismo de Nietzsche, segundo Sérgio Buarque de Holanda."

22. Forbes, "O homem cordial e a psicanálise."

23. See Calligaris, "O verdadeiro petista."

24. Salles's documentary poses an interesting contrast to the melodramatic narrative of the recent film directed by Fábio Barreto, with a screenplay by Fernando Bonassi and Denise Paraná, in which Lula's father is little more than a violent drunk abandoned by his family. See Barreto, *Lula, o filho do Brasil*.

25. Quoting Saint-Hilaire, Buarque de Holanda recalls the liberalist turmoil preceding Brazilian independence in 1822, suggesting in the end that the "mass of the people" had been left asking, "'Like the donkey in the fable: Will I not have to carry a heavy load all my life?'" S. Holanda, *Roots of Brazil*, 130. For a better understanding of the formation of a long-lasting republican oligarchy, readers should turn to S. Holanda, *Do Império à República* [From the Empire to the Republic], the first edition dating from 1972. It is interesting to see how the problematic space of the "people" (or "public opinion," as the liberal phrase from the era of the Brazilian Empire went) in the imagination of the elites is the one topic that, while present in *Roots of Brazil*, would be most completely developed in a book (*Do Império à República*) on Brazilian political and parliamentary history, written under the dictatorship, as I have already observed.

26. See Calligaris, "Do homem cordial ao homem vulgar."

27. The topic is evidently still evolving, as the mass of new consumers seems perhaps to be here to stay. On that note, in an arc that stretches from the direct beneficiaries of social programs during the Lula administration to the emergence of new consumers in Brazil, on a pitch that oscillates between optimism as to the emancipatory nature of minimum income [*renda mínima*] programs to distrust of the economicist nature of notions of a "new

middle class," see Rego and Pinzani, *Vozes do bolsa-família*. See also J. Souza, *Os batalhadores brasileiros*.
28. C. Veloso, *Cê*.

Chapter 8. Sérgio Buarque de Holanda and Words, or Evoking Wittgenstein

1. Eco, "Interpretation and History," 23.
2. Montaigne, *Essays*, 159.
3. See Dias, "Estilo e método na obra de Sérgio Buarque de Holanda"; Dias, "Sérgio Buarque de Holanda, historiador"; Dias, "Negação das negações."
4. Not coincidentally, the idea of ethnography as an act of reading, and thus of culture as text, would be developed by Clifford Geertz out of a Weberian principle. See Geertz, "Thick Description: Toward an Interpretive Theory of Culture," in *The Interpretation of Cultures*.
5. Alfredo Bosi was also part of the polemic, almost against his will— his name was brought up by Mota in one of the articles that make up the bulk of the discussions. A letter from Bosi to Buarque de Holanda, dated 1980, seeks to undo any misunderstandings as to the personal feelings of the literary critic toward the author of *Roots of Brazil*, his works, and his ideological positions. See this letter in Arquivo Central do Sistema de Arquivos (hereafter SIARQ) da Unicamp, Fundo Privado SBH, Campinas (São Paulo State), Brazil. It is true that Bosi's critiques of Buarque de Holanda, present in the preface to a book of Mota's, resurface in *Colony, Cult, and Culture*, where Bosi takes aim at the author of *Roots of Brazil*: "In Buarque's highly erudite texts, a subtle sublimation of bandeirante activity, presented as the natural outgrowth of the processes of Portuguese acclimatization to Brazil, downplays the aggression and conflict that objectively characterized the paulista incursions into the interior and the indigenous and Jesuit opposition they faced." Bosi, *Colony, Cult, and Culture*, 48. See also Bosi, "Homenagem a Sérgio Buarque de Holanda," in *Céu, inferno*.
6. Letters both to and from Buarque de Holanda may be consulted at SIARQ da Unicamp, Fundo Privado SBH, folders 5–11 (subseries Ca and Cp).
7. See C.G. Mota, "Formas de pensamento intermediárias," in his *Idéia de revolução no Brasil (1789–1801)*.
8. The article by Sérgio Buarque de Holanda, "Sobre uma doença infantil da historiografia," appeared in the literary supplement of *O Estado de*

S.Paulo on June 17, 1973. It may be found in S. Holanda, *Para uma nova história*, 113–27.

9. See C.G. Mota, "Fazendeiros do ar"; "A perspectiva do historiador"; and "Uma visão ideológica." Lastly, readers should consult a review by Antonio Candido, in which he responds indirectly to the latest, most virulent article from Mota. A.C. Souza, "As 'Tentativas de Mitologia' de Sérgio Buarque de Holanda."

10. S. Holanda, *O espírito e a letra*, 1:214. On *Estética*, see Leonel, *Estética (revista trimensal) e modernismo*.

11. S. Holanda, *Para uma nova história*, 115–16.

12. G. Mota, "Historiografia. Bibliografia. Documentos."

13. S. Holanda, "O atual e o inatual na obra de Leopold von Ranke." Years later, the essay would open a volume on Leopold von Ranke, which Buarque de Holanda edited for Florestan Fernandes's series titled Great Social Scientists. See also Pesavento, "Cartografias do tempo, palimpsestos na escrita da história."

14. SIARQ da Unicamp, Fundo Privado SBH, Cp 349 P11.

15. Wittgenstein, *Philosophical Investigations*, 5e (§7).

16. Ibid., 128e (§§431–32).

17. SIARQ da Unicamp, Fundo Privado SBH, Cp 349 P11.

18. Ibid.

19. Ibid.

20. In addition to the reflections of Maria Odila Leite da Silva Dias, readers may consult the commentary from Flora Süssekind, who has sought to understand the interaction between the "literary" and "objective" registers in the prose of Buarque de Holanda. See Süssekind, "Comentário ao texto 'Nota breve sobre Sérgio crítico,' de Antonio Arnoni Prado."

21. Gombrich, *The Story of Art*, 219.

22. Adorno, "The Essay as Form," 160.

Chapter 9. In a Thread of Time

1. Cunha Júnior, "Chico Buarque fala sobre seu pai." The topic would resurface in *Raízes do Brasil: Uma cinebiografia de Sérgio Buarque de Hollanda* (Brazil, 2004), a documentary about the writer by Nelson Pereira dos Santos, in the recollections of Chico and his sister Miúcha. For a look at essay and song, side by side, see Starling, "O tempo da delicadeza perdida." For an expanded version of this argument, see Starling, *Uma pátria para todos*. So

as to differentiate father from son, in this chapter I will refer to Francisco Buarque de Holanda as "Chico" or "Chico Buarque."
2. See J.G. Couto, "Sonho e realidade se confundem na narrativa."
3. See García Márquez, *Cien años de soledad*.
4. F. Holanda, *Benjamin*, 3–4.
5. Paes, "O olhar hiper-realista."
6. S. Holanda, "O atual e o inatual na obra de Leopold von Ranke."
7. Starling, *Uma pátria para todos*, 14.
8. S. Holanda, "O atual e o inatual na obra de Leopold von Ranke," 473–74.
9. It is always tempting to associate the crisis of the narrator, as it appears in the fiction of Chico Buarque, with the now-classic concept of the "death of the author." This being the case, we might well revisit Barthes and Foucault. See Barthes, "La mort de l'auteur," in *Le bruissement de la langue*; Foucault, "Qu'est-ce qu'un auteur?" in *Dits et Écrits*, vol. 1.
10. F. Holanda, *Benjamin*, 71.
11. Ibid., 48.
12. Ibid., 48–49.
13. See Ridenti, "Visões do paraíso perdido."
14. See F. Holanda, *Spilt Milk*. It is interesting to contemplate the narrative focus that takes in the tangled memories of the dying landholder in *Spilt Milk*, in contrast with the flawed lyrical voice in a song like "Bancarrota blues" [Bankruptcy Blues], composed with Edu Lobo for Augusto Boal's play *O corsário do rei* [The King's Corsair] and later included on the 1987 *Francisco*, where another song, "O velho Francisco" [Old Francisco] follows along similar lines. Chico himself has said that the latter song was born of a dream of "an old black woman telling a story from the back of the kitchen, and who was saying, with a deep and drawling voice, 'Close the door! Close the door!'" Homem, *Histórias de canções*, 251. The imagination opens up to the subject who finds himself before the ruinous result of history, discovering himself as a ruin in turn. In this sense, we might look to the critical work of Idelber Avelar, who has investigated mourning in the fictional context of the postdictatorship period in Latin America. See Avelar, *The Untimely Present*. I might also evoke the possibility of comparing the fragmented "speech" of these narrators on the brink of death to the fevered writing of the priest who narrates Roberto Bolaño's *By Night in Chile*. Bolaño, *By Night in Chile*.
15. I shall refrain from remarking on the 2014 novel *O irmão alemão* [The German Brother], previously referenced and published while my book

was being finished up. However, it is important to note that Chico Buarque's fictional work is still haunted by his father's name. On this, see Meira Monteiro, "O pai, lá em cima."

16. S. Holanda, "Perspectivas," in *O espírito e a letra*, 1:214. On the night of the release for *O espírito e a letra*, publishers distributed a notebook containing two articles to be read by Chico Buarque. S. Holanda, *O espírito e a letra: Trechos lidos por Chico Buarque*. Onstage in the main MASP auditorium, in addition to Chico Buarque, were critics Antonio Arnoni Prado and Antonio Candido, as well as publisher Luiz Schwarcz.

17. F. Holanda, *Budapest*.

Epilogue. Roots of the Twenty-First Century

1. Wisnik, *Veneno remédio*.
2. I briefly discussed the specter of populism in *Roots of Brazil* in the preface to the recent (2012) North American edition of the book. Cf. Meira Monteiro, "Why Read *Roots of Brazil* Today?"
3. For an approach of the notion in Derrida, see Meira Monteiro, "O modernismo entra em campo." Cordiality as an "undecidable" concept would produce, in Silviano Santiago's terms, "a *halved* effect: halved, as an element that still contains two poles (friendship/enmity), and halved, in that the meaning remains between two poles (concord/discord). Philosophically, the undecidable is not comprehensible by means of a binary opposition, but it nonetheless inhabits it, resisting and disorganizing it, without ever forming a third pole or giving way to a solution in the form of a speculative dialectic." Santiago, *As raízes e o labirinto da América Latina*, 243.
4. Wisnik, *Veneno remédio*, 13.
5. I am referring to the movement that, begun in the 1960s by musicians like Caetano Veloso and Gilberto Gil, then spread to other arts and philosophy, becoming one of the most important vectors of Brazil's counterculture. See Dunn, *Brutality Garden*.
6. Wisnik, *Veneno remédio*, 430.
7. Ibid., 155. The phrase *stoplight jugglers* refers to the people, often youths and children, who take advantage of the time at the red light to put on a brief juggling show and then ask the stopped drivers for spare change before the light changes. The phenomenon is quite common in large Brazilian cities.
8. Ibid., 149.

9. Ibid., 235.
10. Here I am referring to Mário de Andrade's antihero, the title character of one of the most important works of Brazilian modernism, published in 1928. Macunaíma contains within himself the ethnic mixture and the winking slyness of Brazil, perennially failing to devote himself to a single project as he wanders from the forest to the city in search of a mythical stone of which he has been robbed. M. Andrade, *Macunaíma*. On the topic of Macunaímian "laziness," in a productive comparison with Melville, see Dieleke, "Genealogies and Inquiries into Laziness from *Macunaíma*."
11. Wisnik, *Veneno remédio*, 270.
12. Ibid., 291.
13. A.C. Souza, "Dialectic of Malandroism," 90.
14. Wisnik, *Veneno remédio*, 424.
15. As Wisnik writes, "This is what we may recognize in Fernando Novais's take on Sérgio Buarque's book: *if Brazil remains Brazil it cannot modernize, and if it modernizes, it will no longer be Brazil.*" Ibid., 418. Here I might recall Sérgio Costa's provocative evaluation in an afterword to a recent German edition of *Roots of Brazil*:

> We know that *Roots of Brazil* did not emerge from a poststructuralist colloquium on the verge of the twenty-first century. Rather, it is a response to the political challenges of its time—and, for that matter, quite probably the best possible answer. From this angle, Buarque de Holanda deconstructs the discourses of power of oligarchs, racists, and nationalist Romantics. In this process, the idealization of Europe is the inevitable price to be paid for the position he adopts: "hyper-real Europe" was the necessary vanishing point by which to orient the project of constructing a modern society where colonialism, slavery, and the rural patriarchy had left so much destruction in their wake.

My thanks to the author for ceding a translation (by Iasmin Goes) from the original German to Portuguese. See Costa, "Nachtwort." Beyond the idea of the idealization of Europe as a sort of "inevitable price" placed on a critique of "wreckage" in *Roots of Brazil*, it is interesting to note that the problem may emerge in the form of an impasse here as well: a critique of local experience reinforces the foreign solution, leaving the reader with an answer that is constantly put off, since solutions are to be found neither here nor there.
16. C. Veloso, *Circuladô Vivo*.

17. For a sort of tour through the "malaise" of cordiality, in a spectrum that ranges from Brazilian domestic politics to the "miasma of Nazism," see Rosenfield, "Cordialidades austro-brasileiras."

18. See, on this, C. Veloso, *Verdade tropical*.

19. Wisnik, *Veneno remédio*, 409–11.

20. See, on this note, the recent spat between Caetano Veloso and Roberto Schwarz, which brings to light the impasses of Tropicalism and counterculture in Brazil: Meira Monteiro, "O que é isso, Caetano?"

21. A.C. Souza, "The Significance of *Roots of Brazil*."

22. In Portuguese, Wisnik inverts the famous expression from Roberto Schwarz (*ideias fora do lugar* or "ideas out of place," translated as "misplaced ideas"), speaking of a *lugar fora das ideias* (a place outside ideas). Schwarz was referring to the disconnect between bourgeois norms and slaveholding practices in nineteenth-century Brazil, while Wisnik's turn of phrase points to the agency and subjectivity of slaves, whose cultural production refuses to fit into an analytical framework that engages only with the logic of productivity and the ideologies that sustain or mask it.

23. Wisnik, *Veneno remédio*, 412.

24. Ibid., 414.

25. Wisnik, *Sem receita*, 83. Also, Wisnik, "The Gay Science," 191–202. Finally, Wisnik, "The Riddle of Brazilian Soccer."

26. Wisnik, *Sem receita*, 60.

27. Wisnik, *Veneno remédio*, 415.

28. Ibid., 416.

29. Ibid.

30. Ibid., 424. In situating the debates around religious principles and society, referring to the "ambiguity of the democratic principles of the sect," Jessé Souza discusses the Weberian distinction between sect and church, noting that the

> emphasis on purity—ultimately responsible for sects' enormous energy in pursuing their associative ends—simultaneously sets up an insurpassable opposition between sectarians, considered "pure," and nonsectarians, considered "impure." The difference in relation to the church is not the paradigmatic position on the concept of purity, as this is fundamental in both the church and the sect. The hierarchical nature of the church, however, allows for one to *accept* the impure, while the sect *rejects* it. In this sense—and hence the importance of cultural ambiguities in the study of universal issues—the "democratic" elective affinity of the base value of the political liberalism of *tolerance* is inherent to the

hierarchy of the church, which embraces all and guarantees space for each, while it is absent from the exclusive nature of the sect. The sect, in drawing an unsurpassable dividing line between the saint and the reprobate, eliminates any possibility of exchange between the two. The emphasis here is on the *intolerance of the Other*. With the secularization of the principle of tolerance, this Other may be any one who is different, not solely the infidel. (J. Souza, *O malandro e o protestante*, 49–50)

31. Schwarz, *Que horas são?*, 129–55. In late 1968, Institutional Act No. 5 (AI-5, in Portuguese) abolished habeas corpus in Brazil and opened the way for the tightening of dictatorial rule in the years to come, as well as for the subsequent emergence of countless hubs of guerrilla resistance, both rural and urban. On the opposition to the Brazilian dictatorship in the United States, see Green, *We Cannot Remain Silent*.

32. Oddly enough, in moving the cordial man closer to Simmelian typology, André Goldfeder and Leopoldo Waizbort's approach meets up directly with Wisnik's reflections on a more spontaneous form of sociability: "Cordiality consists, almost paradoxically, of a sort of sociability whose content resists becoming completely formalized, to an extent; rather, it consists of a social form that is crystallized but whose composition includes a certain element of spontaneity, a vital flow, that persists and refuses to be completely dammed up by its being directed into fixed forms." André Goldfeder and Leopoldo Waizbort, "Sobre os 'tipos' em *Raízes do Brasil*,"
34. What I am proposing here is unlike Paulo Niccoli Ramirez's reading of Walter Benjamin alongside Sérgio Buarque de Holanda, where cordiality is cast as "sovereign in Brazil, as it decides our state of exception, such that our institutions and laws are made obsolete and annulled by it." Ramirez, *Sérgio Buarque de Holanda e a dialética da cordialidade*, 155. For a nuanced understanding of the revolutionary principle (the possibility of *revolvere*), also in dialogue with Benjamin and Agamben, see Vecchi, "Atlas intersticial do tempo do fim," particularly 169–71.

33. Wisnik, *Veneno remédio*, 240.
34. Ibid., 408.
35. See Nobre, "Depois da 'formação.'"
36. Zambrano, *Islas*, 4.

Works Cited

Books, Articles, Digital Sources

Abelard, Peter. Incipiunt Glossae Secundum Magistrum Petrum Abaelardum Super Porphyrium. http://www.documentacatholicaomnia.eu.
———. "On Universals." In *Readings in Medieval Philosophy*, edited by Andrew B. Schoedinger, 529–38. Oxford: Oxford University Press, 1996.
Adorno, Theodor. "The Essay as Form." Translated by Bob Hullot-Kentor and Frederic Will. *New German Critique*, no. 32 (Spring–Summer, 1984): 151–71.
Agamben, Giorgio. *Stanzas: Word and Phantasm in Western Culture*, translated by Ronald L. Martinez. Minneapolis and London: University of Minnesota Press, 1993.
Aguiar, Flávio. "A moldura e o espelho." In *Pelas margens: Outros caminhos da história e da literatura*, edited by Edgar Salvadori De Decca and Ria Lemaire, 67–84. Campinas and Porto Alegre, Brazil: Editora da Unicamp, Editora da Universidade-UFRGS, 2000.
Alcides, Sérgio. "O lugar não-comum e a república das letras." *Revista do Arquivo Público Mineiro* 44 (2008): 109–21.
Alencastro, Luiz Felipe de. "Introdução: Modelos de história e da historiografia imperial." In *História da vida privada no Brasil: Império*. São Paulo: Companhia das Letras, 1997.
Alighieri, Dante. *The Inferno of Dante*. Translated by Robert Pinsky. New York: Farrar, Straus and Giroux, 1994.
Andrade, Mário de. *Macunaíma: O herói sem nenhum caráter*. Edited by Telê Porto Ancona Lopez. Madrid: ALLCA XX, 1996.
Andrade, Olímpio de Souza. *Joaquim Nabuco e o Brasil na América*. São Paulo: Companhia Editora Nacional, 1978.
Andrade, Oswald de. *A utopia antropofágica*. São Paulo: Globo/Secretaria de Estado da Cultura, 1990.

———. "Manifesto of Pau-Brasil Poetry." Translated by Stella M. de Sá Rego. *Latin American Literary Review* 14, no. 27 (January–June 1986): 184–87.

———. *Pau-brasil*. São Paulo: Globo, 2003.

Antelo, Raúl. "Rizomas del Brasil." *The Colorado Review of Hispanic Studies* 5 (2007): 211–25.

Antunes, António Lobo. *The Return of the Caravels*. Translated by Gregory Rabassa. New York: Grove Press, 2002.

Aquinas, Thomas, Saint. *Summa theologiae*. Edited by Petri Caramello. 5 vols. Turin, Italy: Marietti, 1952–1956.

Arantes, Paulo Eduardo. *Sentimento da dialética na experiência intelectual brasileira: Dialética e dualidade segundo Antonio Candido e Roberto Schwarz*. Rio de Janeiro: Paz e Terra, 1992.

Araújo, Ricardo Benzaquen de. *Guerra e paz:* Casa-grande & senzala *e a obra de Gilberto Freyre nos anos 30*. Rio de Janeiro: Editora 34, 1994.

Arocena, Felipe. "Ariel, Caliban e Próspero: Notas sobre a cultura latino-americana." *Presença*, no. 15 (1990): 92–109.

Arroyo, Jossianna. *Travestismos culturales: Literatura y etnografía en Cuba y Brasil*. Pittsburgh: University of Pittsburgh Press/Instituto Internacional de Literatura Iberoamericana, 2003.

Assis, Arthur. "A teoria da história como hermenêutica da historiografia: Uma interpretação de *Do Império à República*, de Sérgio Buarque de Holanda." *Revista Brasileira de História* 30, no. 59 (2010): 91–120.

Augustine, Saint, Bishop of Hippo. *Against the Academicians and the Teacher*. Translated by Peter King. Indianapolis, IN: Hackett, 1995.

Avelar, Idelber. *The Untimely Present: Postdictatorial Latin American Fiction and the Task of Mourning*. Durham, NC: Duke University Press, 1999.

Avelino Filho, George. "As raízes de *Raízes do Brasil*." *Novos Estudos* 18 (September 1987): 33–41.

———. "Cordialidade e civilidade em *Raízes do Brasil*." *Revista Brasileira de Ciências Sociais* 5, no. 12 (February 1990): 5–14.

Bandeira, Manuel. "Introdução." In *Raízes de Sérgio Buarque de Holanda*, by Sérgio Buarque de Holanda, edited by Francisco de Assis Barbosa, 291–93. Rio de Janeiro: Rocco, 1988.

Baptista, Maria Manuel. "A lusofonia não é um jardim ou da necessidade de 'perder o medo às realidades e aos mosquitos.'" *ellipsis: The Journal of the American Portuguese Studies Association* 4 (2006): 99–129.

Barbosa, Francisco de Assis. "Verdes anos de Sérgio Buarque de Holanda: Ensaio sobre sua formação intelectual até *Raízes do Brasil*." In *Sérgio Buarque de Holanda: Vida e obra*, edited by Arlinda Rocha Nogueira,

Floripes de Moura Pacheco, Marcia Pilnik, and Rosemarie Erika Horch, 27–54. São Paulo: Secretaria de Estado da Cultura/Arquivo do Estado/ Universidade de São Paulo/Instituto de Estudos Brasileiros, 1988.

Barthes, Roland. *Le bruissement de la langue*. Paris: Seuil, 1984.

Bary, Leslie. "Oswald de Andrade's 'Cannibalist Manifesto.'" *Latin American Literary Review* 19, no. 38 (1991): 35–47.

Bastos, Elide Rugai. *As criaturas de Prometeu: Gilberto Freyre e a formação da sociedade brasileira*. São Paulo: Global, 2006.

———. *Gilberto Freyre e o pensamento hispânico: Entre Dom Quixote e Alonso El Bueno*. Bauru, Brazil: EDUSC, 2003.

———. "*Raízes do Brasil*—*Sobrados e mucambos*: Um diálogo." In *Sérgio Buarque de Holanda: Perspectivas*, edited by Pedro Meira Monteiro and João Kennedy Eugênio, 227–44. Rio de Janeiro/Campinas: EdUERJ/ Editora da Unicamp, 2008.

———. "Região e nação: Velhos e novos dilemas." In *Agenda brasileira: Temas de uma sociedade em mudança*, edited by André Botelho and Lilia Moritz Schwarcz, 444–57. São Paulo: Companhia das Letras, 2011.

Bataille, Georges. *L'érotisme*. Paris: Éditions de Minuit, 1957.

Baudelaire, Charles. *Curiosités esthétiques et l'art romantique et autres oeuvres critiques*. Paris: Bordas, 1990.

Baudrillard, Jean. *Oublier Foucault*. Paris: Éditions Galilée, 1977.

Benjamin, Walter. *Illuminations: Essays and Reflections*. Translated by Harry Zohn. New York: Schocken, 1969.

Bertolli Filho, Claudio. "Sérgio Buarque e Cassiano Ricardo: Confrontos sobre a cultura e o Estado brasileiro." In *Leituras cruzadas: Diálogos da história com a literatura*, edited by Sandra Jatahy Pesavento, 237–54. Porto Alegre, Brazil: Editora da Universidade/UFRGS, 2000.

Bhabha, Homi K. *Nation and Narration*. London: Routledge, 1990.

Blaj, Ilana. "Sérgio Buarque de Holanda: Historiador da cultura material." In *Sérgio Buarque de Holanda e o Brasil*, edited by Antonio Candido de Mello e Souza, 29–48. São Paulo: Editora Fundação Perseu Abramo, 1998.

Bolaño, Roberto. *By Night in Chile*. Translated by Christopher Andrews. New York: New Directions, 2003.

Bomeny, Helena. "Saudades do Brasil de Richard Morse." In *O código Morse: Ensaios sobre Richard Morse*, edited by Beatriz H. Domingues and Peter L. Blasenheim, 119–39. Belo Horizonte, Brazil: Editora UFMG, 2010.

Bosi, Alfredo. *Céu, inferno: Ensaios de crítica literária e ideológica*. São Paulo: Ática, 1988.

———. *Colony, Cult, and Culture.* Translated by Robert P. Newcomb. Dartmouth: University of Massachusetts Dartmouth, 2008.
———. *Entre a literatura e a história.* São Paulo: Editora 34, 2013.
———. "Um testemunho do presente." In *Ideologia da cultura brasileira (1933–1974): Pontos de partida para uma revisão histórica*, by Carlos Guilherme Mota, i–xvii. São Paulo: Ática, 1977.
Botelho, André. *O Brasil e os dias: Estado-nação, modernismo e rotina intelectual.* Bauru, Brazil: EDUSC, 2005.
———. "Público e privado no pensamento social brasileiro." In *Cidadania: Um projeto em construção*, edited by André Botelho and Lilia Moritz Schwarcz, 48–59. São Paulo: Companhia das Letras, 2012.
Bottmann, Denise. *A propósito de Capistrano.* Campinas, Brazil: IFCH-Unicamp, 1989.
Brasil Jr, Antonio, and André Botelho. "Próximo distante: Rural e urbano em *Populações meridionais* e *Raízes do Brasil.*" In *Revisão do pensamento conservador: Ideias e política no Brasil*, edited by Gabriela Nunes Ferreira and André Botelho, 233–72. São Paulo: Hucitec, 2010.
Brioso, Jorge. "De la desaparición de los oráculos y de la muerte y resurrección de los dioses: Lo sagrado y lo profano en la obra de Rubén Darío." In *Hacia una historia de las literaturas centroamericanas*, edited by Ricardo Roque Baldovinos and Valeria Grinberg Pla, 85–118. Guatemala City: F&G Editores, 2009.
Caldeira, João Ricardo de Castro. "Sérgio Buarque de Holanda e a criação do Instituto de Estudos Brasileiros da USP." In *Sérgio Buarque de Holanda: Perspectivas*, edited by Pedro Meira Monteiro and João Kennedy Eugênio, 83–101. Rio de Janeiro/Campinas, Brazil: EdUERJ/Editora da Unicamp, 2008.
Calligaris, Contardo. "Do homem cordial ao homem vulgar." In *Cordialidade à brasileira: Mito ou realidade?*, edited by João Cezar de Castro Rocha, 39–53. Rio de Janeiro: Museu da República, 2005.
———. *Hello Brasil! Notas de um psicanalista europeu viajando ao Brasil.* São Paulo: Escuta, 2000.
———. "O verdadeiro petista." *Folha de S.Paulo*, Ilustrada, April 13, 2006.
Camões, Luís de. *The Lusiads.* Translated by William C. Atkinson. New York: Penguin, 1952.
Carvalho, Marcus Vinicius Corrêa. "1936: Tradição, cultura e vida." Master's thesis, IFCH/Unicamp, 1997.
———. "Outros Lados: Sergio Buarque de Holanda, crítica literária, história e política (1920–1940)." PhD diss., IFCH/Unicamp, 2003.

Carvalho, Maria Alice Rezende de. *Quatro vezes cidade*. Rio de Janeiro: 7 Letras, 1994.
Castro, Belén. Introduction to *Ariel*, by José Enrique Rodó, 9–135. Madrid: Cátedra, 2004.
Castro, Conrado Pires de. "Com tradições e contradições: Contribuição ao estudo das raízes modernistas do pensamento de Sergio Buarque de Holanda." Master's thesis, IEL/Unicamp, 2002.
Cervantes, Miguel de. *Don Quijote de la Mancha*. Edited by Francisco Rico. Barcelona: Editorial Crítica, 2001.
Chaves, Ernani. "O Historicismo de Nietzsche segundo Sérgio Buarque de Holanda." In *Sérgio Buarque de Holanda: Perspectivas*, edited by Pedro Meira Monteiro and João Kennedy Eugênio, 397–412. Rio de Janeiro/Campinas, Brazil: EdUERJ/Editora da Unicamp, 2008.
———. "*Raízes do Brasil* e Nietzsche." *Cult* (August 2000): 52–55.
Cicalo, André. *Urban Encounters: Affirmative Action and Black Identities in Brazil*. New York: Palgrave, 2012.
Coelho, João Marcos. "Entrevista: Sérgio Buarque de Holanda. A democracia é difícil: As observações e as conclusões de um especialista com base no exame da história." *Veja*, January 28, 1976.
Cohen, Thomas, and Dain Borges, eds. "Culture and Ideology in the Americas: Essays in Honor of Richard M. Morse." Special issue, *Luso-Brazilian Review* 32, no. 2 (1995).
Cohn, Gabriel. *Crítica e resignação: Fundamentos da sociologia de Max Weber*. São Paulo: T.A. Queiroz, 1979.
———. "O pensador do desterro." *Folha de S.Paulo*, mais!, June 23, 2002, 10–11.
Coli, Jorge. "Primeira missa e invenção da descoberta." In *A descoberta do homem e do mundo*, edited by Adauto Novaes, 107–21. São Paulo: Companhia das Letras, 1998.
Costa, Sérgio. "Nachtwort." In *Die Wurzeln Brasiliens*, by Sérgio Buarque de Holanda, 235–69. Berlin: Suhrkamp, 2013.
Couto, José Geraldo. "Sonho e realidade se confundem na narrativa." *Folha de S.Paulo*, December 2, 1995.
Couto, Rui Ribeiro. "El hombre cordial, producto americano." In *Raízes do Brasil*, by Sérgio Buarque de Holanda, edited by Ricardo Benzaquen de Araújo and Lilia Moritz Schwarcz, 397–98. São Paulo: Companhia das Letras, 2006.
Cunha, Euclides da. *Rebellion in the Backlands*. Translated by Samuel Putnam. Chicago: University of Chicago Press, 1944.

Cunha Júnior, Melquíades. "Chico Buarque fala sobre seu pai." *Folha da Manhã*, July 5, 1992.
DaMatta, Roberto. *Carnivals, Rogues, and Heroes: An Interpretation of the Brazilian Dilemma*. Notre Dame, IN: University of Notre Dame Press, 1991.
D'Andrea, Moema Selma. *A tradição re(des)coberta: Gilberto Freyre e a literatura regionalista*. Campinas, Brazil: Editora da Unicamp, 1992.
Dantas, Luiz. "Prefácio." In *A queda do aventureiro: Aventura, cordialidade e os novos tempos em Raízes do Brasil*, by Pedro Meira Monteiro, 15–20. Campinas, Brazil: Editora da Unicamp, 1999.
Darío, Rubén. *Los raros*. Buenos Aires: Espasa-Calpe, 1952.
———. *Selected Writings*. Translated by Andrew Hurley. New York: Penguin, 2005.
De Decca, Edgar Salvadori. "Decifra-me ou te devoro: As metáforas em *Raízes do Brasil*." In *Sérgio Buarque de Holanda: Perspectivas*, edited by Pedro Meira Monteiro and João Kennedy Eugênio, 209–26. Rio de Janeiro/Campinas: EdUERJ/Editora da Unicamp, 2008.
Derrida, Jacques. *Dissemination*. Translated by Barbara Johnson. Chicago: University of Chicago Press, 1981.
Descartes, René. *Meditations on First Philosophy*. Translated by John Veitch, edited by David B. Manley and Charles S. Taylor. http://www.wright.edu
Dias, Maria Odila Leite da Silva. "Estilo e método na obra de Sérgio Buarque de Holanda." In *Sérgio Buarque de Holanda: Vida e obra*, edited by Arlinda Rocha Nogueira, Floripes de Moura Pacheco, Marcia Pilnik, and Rosemarie Erika Horch, 71–79. São Paulo: Secretaria de Estado da Cultura/Arquivo do Estado/Universidade de São Paulo/Instituto de Estudos Brasileiros, 1988.
———. "Negação das negações." In *Sérgio Buarque de Holanda: Perspectivas*, edited by Pedro Meira Monteiro and João Kennedy Eugênio, 317–47. Rio de Janeiro/Campinas, Brazil: EdUERJ/Editora da Unicamp, 2008.
———. "Sérgio Buarque de Holanda, historiador." In *Sérgio Buarque de Holanda*, 5–64. Coleção Grandes Cientistas Sociais [Great Social Scientists Collection], no. 51. São Paulo: Ática, 1985.
Díaz-Quiñones, Arcadio. *Sobre los principios: Los intelectuales caribeños y la tradición*. Bernal, Brazil: Universidad Nacional de Quilmes, 2006.
Dieleke, Edgardo. "Genealogies and Inquiries into Laziness from Macunaíma." *ellipsis: The Journal of the American Portuguese Studies Association* 5 (2007): 9–24.
Dimas, Antonio. "Um manifesto guloso." In *Gilberto Freyre em quatro tempos*, edited by Ethel Volfzon Kosminsky, Claude Lépine, and Fernanda

Arêas Peixoto, 327–46. São Paulo/Bauru, Brazil: Editora Unesp/ EDUSC, 2003.

Diniz, Dilma Castelo Branco. "O conceito de América Latina: Uma perspectiva francesa." *Anais do XI Encontro Regional da ABRALIC.* São Paulo: Abralic, 2007.

Domingues, Beatriz H., and Peter L. Blasenheim, eds. *O código Morse: Ensaios sobre Richard Morse.* Belo Horizonte, Brazil: Editora UFMG, 2010.

Draper, Susana. "Entre política y crítica cultural: Rodó y la microsociología de Proteo." *Latin American Literary Review* 34, no. 67 (2006): 50–74.

Dreyfus, Hubert L., and Paul Rabinow. *Michel Foucault: Beyond Structuralism and Hermeneutics.* Chicago: University of Chicago Press, 1982.

Dunn, Christopher. *Brutality Garden: Tropicália and the Emergence of a Brazilian Counterculture.* Chapel Hill: University of North Carolina Press, 2001.

Eco, Umberto. "Interpretation and History." In *Interpretation and Overinterpretation,* edited by Stefan Collini, 23–43. Cambridge: Cambridge University Press, 1992.

———. *The Name of the Rose.* Translated by William Weaver. San Diego: Harvest Brace, 1994.

Esteves, Paulo Luiz Moreaux Lavigne. "Cordialidade e familismo amoral: Os dilemas da modernização." *Revista Brasileira de Ciências Sociais* 13, no. 36 (February 1998), http://www.scielo.br/scielo.php?script=sci _arttext&pid=S0102-69091998000100006.

Eugênio, João Kennedy. *Ritmo espontâneo: Organicismo em* Raízes do Brasil *de Sérgio Buarque de Holanda.* Teresina, Brazil: EDUFPI, 2011.

———. "Um horizonte de autenticidade. Sérgio Buarque de Holanda: Monarquista, modernista, romântico (1920–1935)." In *Sérgio Buarque de Holanda: Perspectivas,* edited Pedro Meira Monteiro and João Kennedy Eugênio, 425–59. Rio de Janeiro/Campinas, Brazil: EdUERJ/ Editora da Unicamp, 2008.

Eulalio, Alexandre. *A aventura brasileira de Blaise Cendrars.* Edited by Carlos Augusto Calil. São Paulo: Edusp, 2001.

———. "Antes de tudo, escritor." In *Raízes do Brasil,* by Sérgio Buarque de Holanda, edited by Ricardo Benzaquen de Araújo and Lilia Moritz Schwarcz, 253–68. São Paulo: Companhia das Letras, 2006.

Faoro, Raymundo. "A aventura liberal numa ordem patrimonialista." *Revista USP,* no. 17 (March–May 1993): 14–29.

———. "A questão nacional: A modernização." *Estudos Avançados* 6, no. 14 (1992): 7–22.

Feldman, Luiz. "Um clássico por amadurecimento: *Raízes do Brasil.*" *Revista Brasileira de Ciências Sociais* 28, no. 82 (2013): 119–254.
Fernández Retamar, Roberto. *Todo Caliban.* Buenos Aires: CLACSO, 2004.
Finazzi-Agrò, Ettore. "Caminhando entre fronteiras: A lógica 'trivial' em Sérgio Buarque de Holanda." In *Sérgio Buarque de Holanda: Perspectivas,* edited by Pedro Meira Monteiro and João Kennedy Eugênio, 413–23. Rio de Janeiro/Campinas, Brazil: EdUERJ/Editora da Unicamp, 2008.

———. *Um lugar do tamanho do mundo: Tempos e espaços da ficção em João Guimarães Rosa.* Belo Horizonte, Brazil: Editora UFMG, 2001.
Firbas, Paul, and Pedro Meira Monteiro, eds. *Andrés Di Tella: Cine documental y archivo personal: Conversación en Princeton.* Buenos Aires: Siglo XXI Editora Iberoamericana, 2006.
Fonseca, Edson Nery da. "Arquitetura e paisagismo." *Diário de Pernambuco,* April 17, 2007.
Forbes, Jorge. "O homem cordial e a psicanálise." In *Sérgio Buarque de Holanda: Perspectivas,* edited by Pedro Meira Monteiro and João Kennedy Eugênio, 277–82. Rio de Janeiro/Campinas, Brazil: EdUERJ/Editora da Unicamp, 2008.
Foucault, Michel. *Dits et Écrits,* vol. 1, *1954–1975.* Paris: Gallimard, 2001.

———. "Nietzsche, Freud, Marx." Translated by Jon Anderson and Gary Hentzi. In *Aesthetics, Method, and Epistemology,* edited by James D. Faubion, 269–78. New York: The New Press, 1998.
Franco, Maria Sylvia Carvalho. "*Visão do Paraíso*: Romantismo e História." In *Sérgio Buarque de Holanda: Perspectivas,* edited by Pedro Meira Monteiro and João Kennedy Eugênio, 535–46. Rio de Janeiro/Campinas, Brazil: EdUERJ/Editora da Unicamp, 2008.
Françozo, Mariana de Campos. "Um outro olhar: A etnologia alemã na obra de Sérgio Buarque de Holanda." Master's thesis, IFCH-Unicamp, 2004.

———. "Os outros alemães de Sérgio: Etnografia e povos indígenas em *Caminhos e fronteiras.*" *Revista Brasileira de Ciências Sociais* 22, no. 63 (2007): 137–74.
Freud, Sigmund. *General Pyschological Theory: Papers on Metapsychology.* Translated by Philip Rieff. New York: Simon & Schuster, 1991.
Freyre, Gilberto. "Camerado Whitman." Translated by Benjamin M. Woodbridge Jr. In *Walt Whitman Abroad: Critical Essays from Germany, France, Scandinavia, Russia, Italy, Spain and Latin America, Israel, Japan, and India,* edited by Gay Wilson Allen, 223–24. Syracuse, NY: Syracuse University Press, 1955.

———. "Documentos brasileiros." In *Raizes do Brasil*, by Sérgio Buarque de Holanda, v–ix. Rio de Janeiro: José Olympio, 1936.

———. *The Masters and the Slaves: A Study in the Development of Brazilian Civilization*. Translated by Harriet de Onis. New York: Knopf, 1956.

———. *Seis conferências em busca de um leitor*. Rio de Janeiro: José Olympio, 1965.

———. "Sergio, mestre dos mestres." *Revista do Brasil* 6 (1987): 117.

———. *Sobrados e mucambos: Decadência do patriarcado rural e desenvolvimento do urbano*. São Paulo: Global, 2003.

Galvão, Walnice Nogueira. *Mitológica rosiana*. São Paulo: Ática, 1978.

———. "Presença da literatura na obra de Sérgio Buarque de Holanda." In *Sérgio Buarque de Holanda: Perspectivas*, edited by Pedro Meira Monteiro and João Kennedy Eugênio, 117–34. Rio de Janeiro/Campinas, Brazil: EdUERJ/Editora da Unicamp, 2008.

García Márquez, Gabriel. *Cien años de soledad*. Buenos Aires: Editorial Sudamericana, 1967.

Garramuño, Florencia. *Primitive Modernities: Tango, Samba, and Nation*. Translated by Anna Kazumi Stahl. Stanford, CA: Stanford University Press, 2011.

Gaspari, Elio. "Uma cabeça que bate contra a maré: Wanderley Guilherme dos Santos, elitista e marginal, vencedor de causas perdidas." *Veja*, May 18, 1994, 40–43.

Geertz, Clifford. *The Interpretation of Cultures*. New York: Basic Books, 1973.

Gelado, Viviana. *Vanguarda e cultura popular nos anos 20 na América Latina*. Rio de Janeiro/São Carlos, Brazil: 7 Letras/EdUFSCar, 2006.

Glissant, Édouard. *Introduction à une Poétique du Divers*. Paris: Gallimard, 1996.

Goldfeder, André, and Leopoldo Waizbort. "Sobre os 'tipos' em *Raízes do Brasil*": *Revista do Instituto de Estudos Brasileiros* 48 (March 2009): 13–35.

Goldman, Harvey. *Politics, Death and the Devil: Self and Power in Max Weber and Thomas Mann*. Berkeley: University of California Press, 1992.

Goldmann, Lucien. *Le Dieu caché: Étude sur la vision tragique dans les* Pensées *de Pascal et dans le théatre de Racine*. Paris: Gallimard, 1975.

Goldsmith, Oliver. *The Complete Poetical Works of Oliver Goldsmith*. Edited with an introduction and notes by Austin Dobson. Project Gutenberg. Reprint of *Selected Poems*, Oxford: Clarendon Press, 1887.

Gombrich, E.H. *The Story of Art*. London: Phaidon, 1950.

Gomes, Angela de Castro. "Dialética da tradição." *Revista Brasileira de Ciências Sociais* 5, no. 12 (1988): 15–27.

Graham, Richard. "Dr. Sérgio: A coerência do homem e do historiador." In *Sérgio Buarque de Holanda: Perspectivas*, edited by Pedro Meira Monteiro and João Kennedy Eugênio, 103–16. Rio de Janeiro/Campinas, Brazil: EdUERJ/Editora da Unicamp, 2008.

———. "An Interview with Sérgio Buarque de Holanda." *The Hispanic American Historical Review* 62, no. 1 (February 1982): 3–17.

———. "O teatro das eleições no Brasil imperial." In *Atualidade de Sérgio Buarque de Holanda*, edited by Stelio Marras, 133–50. São Paulo: Edusp/Instituto de Estudos Brasileiros, 2012.

Green, James N. *We Cannot Remain Silent: Opposition to the Brazilian Military Dictatorship in the United States*. Durham, NC: Duke University Press, 2010.

Guimarães, Antônio Sérgio. *Classes, raças e democracia*. São Paulo: Editora 34, 2012.

———. "Racial Democracy." In *Imagining Brazil*, edited by Jessé Souza and Valter Sindler, 119–40. Lanham, MD: Lexington, 2005.

Hegel, Georg W.F. *Phenomenology of Spirit*. Translated by A.V. Miller. Oxford: Clarendon Press, 1977.

Henríquez Ureña, Pedro. *Obra crítica*. Edited by Emma Susana Speratti Piñero. Mexico City: Fondo de Cultura Económica, 2001.

Hertzman, Marc. *Making Samba: A New History of Race and Music in Brazil*. Durham, NC: Duke University Press, 2013.

Holanda, Francisco Buarque de. *Benjamin*. Translated by Clifford E. Landers. London: Bloomsbury, 1997.

———. *Budapest: A Novel*. Translated by Alison Entrekin. New York: Grove Press, 2004.

———. *O irmão alemão*. São Paulo: Companhia das Letras, 2014.

———. *Spilt Milk*. Translated by Alison Entrekin. New York: Grove Press, 2012.

Holanda, Sérgio Buarque de. "A Chiméra do Monroismo." *A Cigarra*, July 1, 1920.

———. *Caminhos e fronteiras*. São Paulo: Companhia das Letras, 1994.

———. *Capítulos de história do Império*. Edited by Fernando Novais. São Paulo: Companhia das Letras, 2010.

———. *Capítulos de literatura colonial*. Edited and with introduction by Antonio Candido. São Paulo: Brasiliense, 1991.

———. *Cobra de vidro*. São Paulo: Perspectiva, 1978.

———. *Do Império à República*. Tome 2, vol. 5, of História Geral da Civilização Brasileira. São Paulo: Difel, 1985.

———. *Monções*. São Paulo: Brasiliense, 1992.

———. "O atual e o inatual na obra de Leopold von Ranke." *Revista de História* 50, no. 100 (October–December 1974): 431–82.

———. *O espírito e a letra: Estudos de crítica literária.* Edited by Antonio Arnoni Prado. 2 vols. São Paulo: Companhia das Letras, 1996.

———. *O espírito e a letra: Trechos lidos por Chico Buarque em 22 de novembro de 1996, no auditório do MASP.* São Paulo: Companhia das Letras, 1996.

———. "O pensamento histórico no Brasil nos últimos 50 anos." In *Sérgio Buarque de Holanda: Perspectivas*, edited by Pedro Meira Monteiro and João Kennedy Eugênio, 601–15. Rio de Janeiro/Campinas, Brazil: EdUERJ/Editora da Unicamp, 2008.

———. *Para uma nova história: Textos de Sérgio Buarque de Holanda.* Edited by Marcos Costa. São Paulo: Editora Fundação Perseu Abramo, 2004.

———. *Racines du Brésil.* Translated by Marlyse Meyer. Paris: Gallimard, Unesco, 1998.

———. *Raízes de Sérgio Buarque de Holanda.* Edited by Francisco de Assis Barbosa. Rio de Janeiro: Rocco, 1988.

———. *Raízes do Brasil.* Edited by Ricardo Benzaquen de Araújo and Lilia Moritz Schwarcz. São Paulo: Companhia das Letras, 2006.

———. *Raizes do Brasil.* Rio de Janeiro: José Olympio, 1936.

———. *Roots of Brazil.* Translated by G. Harvey Summ. Notre Dame, IN: University of Notre Dame Press, 2012.

———. *Sérgio Buarque de Holanda: Escritos coligidos.* Edited by Marcos Costa. 2 vols. São Paulo: Editora Unesp/Editora Fundação Perseu Abramo, 2011.

———. *Tentativas de mitologia.* São Paulo: Perspectiva, 1979.

———. *Visão do paraíso: Os motivos edênicos no descobrimento e colonização do Brasil.* São Paulo: Brasiliense, 1992.

Homem, Wagner. *Histórias de canções: Chico Buarque.* São Paulo: Leya, 2009.

Ianni, Octavio. "A crise dos paradigmas na sociologia: Problemas de explicação." *Revista Brasileira de Ciências Sociais* 5, no. 13 (1990): 90–100.

Jáuregui, Carlos. "Calibán: Ícono del 98. A propósito de un artículo de Rubén Darío." *Revista Iberoamericana* 64, nos. 184–85 (1998): 441–49.

Joyce, James. *Ulysses.* New York: The Modern Library, 1992.

Lacan, Jacques. *L'Angoisse: Le Séminaire livre X.* Edited by Jacques-Alain Miller. Paris: Éditions du Seuil, 2004.

Lafetá, João Luiz. *1930: A crítica e o modernismo.* São Paulo: Livraria Duas Cidades/Editora 34, 2000.

Lamounier, Bolívar. "Sérgio Buarque e os 'grilhões do passado.'" In *Raízes do Brasil*, by Sérgio Buarque de Holanda, edited by Ricardo Benzaquen de Araújo and Lilia Moritz Schwarcz, 275–93. São Paulo: Companhia das Letras, 2006.

Leenhardt, Jacques. "Frente ao presente do passado: As raízes portuguesas do Brasil." In *Um historiador nas fronteiras: O Brasil de Sérgio Buarque de Holanda*, edited by Sandra Jatahy Pesavento, 81–105. Belo Horizonte, Brazil: Editora UFMG, 2005.

Leite, Dante Moreira. *O caráter nacional brasileiro: História de uma ideologia*. São Paulo: Pioneira, 1983.

Leonel, Maria Célia de Moraes. *Estética (revista trimensal) e modernismo*. São Paulo: Hucitec, 1984.

Lezama Lima, José. *La expresión americana*. Edited by Irlemar Chiampi. Mexico City: Fondo de Cultura Económica, 1993.

Lourenço, Eduardo. *A Nau de Ícaro e Imagem e miragem da lusofonia*. São Paulo: Companhia das Letras, 2001.

Lund, Joshua, and Malcolm McNee, eds. *Gilberto Freyre e os estudos latino-americanos*. Pittsburgh: University of Pittsburgh/Instituto Internacional de Literatura Iberoamericana, 2006.

Machado, Brasil Pinheiro. "*Raízes do Brasil*: Uma releitura." In *Sérgio Buarque de Holanda: Perspectivas*, edited by Pedro Meira Monteiro and João Kennedy Eugênio, 155–80. Rio de Janeiro/Campinas, Brazil: EdUERJ/Editora da Unicamp, 2008.

Machado de Assis, Joaquim Maria. *Epitaph of a Small Winner*. Translated by William Grossman. New York: Farrar, Straus and Giroux, 2008.

———. *Obras completas*. 3 vols. Rio de Janeiro: Nova Aguilar, 1997.

Mainwaring, Scott, and Aníbal Pérez-Liñán. *Democracies and Dictatorships in Latin America: Emergence, Survival, and Fall*. New York: Cambridge University Press, 2013.

Martí, José. *En los Estados Unidos: Periodismo de 1881 a 1892*. Edited by Roberto Fernández Retamar and Pedro Pablo Rodríguez. Madrid: ALLCA XX, 2003.

Mattos, Hebe. "A vida política." In *A abertura para o mundo: 1889–1930*, edited by Lilia Moritz Schwarcz, 85–131. Rio de Janeiro: Objetiva, 2012.

Meira Monteiro, Pedro. "A cordialidade evanescente em *Raízes do Brasil*." *Ethnos Brasil*, no. 2 (September 2002): 97–104.

———. *A queda do aventureiro: Aventura, cordialidade e os novos tempos em Raízes do Brasil*. Campinas, Brazil: Editora da Unicamp, 1999.

———. "Coisas sutis *ergo* profundas: O diálogo entre Mário de Andrade e Sérgio Buarque de Holanda." In *Mário de Andrade e Sérgio Buarque de Holanda: Correspondência*, edited by Pedro Meira Monteiro,

169–360. São Paulo: Companhia das Letras/Edusp/Instituto de Estudos Brasileiros, 2012.

———. "Desfazendo gênero: Sérgio Buarque de Holanda, entre poesia e história." *Rassegna Iberistica*, nos. 99–100 (October 2013): 157–65.

———. "The Dialetic of Resistance: Alfredo Bosi, Literary Critic." In *Colony, Cult, and Culture*, by Alfredo Bosi, translated by Robert P. Newcomb, 7–17. Dartmouth: University of Massachusetts Dartmouth, 2008.

———. "The Impertinence of Belonging." *Review: Literature and Arts of the Americas* 41, issue 77, no. 2 (2008): 283–93.

———. "Literatura e resistência: Alfredo Bosi e a crítica (fora do Brasil)." *Luso-Brazilian Review* 50, no. 2 (2013): 64–75.

———. "O modernismo entra em campo: O caso Wisnik." *Tempo Social: Revista de Sociologia da USP* 22, no. 2 (2010): 187–216.

———. "O pai, lá em cima." Blog da Companhia.

———. "O que é isso, Caetano? Revolução, culpa e desejo." *Serrote: Uma revista de ensaios, artes visuais, ideias e literatura*, no. 12 (2012): 7–19.

———. "The Other Roots: Sérgio Buarque de Holanda and the Portuguese." *ellipsis: The Journal of the American Portuguese Studies Association* 6 (2008): 73–81.

———. "Richard Morse: A paixão latino-americana." In *Um enigma chamado Brasil: 29 intérpretes e um país*, edited by André Botelho and Lilia Moritz Schwarcz, 352–63. São Paulo: Companhia das Letras, 2009.

———. "Why Read *Roots of Brazil* Today?" In *Roots of Brazil*, by Sérgio Buarque de Holanda, xi–xix. Notre Dame, IN: University of Notre Dame Press, 2012.

Mello, Evaldo Cabral de. "*Raízes do Brasil* e depois." In *Raízes do Brasil*, by Sérgio Buarque de Holanda, edited by Ricardo Benzaquen de Araújo and Lilia Moritz Schwarcz, 269–74. São Paulo: Companhia das Letras, 2006.

Melo, Alfredo Cesar. "Lusitanian Roots and Iberian Heritage in *Raízes do Brasil*." *Portuguese Studies* 27, no. 1 (2011): 78–95.

———. "Os mundos misturados de Gilberto Freyre." *Luso-Brazilian Review* 43, no. 2 (2006): 27–44.

Merquior, José Guilherme. "O outro Ocidente." *Presença*, no. 15 (1990): 67–91.

Miceli, Sergio. *Intelectuais à brasileira*. São Paulo: Companhia das Letras, 2001.

Monasterio, José Ortiz. "*Raízes do Brasil* y *El laberinto de la soledad*: Una comparación." In *Sérgio Buarque de Holanda: Perspectivas*, edited by

Pedro Meira Monteiro and João Kennedy Eugênio, 283–316. Rio de Janeiro/Campinas, Brazil: EdUERJ/Editora da Unicamp, 2008.

Montaigne, Michel de. *Essays.* Translated by J.M. Cohen. New York: Penguin, 1958.

Moraes, Ricardo Gaiotto de. "Críticas cruzadas: Mário de Andrade e Sérgio Buarque de Holanda." PhD diss., IEL/Unicamp, 2014.

More, Thomas. *De optimo statu reipublicae deque nova insula Utopia.* Basel, 1518. Facsimile, Bibliotheca Augustana.

———. *Utopia.* Edited by Henry Morley. Project Gutenberg.

Moreira, Luiza Franco. *Meninos, poetas e heróis: Aspectos de Cassiano Ricardo do modernismo ao Estado Novo.* São Paulo: Edusp, 2001.

Moreira, Paulo. *Literary and Cultural Relations between Brazil and Mexico: Deep Undercurrents.* New York: Palgrave, 2013.

Moreira, Roberto S.C. "Weber e o mal-estar colonial." In *O malandro e o protestante: A tese weberiana e a singularidade cultural brasileira,* edited by Jessé Souza, 195–210. Brasília: Editora Universidade de Brasília, 1999.

Morse, Richard. "Balancing Myth and Evidence: Freyre and Sérgio Buarque." *Luso-Brazilian Review* 32, no. 2 (1995): 47–57.

———. "A miopia de Schwartzman." *Novos Estudos Cebrap,* no. 24 (July 1989): 166–78.

———. *New World Soundings: Culture and Ideology in the Americas.* Baltimore: The Johns Hopkins University Press, 1989.

———. "Prospero's Mirror: A Study in New World Dialectic." Unpublished manuscript, 1982.

———. "Sérgio Buarque de Holanda (1902–1982)." *Hispanic American Historical Review* 63, no. 1 (1983): 147–50.

———, ed. *The Bandeirantes: The Historical Role of the Brazilian Pathfinders.* New York: Alfred A. Knopf, 1965.

Mota, Carlos Guilherme. "A perspectiva do historiador." *Opinião,* June 8, 1976.

———. "Fazendeiros do ar." *O Estado de S.Paulo,* Suplemento Literário, September 2, 1975.

———. *Idéia de revolução no Brasil (1789–1801): Estudo das formas de pensamento.* São Paulo: Cortez, 1989.

———. *Ideologia da cultura brasileira (1933–1974): Pontos de partida para uma revisão histórica.* São Paulo: Ática, 1977.

———. "Uma visão ideológica." *O Escritor* 5 (August–September 1980).

Mota, Giselda. "Historiografia. Bibliografia. Documentos." In *1822: Dimensões,* edited by Carlos Guilherme Mota, 377–464. São Paulo: Perspectiva, 1972.

Newcomb, Robert P. *"Nossa" and "Nuestra América": Inter-American Dialogues*. West Lafayette, IN: Purdue University Press, 2012.
Nicodemo, Thiago Lima. "Sérgio Buarque de Holanda e a dinâmica das instituições culturais no Brasil 1930–1960." In *Atualidade de Sérgio Buarque de Holanda*, edited by Stelio Marras, 109–32. São Paulo: Edusp/Instituto de Estudos Brasileiros, 2012.
———. *Urdidura do vivido: Visão do Paraíso e a obra de Sérgio Buarque de Holanda nos anos 1950*. São Paulo: Edusp, 2008.
Nobre, Marcos. "Depois da 'formação.'" *piauí*, November 2012, 74–77.
Nogueira, Arlinda Rocha, Floripes de Moura Pacheco, Marcia Pilnik, and Rosemarie Erika Horch, eds. *Sérgio Buarque de Holanda: Vida e obra*. São Paulo: Secretaria de Estado da Cultura/Arquivo do Estado/Universidade de São Paulo/Instituto de Estudos Brasileiros, 1988.
Novais, Fernando. "Prefácio." In *Caminhos e fronteiras*, by Sérgio Buarque de Holanda, 7–8. São Paulo: Companhia das Letras, 1994.
Oliveira, Lucia Lippi de. "Anotações sobre um debate." *Presença*, no. 16 (April 1991): 26–41.
Paes, José Paulo. "O olhar hiper-realista." *Folha de S.Paulo, mais!*, December 31, 1995.
Pallares-Burke, Maria Lúcia. *Gilberto Freyre: Um vitoriano nos trópicos*. São Paulo: Editora UNESP, 2005.
Palti, Elías José. "The Problem of 'Misplaced Ideas' Revisited: Beyond the 'History of Ideas' in Latin America." *Journal of the History of Ideas* 67, no. 1 (January 2006): 149–79.
Panizza, Francisco, ed. *Populism and the Mirror of Democracy*. London: Verso, 2005.
Pareto, Vilfredo. *The Mind and Society*. Edited by Arthur Livingston. Translated by Andrew Bongiorno and Arthur Livingston. London: Jonathan Cape, 1935.
Park, Robert Ezra, and Ernest W Burgess. *Introduction to the Science of Sociology*. Chicago: University of Chicago Press, 1924.
Pascal, Blaise. "Pensées." Edited by Philippe Sellier. *Moralistes du XVIIe siècle*. Paris: Robert Laffont, 1992.
Pécora, Alcir. "A importância de ser prudente." In *Sérgio Buarque de Holanda: Perspectivas*, edited by Pedro Meira Monteiro and João Kennedy Eugênio, 23–27. Rio de Janeiro/Campinas, Brazil: EdUERJ/Editora da Unicamp, 2008.
Pereira, Lawrence Flores. "Cordialidade, ressentimento e lírica." In *Cordialidade à brasileira: Mito ou realidade?*, edited by João Cezar de Castro Rocha, 87–102. Rio de Janeiro: Museu da República, 2005.

Pesavento, Sandra Jatahy. "Cartografias do tempo, palimpsestos na escrita da história." In *Um historiador nas fronteiras: O Brasil de Sérgio Buarque de Holanda*, 17–79. Belo Horizonte, Brazil: Editora UFMG, 2005.
Pessoa, Fernando. *Message*. Translated by Jonathan Griffin. London: Menard, 1992.
Pierucci, Antônio Flávio. *O desencantamento do mundo: Todos os passos do conceito em Max Weber*. São Paulo: Editora 34, 2003.
Piglia, Ricardo. *El último lector*. Barcelona: Anagrama, 2005.
Pinto, Edith Pimentel, ed. *A gramatiquinha de Mário de Andrade: Texto e contexto*. São Paulo: Duas Cidades/Secretaria de Estado da Cultura, 1990.
Piva, Luiz Guilherme. *Ladrilhadores e semeadores: A modernização brasileira no pensamento político de Oliveira Vianna, Sérgio Buarque de Holanda, Azevedo Amaral e Nestor Duarte (1920–1940)*. São Paulo: Editora 34/ Departamento de Ciência Política da USP, 2000.
Prado, Antonio Arnoni. "Introdução." In *O espírito e a letra: Estudos de crítica literária*, by Sérgio Buarque de Holanda, 1:21–32. São Paulo: Companhia das Letras, 1996.
———. "Sérgio e Mário: Um diálogo entre críticos." In *Atualidade de Sérgio Buarque de Holanda*, edited by Stelio Marras, 79–90. São Paulo: Edusp/ Instituto de Estudos Brasileiros, 2012.
———. *Trincheira, palco e letras: crítica, literatura e utopia no Brasil*. São Paulo: Cosac Naify, 2004.
Prado, Paulo. "Poesia pau-brasil." In *Pau-Brasil*, by Oswald de Andrade, 57–60. São Paulo: Globo/Secretaria de Estado da Cultura, 1990.
———. *Retrato do Brasil: Ensaio sobre a tristeza brasileira*. Edited by Carlos Augusto Calil. São Paulo: Companhia das Letras, 1997.
Prado Jr, Caio. *The Colonial Background of Modern Brazil*. Translated by Suzette Macedo. Berkeley: University of California Press, 1967.
Pratt, Mary Louise. "Arts of the Contact Zone." *Profession*, no. 91 (1991): 33–40.
Rama, Ángel. *La ciudad letrada*. Hanover, NH: Ediciones del Norte, 1984.
———. "La riesgosa navegación del escritor exilado." *Nueva Sociedad*, no. 35 (March–April 1978): 5–15.
Ramirez, Paulo Niccoli. *Sérgio Buarque de Holanda e a dialética da cordialidade*. São Paulo: Educ, 2011.
Renan, Ernest. *Caliban, suite de La Tempête*. Paris: Calmann Levy, 1878.
Rego, Rubem Murilo Leão. *Sentimento do Brasil. Caio Prado Junior: Continuidades e mudanças no desenvolvimento da sociedade brasileira*. Campinas, Brazil: Editora da Unicamp, 2000.

Rego, Walquiria Domingues Leão, and Alessandro Pinzani. *Vozes do bolsafamília: Autonomia, dinheiro e cidadania*. São Paulo: Editora Unesp, 2013.
Reyes, Alfonso. *Antología de Alfonso Reyes*. Edited by José Luis Martínez. Mexico City: B. Costa-Amic, 1965.
———. *Capítulos de Literatura Española (Primera serie)*. Mexico City: La Casa de España en México, 1939.
Ribeiro, Maria Aparecida. *A carta de Caminha e seus ecos: Estudo e antologia*. Coimbra, Portugal: Angelus Novus, 2003.
Ricardo, Cassiano. *O homem cordial e outros pequenos estudos brasileiros*. Rio de Janeiro: Instituto Nacional do Livro, 1959.
Ricupero, Bernardo. *Caio Prado Jr. e a nacionalização do marxismo no Brasil*. São Paulo: Editora 34, 2000.
———. "Celso Furtado e o pensamento social brasileiro." *Estudos Avançados* 19, no. 53 (2005): 371–77.
Ridenti, Marcelo. *Em busca do povo brasileiro: Artistas da revolução, do CPC à era da TV*. Rio de Janeiro: Record, 2000.
Rimbaud, Arthur. *Correspondance*. Edited by Jean-Jacques Lefrère. Paris: Fayard, 2007.
Rocha, João Cezar de Castro, ed. *Brazil 2001: A Revisionary History of Brazilian Literature and Culture*. Dartmouth, MA: Tagus Books, 2000.
———. *Crítica literária: Em busca do tempo perdido?* Chapecó, Brazil: Argos, 2011.
———. "'Nenhum Brasil existe': Poesia como história cultural." In *Nenhum Brasil existe: Pequena enciclopédia*, 17–32. Rio de Janeiro: Topbooks Editora/UniverCidade, 2003.
———. *O exílio do homem cordial: Ensaios e revisões*. Rio de Janeiro: Museu da República, 2004.
———. "*Raízes do Brasil*: Biografia de um Livro-Problema." In *Atualidade de Sérgio Buarque de Holanda*, edited by Stelio Marras, 19–37. São Paulo: Edusp/Instituto de Estudos Brasileiros, 2012.
Rodó, José Enrique. *Ariel*. Translated by Margaret Sayes Peden. Austin: University of Texas, 1988.
Romero, Simon. "Richard McGee Morse, 78, Latin America Expert." *New York Times*, April 28, 2001.
Rosa, João Guimarães. *The Third Bank of the River and Other Stories*. Edited and translated by Barbara Shelby. New York: Knopf, 1968.
Rosenfield, Kathrin Holzermayr. "Cordialidades austro-brasileiras." In *Cordialidade à brasileira: Mito ou realidade?*, edited by João Cezar de Castro Rocha, 67–86. Rio de Janeiro: Editora Museu da República, 2005.

Rothwell, Phillip. *A Canon of Empty Fathers: Paternity in Portuguese Narrative*. Lewisburg, PA: Bucknell, 2007.
Said, Edward W. *Orientalism*. New York: Pantheon Books, 1978.
Sallum Jr, Brasilio. "Sobre a noção de democracia em *Raízes do Brasil*." In *Atualidade de Sérgio Buarque de Holanda*, edited by Stelio Marras, 51–61. São Paulo: Edusp/Instituto de Estudos Brasileiros, 2012.
Santí, Enrico Mario. "Esta edición." In *Contrapunteo cubano del tabaco y el azúcar*, by Fernando Ortiz, 105–10. Madrid: Cátedra, 2002.
Santiago, Silviano. *As raízes e o labirinto da América Latina*. Rio de Janeiro: Rocco, 2006.
Santos, Boaventura de Sousa. "Entre Próspero e Caliban: Colonialismo, pós-colonialismo e interidentidade." *Novos Estudos Cebrap*, no. 66 (July 2003): 23–52.
Santos, Laymert Garcia dos. *Tempo de ensaio*. São Paulo: Companhia das Letras, 1989.
Santos Jr, Valdir Donizete dos. *A trama das ideias: Intelectuais, ensaios e construção de identidades na América Latina (1898–1914)*. São Paulo: Intermeios, 2016.
Saramago, José. *The Stone Raft*. Translated by Giovanni Pontiero. New York: Harcourt Brace, 1995.
Saussure, Ferdinand de. *Words Upon Words: The Anagrams of Ferdinand de Asussure*. Edited by Jean Starobinski. Translated by Olivia Emmet. New Haven, CT: Yale University Press, 1979.
Schwarcz, Lilia Moritz. "Sérgio Buarque de Holanda e essa tal de 'cordialidade.'" *IDE: Psicanálise e cultura* 31, no. 46 (2008): 83–89.
———. *The Spectacle of the Races: Scientists, Institutions, and the Race Question in Brazil, 1870–1930*. New York: Hill and Wang, 1999.
Schwartz, Jorge. "Abaixo Tordesilhas!" In *Nenhum Brasil existe: Pequena enciclopédia*, edited by João Cezar de Castro Rocha, 845–61. Rio de Janeiro: Topbooks/ UniverCidade, 2003.
———. *Vanguardas latino-americanas: Polêmicas, manifestos e textos críticos*. São Paulo: Edusp, 2008.
Schwartzman, Simon. "O espelho de Morse." *Novos Estudos Cebrap*, no. 22 (October 1988): 185–92.
———. "O gato de Cortázar." *Novos Estudos Cebrap*, no. 25 (October 1989): 191–203.
Schwarz, Roberto. *Misplaced Ideas: Essays on Brazilian Culture*. Edited by John Gledson. London: Verso, 1992.
———. *Que horas são?* São Paulo: Companhia das Letras, 1987.

Sevcenko, Nicolau. *Orfeu extático na metrópole: São Paulo, sociedade e cultura nos frementes anos 20*. São Paulo: Companhia das Letras, 1992.
Simmel, Georg. *On Individuality and Social Forms*. Translated by Donald Levine. Chicago: University of Chicago Press, 1971.
Sommer, Doris. *Foundational Fictions: The National Romances of Latin America*. Berkeley: University of California Press, 1991.
Sophocles. *Antigone*. Translated by R.C. Jebb. Internet Classics Archive.
Souza, Antonio Candido de Mello e. "Amizade com Sergio." *Revista do Brasil*, no. 6 (1987): 132–33.
———. "As 'Tentativas de Mitologia' de Sérgio Buarque de Holanda." *O Escritor*, no. 6 (October–November 1980): 12.
———. "A visão política de Sérgio Buarque de Holanda." In *Sérgio Buarque de Holanda e o Brasil*, 81–88. São Paulo: Editora Fundação Perseu Abramo, 1998.
———. "Dialectic of Malandroism." In *On Literature and Society*, edited and translated by Howard S. Becker, 79–103. Princeton, NJ: Princeton University Press, 1995.
———. *Formação da literatura brasileira: Momentos decisivos*. Belo Horizonte, Brazil: Itatiaia, 1981.
———. "Introdução." In *Capítulos de literatura colonial*, by Sérgio Buarque de Holanda, 7–23. São Paulo: Brasiliense, 1991.
———. "O portador." In *Obras incompletas*, by Friedrich Nietzsche, edited by Gerard Lebrun, translated by Rubens Rodrigues Torres Filho, 417–24. São Paulo: Abril Cultural, 1974.
———. *Os parceiros do Rio Bonito: Estudo sobre os caipiras paulistas e a transformação dos seus meios de vida*. São Paulo: Livraria Duas Cidades, 1971.
———. "Prefácio." In *Intelectuais à brasileira*, by Sergio Miceli, 71–75. São Paulo: Companhia das Letras, 2001.
———. "Radicalismos." *Estudos Avançados* 4, no. 8 (January–April 1990): 4–18.
———. "Sérgio em Berlim e depois." In *Raízes de Sérgio Buarque de Holanda*, by Sérgio Buarque de Holanda, edited by Francisco de Assis Barbosa, 119–29. Rio de Janeiro: Rocco, 1988.
———. "Sérgio, o radical." In *Sérgio Buarque de Holanda: Vida e obra*, edited by Arlinda Rocha Nogueira, Floripes de Moura Pacheco, Marcia Pilnik, and Rosemarie Erika Horch, 61–65. São Paulo: Secretaria de Estado da Cultura/Arquivo do Estado/Universidade de São Paulo/Instituto de Estudos Brasileiros, 1988.

———. "The Significance of *Roots of Brazil*." In *Roots of Brazil*, by Sérgio Buarque de Holanda, translated by G. Harvey Summ, xxi–xxxv. Notre Dame, IN: University of Notre Dame Press, 2012.
Souza, Jessé. *Os batalhadores brasileiros: Nova classe média ou nova classe trabalhadora?* Belo Horizonte, Brazil: Editora UFMG, 2012.
———, ed. *O malandro e o protestante: A tese weberiana e a singularidade cultural brasileira.* Brasília: Editora Universidade de Brasília, 1999.
Souza, Laura de Mello e. "Corpo e alma do Brasil: Entrevista com Sérgio Buarque de Holanda." *Novos Estudos*, no. 69 (July 2004): 3–14.
Starling, Heloisa Maria Murgel. "O tempo da delicadeza perdida: Chico, Sérgio e as raízes do homem cordial." In *Atualidade de Sérgio Buarque de Holanda*, edited by Stelio Marras, 63–78. São Paulo: Edusp/Instituto de Estudos Brasileiros, 2012.
———. *Uma pátria para todos: Chico Buarque e as raízes do Brasil.* Rio de Janeiro: Língua Geral, 2009.
Subirats, Eduardo. "Writing and Cities." In *Cruelty & Utopia: Cities and Landscapes of Latin America*, edited by Jean-François Lejeune, 85–97. New York: Princeton Architectural Press, 2003.
Süssekind, Flora. "Comentário ao texto 'Nota breve sobre Sérgio crítico,' de Antonio Arnoni Prado." In *3º Colóquio UERJ: Sérgio Buarque de Holanda*, 136–45. Rio de Janeiro: Imago, 1992.
———. *O Brasil não é longe daqui: O narrador, a viagem.* São Paulo: Companhia das Letras, 1990.
Telles, Edward E. *Race in Another America: The Significance of Skin Color in Brazil.* Princeton, NJ: Princeton University Press, 2004.
Tenorio, Mauricio. "Profissão: Latin Americanist. Richard Morse e a historiografia norte-americana da América Latina." *Estudos Históricos* 2, no. 3 (1989): 104–32.
Thiengo, Mariana. "A crítica entre a literatura e a história: O percurso da crítica literária de Sérgio Buarque de Holanda dos verdes anos à profissionalização do ofício." PhD diss., Faculdade de Letras/UFMG, 2011.
Thomas, William I., and Florian Znaniecki. *The Polish Peasant in Europe and America.* New York: Alfred A. Knopf, 1927.
Turra, Cleusa, and Gustavo Venturi. *Racismo cordial: A mais completa análise sobre o preconceito de cor no Brasil.* São Paulo: Ática, 1995.
Valente, Luiz Fernando. *Mundivivências: Leituras comparativas de Guimarães Rosa.* Belo Horizonte, Brazil: Editora UFMG, 2011.
Vangelista, Chiara. "'Sua vocação estaria no caminho': Espaço, território e fronteira." In *Um historiador nas fronteiras: O Brasil de Sérgio Buarque de*

Holanda, edited by Sandra Jatahy Pesavento, 107–42. Belo Horizonte, Brazil: Editora UFMG, 2005.
Vasconcelos, José. *The Cosmic Race: A Bilingual Edition*. Translated by Didier T. Jaén. Baltimore: Johns Hopkins University Press, 1997.
Vecchi, Roberto. "Atlas intersticial do tempo do fim: 'Nossa revolução.'" In *Um historiador nas fronteiras: O Brasil de Sérgio Buarque de Holanda*, edited by Sandra Jatahy Pesavento, 161–93. Belo Horizonte, Brazil: Editora UFMG, 2005.
———. "Contrapontos à brasileira: *Raízes do Brasil* e o jogo das metáforas." In *Sérgio Buarque de Holanda: Perspectivas*, edited by Pedro Meira Monteiro and João Kennedy Eugênio, 363–84. Rio de Janeiro/Campinas, Brazil: EdUERJ/Editora da Unicamp, 2008.
———. "Ratos cordiais e raízes daninhas." In *Leituras cruzadas: Diálogos da história com a literatura*, edited by Sandra Jatahy Pesavento, 77–105. Porto Alegre, Brazil: Editora da Universidade/UFRGS, 2000.
Velho, Otávio. "O espelho de Morse e outros espelhos." *Estudos Históricos* 2, no. 3 (1989): 94–101.
Veloso, Caetano. *Verdade tropical*. São Paulo: Companhia das Letras, 1997.
Veloso, Mariza, and Angélica Madeira. *Leituras brasileiras: Itinerários no pensamento social e na literatura*. São Paulo: Paz e Terra, 1999.
Vianna, Hermano. "Mestiçagem fora de lugar." *Folha de S. Paulo*, June 27, 2004.
———. *The Mystery of Samba: Popular Music and National Identity in Brazil*. Edited and translated by Charles Chasteen. Chapel Hill: University of North Carolina Press, 1999.
Vianna, Luiz Werneck. *A revolução passiva: Iberismo e americanismo no Brasil*. Rio de Janeiro: Revan, 1997.
———. "Weber e a interpretação do Brasil." In *O malandro e o protestante: A tese weberiana e a singularidade cultural brasileira*, edited by Jessé Souza, 173–93. Brasília: Editora Universidade de Brasília, 1999.
Vianna, Luiz Werneck, and Fernando Perlatto. "Iberismo e americanismo." In *Agenda brasileira: Temas de uma sociedade em mudança*, edited by André Botelho and Lilia Moritz Schwarcz, 246–55. São Paulo: Companhia das Letras, 2011.
Vieira, António. *História do futuro*. Edited by Maria Leonor C. Buescu. Lisbon: Imprensa Nacional/Casa da Moeda, 1992.
Waizbort, Leopoldo. *A passagem do três ao um: Crítica literária, sociologia, filologia*. São Paulo: Cosac Naify, 2007.
———. "O mal-entendido da democracia. Sergio Buarque de Hollanda, *Raízes do Brasil*, 1936." *Revista Brasileira de Ciências Sociais* 26, no. 76 (June 2011): 41–62.

Weber, Max. *The Protestant Ethic and the Spirit of Capitalism*. Translated by Stephen Kalberg. Los Angeles: Roxbury Publishing, 2002.
———. *The Vocation Lectures*. Edited by David Owen and Tracy B. Strong. Translated by Rodney Livingstone. Indianapolis, IN: Hackett Publishing Company, 2004.
Wegner, Robert. *A conquista do oeste: A fronteira na obra de Sérgio Buarque de Holanda*. Belo Horizonte, Brazil: Editora UFMG, 2000.
———. "America, Joy of Man's Desiring." *Portuguese Literary & Cultural Studies*, nos. 4–5 (2000): 369–76.
———. "Criação e crítica literária na trajetória modernista de Sérgio Buarque de Holanda (1921–1926)." In *A crítica literária brasileira em perspectiva*, edited by Rogério Cordeiro, Andréa Sirihal Werkema, Claudia Campos Soares, and Sérgio Alcides, 133–56. Cotia, Brazil: Ateliê Editorial, 2013.
———. "Latas de leite em pó e garrafas de uísque: Um modernista na universidade." In *Sérgio Buarque de Holanda: Perspectivas*, edited by Pedro Meira Monteiro and João Kennedy Eugênio, 481–501. Rio de Janeiro/Campinas: EdUERJ/Editora da Unicamp, 2008.
———. "Os EUA e a fronteira na obra de Sérgio Buarque de Holanda." In *O malandro e o protestante: A tese weberiana e a singularidade cultural brasileira*, edited by Jessé Souza, 237–56. Brasília: Editora Universidade de Brasília, 1999.
———. "Um ensaio entre o passado e o futuro." In *Raízes do Brasil*, by Sérgio Buarque de Holanda, edited by Ricardo Benzaquen de Araújo and Lilia Moritz Schwarcz, 335–64. São Paulo: Companhia das Letras, 2006.
Williams, Raymond. *Marxism and Literature*. Oxford: Oxford University Press, 1977.
Wisnik, José Miguel. "The Gay Science." *Journal of Latin American Cultural Studies* 5, no. 2 (1996): 191–202.
———. "The Riddle of Brazilian Soccer: Reflections on the Emancipatory Dimensions of Culture." *Review: Literature and Arts of the Americas*, issue 73, vol. 39, no. 2 (2006): 198–209.
———. *Sem receita: Ensaios e canções*. São Paulo: Publifolha, 2004.
———. *Veneno remédio: O futebol e o Brasil*. São Paulo: Companhia das Letras, 2008.
Wittgenstein, Ludwig. *Philosophical Investigations*. Translated by G.E.M. Anscombe. Oxford: Blackwell, 2001.
Zabus, Chantal. *Tempests after Shakespeare*. New York: Palgrave, 2002.
Zambrano, María. *Islas*. Madrid: Editorial Verbum, 2007.

Archival Sources

Arquivo Central do Sistema de Arquivos (SIARQ) da Unicamp (University of Campinas), Fundo Privado SBH. Folders 5–11 (subseries Ca and Cp). Campinas (São Paulo State), Brazil.

Films

Barreto, Fábio. *Lula, o filho do Brasil* [Lula, Son of Brazil]. Brazil, 2009.
Coutinho, Eduardo. *Peões* [Metalworkers]. Brazil, 2004.
Landes, Alejandro. *Cocalero* [Coca grower]. Argentina, 2007.
Salles, João Moreira. *Entreatos* [Intermissions]. Brazil, 2004.
Santos, Nelson Pereira dos. *Raízes do Brasil: Uma cinebiografia de Sérgio Buarque de Hollanda* [Roots of Brazil: A Cinebiography of Sérgio Buarque de Hollanda]. Brazil, 2004.

Music

Holanda, Francisco Buarque de. *Francisco*. BMG Ariola, 1987.
Veloso, Caetano. *Cê*. Universal, 2006.
———. *Circuladô Vivo*. Polygram, 1992.
———. *Velô*. Polygram, 1984.

Index

Abelard, Peter, 82–84
Abreu, Capistrano de, 23, 60
Adorno, Theodor, 173, 192
affirmative action, xv, 6, 9, 72, 201
Alencastro, Luiz Felipe de, 56
Alighieri, Dante, 92, 238n35
Almeida, Guilherme de, 105
Almeida, Manuel Antônio de, 192
Almeida, Miguel Vale de, 89
Amado, Gilberto, 73
Amaral, Tarsila do, xiii
"America," 2, 6, 7, 10, 11, 12, 24, 30, 89, 103, 118, 139
the "American," 30, 124
Americanism, 9, 56
and Brazil, 3–4, 91, 132
colonial America, 88, 90
Pan-Americanism, 56, 128
Portuguese America, 62, 97
and Sérgio Buarque de Holanda, 29–30, 86, 101–3, 123, 124, 143–44
and specular poetics, 118–20, 123, 134, 133, 134, 136
Andrade, Carlos Drummond de, 81
Andrade, Mário de, xiii, 87, 113, 187, 190, 191
Andrade, Oswald de, xiii, 20, 39, 146, 187
Antigone, 8, 41–42, 44, 74, 151, 152, 156

Antunes, António Lobo, 91
Aquinas, Thomas, 107, 108
Aranha, José Pereira da Graça, 105
Araújo, Ricardo Benzaquen de, 196
Ariel (1900), 121, 124–25, 131
arielismo, 118, 129, 133, 134
arielista, 11, 125–26
See also Rodó, José Enrique
Ariès, Philippe, 56
Assis, Machado de, 30, 122, 185–86, 189, 197, 202, 243n25
Auerbach, Erich, 19, 34
Augustine, Saint, 82
authoritarianism, xiv, xvi, xvii
Avelino Filho, George, 25
Azevedo, Aluísio, 73

bandeirante, 45, 246n14, 253n5
Barbosa, Francisco de Assis, 24–25
Barreto, Fábio, 252n24
Bastos, Elide Rugai, 56, 217n3, 229n4, 232n24
Bataille, Georges, 42
Batlle y Ordóñez, José, 131
Baudrillard, Jean, 25
Benjamin, Walter, 25
Betto, Frei, 149
Bhabha, Homi K., 235n13
Big House, the, 56, 57, 60, 63, 66, 71

Boethius, Anicius Manlius
  Severinus, 82
Bonfim, Manoel, 12, 123
Bosi, Alfredo, 40, 145, 227n9,
  253n5
Brasília, 63–64
Brazilian "backwardness," 20, 103,
  240n8
Brazilian family, 56, 60, 62
  familial order, 44, 45, 46, 63
  familial privatism, 63
  familial sphere, 37, 41, 57, 67,
    69, 151
  familial vs. public sphere, 13, 37,
    38, 44–45, 46–47, 67, 68
  familial vs. urbanization, 8, 37,
    64, 149
  and intimate history, 53, 56
  and rural roots, 57, 62
Brazilian literature, 2–3, 7, 30, 31,
  32, 87
Brazilian modernism, xiii, xiv,
  14, 32, 34, 49–52, 63, 90, 91,
  104–5, 110, 129, 135, 146,
  166, 192, 229n4
  and Latin American modernism,
    xiii, 49–50, 121, 129–30, 135,
    139
Brazilian way (*jeitinho brasileiro*),
  193
Brioso, Jorge, 139
Bruno, Ernani da Silva, 223n36
Buarque de Holanda, Sérgio
  and ambivalence, 199–200, 204,
    243n30
  in Berlin, xv, 25, 26, 27, 100,
    143–44, 219n12
  between enchantment and
    disenchantment, 116, 139,
    205, 230n12

  "the German phase," 19, 21, 22,
    25, 26, 52, 100, 101, 220n9
  as historian, 9, 14, 43, 51–54,
    58, 90, 99, 104, 144, 163, 166,
    167–68, 170, 177
  and invention, 33, 34, 163,
    220n4, 222n29
  as literary critic, xii, 1, 7, 8, 14,
    31, 32, 33, 34, 90
  and the modern novel, 29–30
  and the political, 20–21, 28,
    30–31, 72, 251n17, 257n15
  reading Gilberto Freyre, 9, 37,
    39, 57–62
  and the rewriting of *Roots of
    Brazil*, 111–12, 144–45
  in Rio de Janeiro, xiii
  the "Romantic," 12, 37, 85,
    100–102, 133, 144
  and *Roots of Brazil* as essay of
    national interpretation, 14, 98,
    183–84
  "Sérgio before Berlin," 24–25
  writing between
    authoritarianisms, xvi–xvii,
    27–28
Burgess, Ernest W., 38
Buenos Aires, 123, 127

Cabral, Pedro Álvares, 88, 146
Caetano, Marcelo, 89
Cairu, Viscount of [José da Silva
  Lisboa], 64, 165
Calligaris, Contardo, 157
Caminha, Pero Vaz de, 88, 146
Camões, Luís de, 91
Camus, Albert, 177
Candido, Antonio, 7, 8, 19–24,
  26–28, 30–32, 43, 45, 139,
  192–93, 204, 222n26

dialectic of malandroism, 15, 192
dialectical sentiment, 19
intellectual radicalism, 26, 31, 43, 111, 229n1
and Max Weber, 19, 26, 40
1967 preface, 8, 19, 20, 21, 26, 145, 195
Cardoso, Fernando Henrique, 153
Carlyle, Thomas, 130
Carnaval, xvii, xv
Carpentier, Alejo, 135
Carvalho, Ronald de, 105
Cascudo, Luís da Câmara, 22
Castro, Belén, 121–22
caudillismo, 131
caudillo, 153
Cendrars, Blaise, 229n4
Cervantes, Miguel de, 126
Césaire, Aimé, 134
Chicago, 8, 38, 39
Chicago School, the, 39
city, the
 the citizen, xxi, 41, 69, 70, 74, 180
 collectivist/personalist architecture, 63, 232n25
 vs. the family, 8, 40, 41, 43, 45, 46
 the house and the street, 65–67
 laws of the City, 41, 42, 44, 152
 and modernity, xiii, 12, 63
 order of the City, 45
 See also lettered city
civic spirit, 43
coffee, 20–21
Cohn, Gabriel, 236n15
Coimbra, 90
collectivity, xi, xx, 11, 28, 41, 74, 79, 118, 124, 132

collective, 16
collectivism, 71
colonial literature, 33, 34, 52, 163–64
colonial period, 90, 103, 163
communism, 20
 and Astrojildo Pereira, 222n30
conservatism, 33, 43, 199, 231n17
conservation, 43
cordiality, xviii, 6, 12, 13, 69, 74, 110, 129, 145, 146, 155
 defined, 110, 147
 genealogy of, 146–48
 reconfigured, 148–49, 151, 157, 158
cordial man, xvi, xvii, xviii, 5, 8, 9, 37, 70, 72, 74, 110, 127, 140, 151, 154, 187
"cordial" power, 41
 defined, xviii, 72, 147–48
 and the "familial phantasm," 13, 156
 genealogy of, 128
 on the heart, 8, 37–38, 41, 69
 as hero, 140, 158. *See also* Veloso, Caetano
 living through others, 155–56, 158
corruption, xix, 150
Costa, Cláudio Manuel da, 229n25
Costa, Lúcio, 64
Costa, Sérgio, 257n15
Counter-Reformist, the. *See under* Protestant Reformation
Coutinho, Eduardo, 148–50, 153
Couto, Rui Ribeiro, 12, 71, 127, 128, 144, 147
Criterion, The (magazine, 1922–1939), xiii, 50, 166
Cuba, 138

Cunha, Euclides da, 20, 91, 101, 102, 197

Dantas, Luiz, 217n3
Darío, Rubén, 12, 117–19, 127–28, 129, 133, 134, 139, 140
da Vinci, Leonardo, 172
Deleuze, Gilles, 26, 221n24
democracy, xvii, 203
  liberal, 74
  racial, xv, 69, 72, 201–2, 233n45
Derrida, Jacques, 256n3
Descartes, René, 223n31
Dias, Antonio Gonçalves, 91
Dias, Maria Odila Leite da Silva, 34
Díaz, Porfirio, 131
Díaz-Quiñones, Arcadio, 122
Dirceu, José, 251n14
disorder, 103, 104, 106, 115, 200, 201, 207
  "organize our disorder," 105–6
  "order" and "disorder," 192, 193
  dis/order, 203. *See also* Wisnik, José Miguel
displacement, 88, 90, 92, 97
Donga [Ernesto Joaquim Maria dos Santos], 51
Dostoevsky, Fyodor, 29, 177
Duby, Georges, 56
Dumont, Louis, 138
Dunlap, Knight, 70

Eco, Umberto, 84, 161
education, 70
Einstein, Albert, 171
Eliot, Thomas Stearns, xiii, 113
Escorel, Ana Luisa, 228n23
Estado Novo (1937–1945), xv, xvi, 9, 111, 187. *See also* Ricardo, Cassiano

Estética (magazine), xiii, 50, 166
Eugênio, João Kennedy, 219n12, 220n4, 222n29
Eulalio, Alexandre, 74
exile, 35, 90, 91, 98, 143, 149, 225n49, 236n15, 238n40, 241n10
  in Brazilian literature 91–92, 241n1
  eternal, 93
  "exiles in our own land", 47, 85, 102, 149
  permanent, 29, 238n40
  voluntary, 90, 143

Fanon, Frantz, 134
fascism, 106, 131, 185
Faulkner, William, 114
Fernández Retamar, Roberto, 133, 134
Filho, Mário, 201
finalist thinking, 84, 234n10
Finazzi-Agrò, Ettore, 97
Fonseca, Edson Nery da, 64
Foucault, Michel, 25, 123
Freud, Sigmund, 94–95, 191
Freyre, Gilberto, xv, 1, 6, 9, 12, 15, 22, 37, 39–40, 49–58, 86, 114, 135, 183, 187, 193, 196, 198–99, 204
  "constellation of regions," 61, 62
  cordial mulatto, 9, 71–74, 197
  Documentos brasileiros [Brazilian Documents], 1, 241n11
  The Masters and the Slaves, 37, 53, 58, 183, 196, 202
  Sobrados e mucambos [The Mansions and the Shanties], 39, 49, 54–56, 63–67, 72–75, 193, 196–97
Furtado, Celso, 103

Galvão, Walnice Nogueira, 32
Gama, Father Lopes, 64, 70–71
García Calderón, Francisco, 125–26
García Márquez, Gabriel, 14, 114, 175
Garrincha [Manuel Francisco dos Santos], 191, 193
George, Stefan, 242n17
Glissant, Édouard, 136, 187
Global South, 12
Gogol, Nicolai, 29
Goldsmith, Oliver, 226n3
Gombrich, Ernst H., 172
Gramsci, Antonio, 116
Groussac, Paul-François, 199
Guattari, Pierre-Félix, 221n24

Hegel, 41, 42, 44
Hegelian themes, 8, 61, 84, 115, 151
See also Sophocles
Henríquez Ureña, Pedro, 247n30
Herculano, Alexandre, 86
Hintze, Otto, 239n1
Hispanic-American modernism, xii, xiii, 49. See also Latin American modernism
hispanism, 122, 132
Hobbes, Thomas, 131
Holanda, Francisco (Chico) Buarque de, 6, 14–15, 175, 178, 179, 181, 182, 189, 255n14
and *Benjamin* (1995), 175–82
impotence of writing, 14
and Sérgio Buarque de Holanda, 15, 181–82, 255n15, 256n16
Holanda, Maria Amélia Alvim Buarque de, 21

Holanda, Sérgio Buarque de. See Buarque de Holanda, Sérgio
Homer, 80
Huizinga, Johan, 114

Ianni, Octavio, 1, 217n3
Iberian Peninsula, xii, xvii, 6, 10, 64, 86, 88–89, 102
  as bridge-territory, 88–89, 91, 102
Iberian roots, 2, 102, 103, 132
  the "adventurer," 38, 40, 44, 103
  character of the Iberian people, 106–7
  "cult of personality," 102, 106, 109
Ibero-America, xvii, 6, 120, 121
Iberoamericans, 123
  Iberian deviation, 6
Iberianism vs. Americanism, 9, 218n7
  solidarity, 208
  the "worker," 38, 40, 103
  See also Morse, Richard
impeachment, xviii–xix
impressionism, 54–55
individualism, 71, 107, 138
Instituto Camões, 87
Instituto Cervantes, 87
Instituto de Estudos Brasileiros (USP), 54
intimacy, xviii, 11, 13, 108, 125

James, Henry, 29, 30
Jáuregui, Carlos, 129
Jesuit missions, 103
João VI, D., King, 64
Johnson, Samuel, 37
Joyce, James, 80

Kafka, Franz, 177
Klages, Ludwig, 100, 219n12

Klaxon (magazine, 1922–1923), xiii
Kubitschek, Juscelino, 63

Lacan, Jacques, 88
Lamounier, Bolívar, 223n36
language
  and ambiguity, 195–96, 221n24
  a battle with words, 4, 52, 93, 169
  the complexity of, 14, 58
  and eclecticism, 14, 53–54, 230n12
  as ideological, 14
  on instability, 181
  and irresolution of conflict, 40, 42
  language game, 168–69, 170
  language of the historian and painting, 172
  language renewal, 50, 54. *See also* Brazilian modernism
  and opposing types, 40
  on unambiguity, 165, 172–73
Latin America, xii, xvi, xvii, xix, 1, 2, 3, 7, 11, 28, 32, 115, 118, 120–23, 124, 127, 129, 130, 133–34, 137, 139, 140, 148
"Latin Americanist" thought, 2, 87, 129
See also Morse, Richard
Latin American modernism, 130, 135–36, 139. *See also* Brazilian modernism
law, xix, xx, xxi, 13, 15, 26
law and order, xix, xx, 33
Le Brun, Charles, 38
Leenhardt, Jacques, 244
Leite, Dante Moreira, 14, 145
lettered city, 24, 221n18
Lezama Lima, José, 136
liberalism, xvii, 12, 20, 44, 102, 104, 111, 131

liberal pact, xviii, 112
Lima, Alceu Amoroso (1893–1983), 105
Lins, Álvaro, 22, 30
Lobato, Monteiro, 123
Loureço, Eduardo, 89
Lourenço, Fernando Antonio, 217n3
Lula era (2003–2010), xix
Lula. *See* Silva, Luiz Inácio Lula da

Malfatti, Anita, xiii
Mallarmé, Stéphane, 188
Mannoni, Dominique-Octave, 134
Manzano, Juan Francisco, 135
Mariátegui, José Carlos, 12
Marroquim, Mário, 50
Martí, José, 123, 124, 128, 133
Mauá, Viscount of, 68–69
medieval mentality, 93, 107
Mello, Evaldo Cabral de, 144–45
Melo, Alfredo Cesar, 222n30
Melville, Herman, 190
Merquior, José Guilherme, 134
Metz, Christian, 138
military dictatorship (1964–1985), xix, 115, 148, 150, 180. *See also* Vargas, Getúlio
Milton, John, 37
miscegenation, xiv, 9, 40, 71, 72, 135, 184, 202, 236n23
  hybridism, 124, 135
Mistral, Frédéric, 125
modern, 29, 46, 72, 116
modernity, 20, 28, 45–47, 70, 108–9, 137, 138, 139
Monroe Doctrine, 132–33
Montaigne, Michel de, 162, 173
Monteiro, Maciel, 133
Moraes Neto, Prudente de, xiii, 50, 51, 166

Morse, Richard, 6, 11, 12, 112–14, 116, 132, 134, 136–39
Mota, Carlos Guilherme, 13, 145, 164–65, 166, 167
Mota, Giselda, 164, 167, 169

Nabuco, Joaquim, 30, 32, 43, 123, 223n35
Napoleon III, 64
national character, xii, 5, 85, 101, 219n13
national discourse, 12, 96, 98, 203, 235n13
Nazism, xv–xvi
New York, 20, 117, 118, 123
Niemeyer, Oscar, 64
Nietzsche, Friedrich, 28, 74, 75, 158, 211
North American academy, 81, 87, 120
and Brazil 81, 87
Northeast, the, 50, 60, 148

oligarchy, xx, xxi
Ortiz, Fernando, 135

Paes, José Paulo, 177
Pallares-Burke, Maria Lúcia, 56
Paoli, Niuvenius Junqueira, 217n3
Paraná, Denise, 252n24
Pareto, Vilfredo, 8, 38
Park, Robert Ezra, 38
Pascal, Blaise, 92
Pasolini, Pier Paolo, 186, 188
patriarchalism, 49, 65, 71, 114
  Brazilian patriarchal society, 54, 58
  the Father, 70, 74, 92, 93
  as fundamental form of sociability, 59
  patriarchal bonds/values, 57, 62

patriarchal family, 46, 56, 61
patriarchal mentality, 57
patriarchal order, 63, 64
the urban and the rural, 67
urban patriarchy, 57
Pécora, Alcir, 224n44
Péladan, Joséphin, 129
Pelé [Edson Arantes do Nascimento], 192
Pereira, Astrojildo, 222n30
Pereira, Lúcia Miguel, 22, 30
Pernambuco, 60
Pessoa, Fernando, 91
Petrone, Maria Tereza, 223n36
Picchia, Menotti del, xiii
Pignatari, Décio, 192
Piratininga highlands, 60
"place outside ideas," 6. *See also* Wisnik, José Miguel
Poe, Edgar Allan, 117, 118, 119
political godparenting, xx, 45
populism, xvii, 28, 152–53, 251n18
Portugal, 87, 89, 90
Prado, Antonio Arnoni, 32–33, 181
Prado, Paulo, 52
Prado, Caio, Júnior, 15, 52, 103, 194–95, 196, 199, 204
Pratt, Mary Louise, 86, 236n17
  contact zone, 86
Princeton, 149, 155
Princeton University, ix
private sphere, 8, 13
Protestant Reformation, 10, 107, 108
  the Protestant, 15, 103, 109, 112, 199
  the Counter-Reformist, 11, 103, 107, 108
Proust, Marcel, 54

public space, xx, 46, 67, 147, 152, 157
public sphere, 8, 149, 151
"pure word," 13. *See also* Mota, Carlos Guilherme

quilombos, 65

racism, xv, 9, 72
Rama, Ángel, 140
Ranke, Leopold von, 15, 167, 177, 178, 239n1
reading public, 23
Rebouças, André 43
Recife, 39, 64, 75
Rego, Rubem Murilo Leão, 217n3
Reyes, Alfonso, 12, 23–24, 127
Ricardo, Cassiano, 9, 69–70, 145, 187
Ridenti, Marcelo, 180–81
Rimbaud, Arthur, 10, 88
Rio de Janeiro, xiii, 50, 179, 180
Rocha, João Cezar de Castro, 31, 81, 241n10, 243n26
Rodó, José Enrique, 11, 12, 118, 121–27, 129, 130–31, 134
Ronaldinho Gaúcho, 189
roots, xi, 10, 26, 29, 30, 31, 32, 85–86, 101, 102
  on ambiguity, 223n36
  on belonging, 87
  the Brazilian aspect of the roots, xii, 31–32, 81, 87, 223n36
  as discomfort, 97
  as feeling of unbelonging, 31
  as ideological, 14, 104
  their indeterminacy, xi–xii, 10, 98, 101–2
  irresolution of conflict, 40, 42
  and literature, 29–30, 97
  and modernization, 240n8
  and orphanhood, 39
  the roots of *Roots of Brazil*, 25, 27–28, 85–86
  "rural roots," 49, 62, 67
  spectral Other, 97
  as *topos*, 30
  transplanting, 86, 90, 112
  "uprooting," 111, 143
Rosa, João Guimarães, 10, 92, 98
  "The Third Bank of the River," 92–96
Rosa, Noel, 190
Rosas, Juan Manuel de, 131
Rosenfeld, Anatol, 201
Rousseau, Jean-Jacques, 131
Rousseff, Dilma, xviii, 251n13

Sáenz Peña, Roque, 127, 128
Said, Edward, 3
Salazar, António de Oliveira, 89, 202
Salles, João Moreira, 6, 13, 148–52, 153, 155, 158, 159
Salvador, Frei Vicente do, 68
Salvador de Bahia, xiii, 164
samba, 50
Santí, Enrico Mario, 135
Santiago, Silviano, 256n3
Santos, Laymert Garcia dos, 217n3
Santos, Wanderley Guilherme dos, 19
São Paulo, xii, xiii, 8, 21, 22, 50, 54, 60, 113, 148, 149
Saramago, José, 91
Sarduy, Severo, 136
Sarmiento, Domingo Faustino, 20
Saussure, Ferdinand de, 10, 81–82, 96
Schmitt, Carl, 111, 115, 132, 152
Schwartzman, Simon, 114, 137
Schwarz, Roberto, 32, 200

sertanejo, 97, 197. *See also* "America," Portuguese America
Sevcenko, Nicolau, 227n7
Shakespeare, William, 89, 120, 134
Silva, Luiz Inácio Lula da, xix, xx, xxi, 6, 13, 137, 148–59, 249n47, 250n12, 251n14, 252n24, 252n27
Simmel, Georg, 61, 100
slavery xiii, 64
  abolition of, xiii, 135, 212
slaves' quarters, 60
soccer, xvii, 15, 153, 184–85, 186, 188, 190, 192, 195, 198, 201–3, 233n43
social contract, xvii
Sophocles, 8, 41–42, 44, 151. See also *Antigone*
Sommer, Doris, 86
Souza, Laura de Mello e, 223n36
Spain, 88
  Generation of '98, 56
  Spanish Black Legend, 146
  Spanish-American War, 127–28
Spengler, Oswald, 12, 130, 219n12
spontaneity, xiv, xv, xvi, 152, 153
Starling, Heloisa Maria Murgel, 178
sugar-cane, 62

Taunay, Affonso, 60, 125
Telles, Edward, 72
Temer, Michel, xix
Tenorio, Mauricio, 137
Thomas, William Isaac, 8, 38–39
Tolstoy, Leo, 40
Tostão [Eduardo Gonçalves de Andrade], 192
totalitarianism, xvi, xvii, 43, 104, 111, 251n17

transcendence, 84, 85, 93, 95, 136, 178
travelling, 79–80
Tropicalism, 195
  the Tropicalist wave, 203
Trotsky, Leon 203

Unamuno, Miguel de, 125
United States of America, xvi, xviii, 7, 12, 30, 81, 89–90, 103, 117, 121, 122, 123, 127, 130, 132, 134, 137, 190
Universidade de São Paulo (USP), 53, 195
Universidade do Distrito Federal, 53
Universidade Estadual de Campinas, 164
urbanization, 8, 37, 49, 52, 57, 64–68

Vargas, Getúlio, xv, 9, 50, 187
Vasconcelos, José, 12, 129
Veblen, Thorstein, 220n7
Velho, Otávio, 138
Veloso, Caetano, 146, 158, 193, 203, 234n9, 249n55
Vianna, Francisco José de Oliveira, 43, 115
Vico, Giambattista, 12, 219n12
Vieira, Father António, 91
Vilhena, Luís dos Santos, 164

Wagner, Richard, 140
Waizbort, Leopoldo, 227, 243n30
Weber, Max, 1, 11, 19, 38, 39, 40, 52, 100, 102–3, 108, 116
Week of Modern Art, xiii, 121
Wegner, Robert, 145, 221n13, 227n5, 241n10

Wenders, Wim, 89
Whitman, Walt, 56
Wisnik, José Miguel, 6, 15, 184,
    187, 188, 202–3, 204
  and American football, 188, 190,
    200
  and dialectic of malandroism 15,
    192–93, 199, 200
  "Garrincha" and Macunaíma,
    190–91, 193
  and Gilberto Freyre, 186, 187,
    196–97, 198–99, 202, 203
  on "nonlinearity," 15, 186,
    188–89, 190, 193
  between "order" and "disorder,"
    192–93, 200, 203
  on poetry and Brazilian soccer,
    186, 188, 203
  poison/cure, 185, 194–95, 199,
    200, 204
  and Sérgio Buarque de Holanda,
    15, 186, 187, 195, 193, 199
  and soccer, 15, 184–85, 186, 188,
    190, 192, 195, 198, 201–3,
    233n43
  Veneno remédio [Poison/Cure:
    Soccer and Brazil] (2008), 15,
    184, 185, 186, 190, 191–92,
    200, 201, 204
  Veneno remédio as essay of
    national interpretation,
    191–92, 193, 204
  the "well-balanced" and the
    "acrobat," 189, 192
Wittgenstein, Ludwig, 14, 168
Wölfflin, Heinrich, 114
Worker's Party, xviii, xix, 137, 156,
    158
World War II, 111
Wright, Frank Lloyd, 190

Zabus, Chantal, 120
Zambrano, María, 205
Znaniecki, Florian, 8, 38–39

Pedro Meira Monteiro is professor of Spanish and Portuguese at Princeton University. He is the author, editor, and co-editor of numerous books, including a critical edition of *Raízes do Brasil*.

www.ingramcontent.com/pod-product-compliance
Lightning Source LLC
Chambersburg PA
CBHW060554230426
43670CB00011B/1820